AF412140

William Blake
Images and Texts

Huntington Library
San Marino, California

Cover illustration: *America a Prophecy*, copy I (Huntington Library), plate 10. Relief etching with white-line etching/engraving; etched and printed 1793.

Simultaneously published as *Huntington Library Quarterly*, vol. 58, nos. 3 & 4

Library of Congress Cataloging-in-Publication Data
William Blake : images and texts.
    p. cm.
Essays presented at a symposium held on October 29, 1994 in honor of the Huntington Library's seventy-fifth anniversary.
Published also as v. 58, no. 3 and 4 of the Huntington Library quarterly.
Includes bibliographical references.
ISBN 0-87328-168-3 (alk. paper)
1. Blake, William, 1757–1827—Criticism and interpretation—Congresses. 2. Literature and society—England—History—18th century—Congresses. 3. Literature and society—England—History—19th century—Congresses. 4. Art and literature—England—History—18th century—Congresses. 5. Art and literature—England—History—19th century—Congresses. 6. Slavery in literature—Congresses. I. Henry E. Huntington Library and Art Gallery. II. Huntington Library quarterly.
PR4147.W47 1997
821'.7—dc21

        97-1401
        CIP

Printed in the United States of America

Henry E. Huntington Library and Art Gallery
1151 Oxford Road, San Marino, California 91108

Contents

List of Figures

Page references for black-and-white illustrations, interspersed throughout the volume, are given below. Color plates, referred to in the text with uppercase roman numerals, follow page 95, where a detailed list of the color plates is given. Measurements are supplied for items designed and printed by Blake.

Introduction

———————————————————————— Robert N. Essick

The Huntington Library, Art Collections, and Botanical Gardens celebrated its seventy-fifth anniversary in 1994. This volume is a product of that signal event. The story, briefly told, of how this collection of essays came together will reveal something of the Huntington's role in preserving cultural treasures, promoting scholarship, and serving larger public interests.

Several years before the anniversary, the Art Division began to consider appropriate ways to honor Henry E. Huntington's generous spirit in founding the institution that bears his name. The collection of British art offered a host of possibilities for a special exhibition to mark the occasion. Dr. Shelley Bennett, Curator of British and European Art, quickly decided that an exhibit of works by William Blake would be appropriate for several reasons. Beginning in 1911, Henry Huntington assembled a remarkable collection of Blake's drawings, watercolors, letters, and illuminated books—the last containing some of Blake's finest poetry and designs. In the years when Huntington was most active, Blake's unique books were considered little more than bibliographic curiosities in collecting circles; his pictorial designs were on the margins of British connoisseurship. Thus, Huntington was extraordinarily prescient in acquiring such a broad range of Blake's productions, graphic and literary. Although only a few major works have been added since Huntington's time, the Blake collection maintained jointly by the Art Gallery and the Library is one of only half a dozen of this caliber in the world. As such, it has contributed much to the development of Blake's canonical status among British Romantic poets and to his popularity as an artist.

Shelley Bennett asked me to curate the Blake exhibition—a task I took on with a mixture of enthusiasm and trepidation. The great series of water colors illustrating John Milton's poems were an obvious choice for presentation, but these had been shown many times in the past. Events in the Library provided an alternative. Most of the Library's copies of Blake's illuminated books had been tightly bound, usually in handsome but now-decaying morocco, late in the last century. In that condition, common to many institutional collections of these books, only one or two pages could be shown from each volume in exhibition cases. Fortunately, the Library was beginning to disbind the illuminated books for conservation. This provided a serendipitous opportunity to present a much larger selection of pages from Blake's most characteristic works than had heretofore been possible. Indeed, the relatively small space reserved for changing exhibitions in the Huntington Art Gallery was capacious enough to mount the largest showing of Blake's illuminated books since the legendary Philadelphia exhibit of 1939. The show also offered the chance, through its display of Library materials in the Art Gallery, to demonstrate the interdisciplinary character of the institution Henry Huntington founded in 1919.

The exhibition, entitled "William Blake's Illuminated Prints," opened festively on 25 September 1994, and ran through 15 January 1995. Visitors were greeted, at the entry to the show, by the two largest images, *Hecate* and *Satan Exulting over Eve*, both color prints designed and first executed by Blake in 1795.[1] The former had been recently, and most successfully, cleaned and restored at the Tate Gallery in London with the assistance of a grant from the National Endowment for the Arts; the latter had been lent by the J. Paul Getty Museum of Art. Cooperation among several institutions, public and private, made significant contributions to the exhibition's success.

For the first time as part of a temporary exhibit at the Huntington, we enlisted the aid of electronic media. The selected original prints on view were complemented by a CD-ROM containing all pictorial images in the Huntington's collection designed and executed by Blake. Visitors could roam at will through hundreds of designs, including complete illuminated books, and enlarge individual images as curiosity dictated. Preparation of the CD led to the publication of *William Blake at the Huntington*, an introduction to the collection with sixty-four full-page color illustrations and facing-page commentaries.[2] Both the book and the CD have made high-quality reproductions of Blake's works available to a large general audience.

The show generated a mild controversy by its presentation of illuminated-book pages in frames hung on the gallery's walls. To some, this violated their bibliographic genre. There is no doubt that Blake created his illuminated books to

---

1. For the last few weeks of the exhibition, *Satan Exulting over Eve* was replaced by *Lamech* (collection of Robert N. Essick), another of the large color prints of 1795.
2. This paperbound volume, published in 1994 by Harry N. Abrams in association with the Huntington, is available from the Huntington Library Press. The CD-ROM can be viewed by scholars working at the Huntington but it is not presently available for sale or rental.

be seen and read as bound volumes, but only the individual framing of pages allowed for viewing by a large audience. Blake had himself established the precedent for the temporary conversion of his books into framed prints by displaying some proofs from his illuminated epic *Jerusalem* at the 1812 exhibition of the Associated Painters in Water-Colours.

Rather than publishing a full catalogue of the exhibit, we decided to offer visitors, without charge, a brief (but nicely illustrated) handlist and husband our resources for a symposium and the publication of the scholarly papers presented. By these means we could forge the final link in a thoroughly integrated tribute to Henry Huntington, one that included art and literature, collecting and conservation, public display and scholarly interpretation.

Generous support from the National Endowment for the Arts helped us realize our plans for the conference. Under the broad umbrella of our symposium title, "William Blake: Images and Texts," we wanted to present a diversity of opinions and approaches at the forefront of contemporary Blake criticism. To achieve that goal, we sought to include not only individuals who had devoted their professional lives to Blake and his circle but also scholar-critics who had begun their careers studying Blake's work and then moved on to broader issues, or who have had notable careers in Romantic studies without a central focus on Blake. We were extremely fortunate in receiving positive responses to our invitations from the distinguished group of literary critics and art historians whose symposium essays are presented here. As the final spice for our recipe, we asked two of the liveliest minds in the study of Romanticism to attend the symposium and respond to the papers. We thereby sought to enlist dialogue in the advancement of humanistic knowledge, and our success is demonstrated in this volume by Morris Eaves's forceful essay, "On Blakes We Want and Blakes We Don't."[3] The keynote address, "Chaosthetics: Blake's Sense of Form," presented by W. J. T. Mitchell, closed a symposium memorable for its mix of solid scholarship, imaginative criticism, and spirited debate.

Each in its own way, the essays published here demonstrate the symbiosis of artifact and idea. While Joseph Viscomi's work is the most heavily invested in the material base, the approaches of the other scholars presented here—whether semiotic, New Historicist, postcolonial, or feminist—also depend on the preservation of Blake's works by collectors such as Henry Huntington and institutions

---

3. At the symposium, held on 29 October 1994, Morris Eaves responded to the presentations by David Bindman and Anne K. Mellor; Jerome McGann responded to the papers by Joseph Viscomi and Tilottama Rajan. We are grateful to Morris Eaves for commenting in written form on all four essays.

such as the Huntington Library. The Library's copy of *Visions of the Daughters of Albion* (1793)—reproduced here complete and in full color for the first time—is but one example of how works from the past speak to issues of present concern. Like the symposium itself, this volume based on the proceedings offers images, texts, and some ways of illuminating their interdependence.

I hope that the foregoing comments give some indication of the Huntington's multiple contributions to the careful maintenance, public presentation, and scholarly understanding of our cultural heritage. Both the essays and illustrations that follow bear more eloquent testimony to the Huntington's dedication to that task.

University of California, Riverside

The Evolution of
The Marriage of Heaven and Hell

——————— Joseph Viscomi

In my end is my beginning.
T. S. Eliot, "East Coker"

The man who never alters his opinion is like
standing water, & breeds reptiles of the mind.
William Blake, *The Marriage of Heaven and Hell*, plate 19

In *The Early Illuminated Books*, volume 3 of the recent Blake Trust series of reproductions, we briefly explained why the genre and structure of *The Marriage of Heaven and Hell* are among the book's "most distinctive, most unsettling primary features." Depending on how one counts, the *Marriage* text is divided into thirteen or more sections or units consisting of one, two, three, and more copper plates[1]—plates with and without illustrations, with and without titles; some of which are "theological or philosophical, others proverbial, others variously narrative (myths of origin, interviews, mock travelogues, conversion stories)," with "few if any characters or settings in common." Moreover, "time and space are freely manipulated: the narrator travels to hell and back, hangs over abysses with an angel, and dines in the approximate present with Isaiah and Ezekiel, while the order of events and the relation of one narrative space to another are seldom specified."[2] Is the book "varied and pregnant fragments"; a mere

I am indebted to my friends and coeditors Morris Eaves and Robert N. Essick for reading earlier versions of this paper and for their many insightful and helpful comments.

1. The thirteen textual units correspond to plates 1, 2, 3, 4, 5–7, 7–10, 11, 12–13, 14, 15, 16–20, 21–24, and 25–27. If one treats the "Notes" on plates 6, 19, and 24 as separate textual units, which I do not, the total number of units is sixteen.
2. For a brief overview of the various classifications given the *Marriage* and the quotations above, see Morris Eaves, Robert N. Essick, and Joseph Viscomi, eds., *The Early Illuminated Books* (Princeton, N.J., 1993), 116–18; page references are given hereafter in the text.

"scrap-book of Blake's philosophy"; a "structureless structure" about "as heterogeneous as one could imagine"?[3] Or is its structure classifiable in terms of genre, as many scholars have attempted to show, perceiving it variously as anatomy, Bible, manifesto, primer, prophecy, or testament? In *The Early Illuminated Books*, we assigned it to a subcategory of Menippean satire identified with the "Greek prose satirist Lucian of Samosata (c. A.D. 125–200), whose works such as *Dialogues of the Dead, Voyage to the Lower World*, and *The True History* (third edition in English, 1781) exemplify the Lucianic 'News from Hell type'" (p. 118).

Clearly, the *Marriage* is an intellectual satire, and its disjointed structure fits reasonably well into the Menippean category. Nevertheless, as I argue here, it would be a mistake to infer from this fit Blake's original intentions for the *Marriage*—to assume that he set out to write a Menippean satire or modeled his book on any one specific work. In this essay, the first of a three-part study on the evolution of the *Marriage*, I argue that the idea of a disjointed, miscellaneous work entitled *The Marriage of Heaven and Hell* emerged only after Blake had written and executed plates 21–24 and planned his "Bible of Hell," and that the structure of the whole work is in some measure the result of a production history in which sections were written and executed at different times.

Narrative discontinuity alone suggests that textual units were not composed in the order in which they are now read. But it only suggests and does not prove disjointed *production*, and it does not provide the clues necessary to establish the sequence in which the textual units were composed. Analysis of the text cannot answer basic questions, such as whether individual units or groups of units were committed to copper plates soon after they were written, or only after the entire manuscript was completed. For clues and for answers, we need to examine technical features unique to illuminated printing; the first printing of plates 21–24; the different lettering styles among the *Marriage* plates; and, most important, the manner in which plates 21–24 and the other plates were supplied from larger sheets of copper. This examination will demonstrate that the four copper plates carrying the text of pages 21–24—which constitute a sustained attack on Swedenborg—were quarters cut from the same sheet of copper, were executed soon after their text was written, and were the first unit produced. They appear to have been written and printed (at least once) as an independent (though probably unissued) pamphlet, but became instead the core of the *Marriage*, generat-

---

3. Descriptions of the form of the *Marriage* from Alexander Gilchrist, *Life of William Blake,* 2 vols. (1863; 2d ed., London, 1880), 1:78; S. Foster Damon, *William Blake: His Philosophy and Symbols* (London, 1924); and Michael Ferber, *The Poetry of William Blake* (London, 1991).

ing twenty of its subsequent twenty-three plates. These plates, also quarters of larger sheets, can be reconfigured into their original sheets; and the sheets, once sequenced by their lettering styles, confirm the textual units as revealed by linguistic codes and identify the larger sections or likely printing sessions to which the units belong. Material evidence provided by the bibliographical codes—by which I mean lettering style as well as reconstructed sheets—establishes the sequence in which the units were most likely written and executed.[4]

When we read the *Marriage* units in this sequence—that is, in a chronology of plate production—we begin to see visual and verbal connections heretofore obscured, connections that illuminate Blake's composing process and the creative logic underlying the book's composition. We can trace the development of key ideas and the relation between unit composition and book production—or, in Blakean parlance, between invention and execution. In this hands-on, workshop style of composing, in which poet and printer could execute plates upon completing autonomous textual units, Blake could think nonlinearly and behave like an artist: ideas and images of a unit already executed could direct the subsequent creative process. We begin to see how Blake interacted with his graphic medium and how such interaction encouraged an ever-evolving (what I have called "organic") mode of composition. Witnessing the *Marriage* unfold through its production enables us to answer basic questions about the *Marriage*'s form and Blake's original and final intentions, as well as general questions about Blake's mode of composing his texts and books. In short, it enables us to see more of Blake's mind at work.

The second essay in my study of the *Marriage* substantiates the claim made here that plates 21–24 were written and executed before the other units, probably as an independent, anti-Swedenborgian pamphlet. I examine their thematic, aesthetic, and rhetorical coherence and date Blake's interest in and disillusionment with Swedenborg, placing the latter within the context of other critiques most likely known to Blake. I identify the primary Swedenborgian texts that Blake satirizes and examine the major themes that figure in and help to generate the subsequent plates and units. The third essay traces these themes and texts through the remaining textual units in the order in which the units were produced. It focuses on Blake's allusions to printmaking and their connection to Swedenborg, examining in detail the image and symbolism of the

---

4. The terms "bibliographical code" and "linguistic code" are Jerome McGann's and refer, respectively, to the material and conceptual dimensions of a book that together constitute textuality. See *The Textual Condition* (Princeton, N.J., 1991), 13–16.

cave. The last essay reveals, in effect, that the *Marriage* is a series of variations on basic themes first raised on plates 21–24.[5]

❧ COMPOSITION IN ILLUMINATED PRINTING ❧

Blake did not date or sign the *Marriage*. Until recently, most scholars dated it circa 1790–93.[6] A set of complex allusions to Swedenborg, Blake, and Christ on plate 3 suggests the beginning date.[7] The "June 5 1793" inscription on *Our End is Come*, an engraving used as a frontispiece in *Marriage* copy B, one of the earliest copies printed, suggests the conventionally accepted end date. The three-year gestation, the perfunctory mention of Swedenborg on plates 3 and 19, and the vociferous attack on plates 21–24 suggest that Blake broke from Swedenborgianism slowly and cautiously, but this conclusion is mistaken. First, the evidence that the composition of the *Marriage* continued beyond 1790 is very weak

---

5. The second essay of this study, entitled "The Lessons of Swedenborg: or, the Origin of William Blake's *The Marriage of Heaven and Hell*," is in Robert Gleckner and Thomas Pfau, eds., *Lessons of Romanticism*, forthcoming from Duke University Press. The third essay, entitled "In the Caves of Heaven and Hell: Swedenborg and Printmaking in Blake's *Marriage*," is in David Worrall and Steve Clark, eds., *Blake in the Nineties*, forthcoming from Macmillan, United Kingdom.

6. *Complete Poetry and Prose of William Blake*, newly rev. ed., ed. David V. Erdman, with commentary by Harold Bloom (New York, 1988), 801 (hereafter cited in the text and in subsequent notes as "E"); and G. E. Bentley Jr., *Blake Books: Annotated Catalogues of William Blake's Writings in Illuminated Printing* (Oxford, 1977).

7. On plate 3, Blake confidently asserts that "it is now thirty-three years since [the] advent" of "a new heaven," echoing Swedenborg's *A Treatise Concerning the Last Judgment and the Destruction of Babylon* (1758; English trans., 1788), n. 61. Closer to home, it echoes propositions 38, 39, and 40 of the *Circular Letter* sent on 7 December 1788 to "all the readers of the Theological Writings of the Hon. Emanuel Swedenborg" (reprinted in *Blake and Swedenborg: Opposition is True Friendship*, ed. Harvey Bellin and Darrell Ruhl [New York, 1985], 122–25). The *Circular Letter's* forty-two propositions were resolved unanimously at the First General conference, held 13–17 April 1789, which Blake and his wife attended; and the thirty-two resolutions were published as part of the conference's *Minutes* by Robert Hindmarsh in 1789 (reprinted in *Blake and Swedenborg*, ed. Bellin and Ruhl; page references to the *Circular Letter* and the *Minutes* are given both in the text and in subsequent notes). Resolution 25, summarizing propositions 38–40, states: "That . . . the Second Advent of the Lord, which is a Coming in the internal sense of his Holy Word, has already commenced, and ought to be announced to all the world. That this Second Advent involves two things, namely, the Last Judgment, or Destruction of the Old Church, which was accomplished in the Spiritual World in the year 1757, and the consequent Formation or Establishment of the New Church" (*Minutes*, 128). Thirty-three years from 1757 dates the "now" of Blake's passage at 1790. The date 1790, to be precise, would apply to the set of plates that plate 3 belongs to (see below); plates produced earlier may have come before 1790, as I speculated in *Blake and the Idea of the Book* (Princeton, N.J., 1993), 237. But this is unlikely because text on plates 21–24 echoes passages from the first issue of *The New Jerusalem Magazine* and in the *Analytical Review*, vol. 5, both of 1790 (see Viscomi, "Lessons of Swedenborg").

(see *Early Illuminated Books,* 113–16). The engraved frontispiece, for example, is not printed on a sheet of paper conjunct with the title page, as thought earlier (see Bentley, *Blake Books,* 287 n. 3). With no documentary evidence to prove otherwise, we should accept the date of 1790, which is implied on plate 3 and, more persuasively, penned-in on plate 3 of copy F—color printed circa 1794 (see *Early Illuminated Books,* 145)—as the end date. Second, the autographic nature of relief etching encouraged moving quickly from text to plate (as I will argue below)—or at the very least did not present any technical obstacles to composition—making it unlikely that a book of twenty-seven small plates would have taken three years to produce, a good deal longer than any of the other books Blake was working on during the same period. The schedule suggested by Blake's professional commitments also supports a 1790 date: the years 1789 and 1790, which saw the first illuminated books, were almost completely void of (known) outside commissions for engravings, whereas during 1791–92 Blake engraved at least seventy plates for book publishers.[8]

The hypothesis that the *Marriage* was in progress for three or more years—and that Blake's feud with Swedenborg was a slow boil, an ambivalence that developed into hostility—is dubious. In fact, as the present essay argues, the evidence that the *Marriage* evolved *from* Blake's hostile attitude toward Swedenborg is very strong. Nevertheless, while the *Marriage* almost certainly did not take three years to compose and execute, neither was it completed overnight; it was in progress for a time, but not in the way, or for as long, as we have thought. As we will see in sections 4 and 5 of this essay, it resulted from four or five distinct and recognizably sequential periods of composition, all presumably taking place in 1790. But before examining the bibliographical evidence indicating chronology, we need to consider what the *Marriage* as a work-in-progress could mean, and that requires clarifying what we already know about Blake's composing and production processes. We need to understand how illuminated printing ensured execution a creative role in the invention of text, illustration, and design.

The suspicion that Blake wrote the units of the *Marriage* out of order is neither new nor surprising. Narrative discontinuity, as noted, has suggested as much to readers of Blake. Logic alone indicates that plates 21–24—which explain the grounds of Blake's attack on Swedenborg—were probably written before plates 3 and 19, where perfunctory mention of Swedenborg appears to rely on information already provided, compositionally speaking. But even those who have seen in Blake's eclectic texts the mind of the *bricoleur,* or a reviser and cobbler

---

8.   Robert N. Essick, *William Blake's Commercial Book Illustrations* (Oxford, 1989).

of fragments, still imagine him pulling the fragments together conventionally.[9] In this view, the narrative's disjointedness is a matter of Blake's drawing on disparate discourses and traditions. When one speaks of Blake writing illuminated texts, even a text as "seemingly ad hoc" as the *Marriage*,[10] one is hard pressed not to envision him writing and rewriting the entire composition on paper before committing it to copper, because one still imagines Blake working as a poet in the manuscript tradition and using illuminated printing subsequently as a mode of reproduction. It is exceedingly difficult to think outside the letterpress paradigm, to conceive of a mode of printing that did not require a finished text or fair copy before execution began; or of a mode of execution in which aesthetic decisions regarding page designs could have an immediate effect on the text, shaping and directing it. In the letterpress paradigm, one simply assumes that a text is written on paper and then set in type, that it is produced and completed before being reproduced, with labor moving determinently—and unidirectionally—from author to compositor. Indeed, authors and compositors were not collaborators, and endings were not set before beginnings.[11]

It is commonplace in Blake studies to assert that illuminated printing united invention and execution, and to view it as a reaction against the division of labor characteristic of letterpress printing; but this assertion has remained mostly theoretical and contradictory. Not much thought has been given to how—let alone exactly where in production—invention and execution intersect, except in the person of Blake himself, as author and printer. But the same laborer does not nec-

9. See Jon Mee, *Dangerous Enthusiasm: William Blake and the Culture of Radicalism in the 1790s* (Oxford, 1992), 3; and Edward Larrissy, *William Blake* (Oxford, 1985), 90.
10. See Robert N. Essick, "Representation, Anxiety, and the Bibliographical Sublime" (forthcoming in *Huntington Library Quarterly*).
11. At the conference on which this volume is based, Jerome McGann questioned these statements about letterpress printing, citing Rossetti's *Poems* (1870): while it was in production, Rossetti altered its text and page order numerous times. I do not doubt it, nor do I doubt that his compositors and publisher acted with restraint and patience. The economics of publishing and printing made legible and finished manuscripts (even in serial publication) self-evidently necessary. Continuous revision is costly: it takes up time, keeps type out of production, and can reduce the number of books the press will produce. Publishers can be forgiven, then, for wanting to prevent authors from using the printing process as we use computer printouts, endlessly proofing and changing our ideas once in material contact with them. McGann, of course, knows this, and so while we did not pursue the full significance of Rossetti's exceptional practice, I must assume that he presented it not to challenge this characterization of the letterpress paradigm but to challenge the idea that letterpress printing and illuminated printing differ only in that the first divides invention from execution while the second combines them. He is right to suspect more essential differences. Although undivided labor indeed provided Blake with creative opportunities unavailable to other writers, what truly differentiates these two modes of production is that one is mechanical and the other is autographic. One requires reconstructing text with discrete pieces of metal type set in formes; the other

essarily mean undivided labor; the acts of writing and printing in the creation of an illuminated book were still perceived as occurring separately. This perception is particularly evident in Ruthven Todd's theory of illuminated printing, which attempts to explain technically how Blake could have avoided writing directly on plates, that is, backward: he must have transferred from paper *first*. Like many before him and since, Todd assumed that Blake produced his books on paper before reproducing them in metal; this effected a modeling relation between text and plate and, furthermore, required fair copies. These are perfectly reasonable assumptions, given that the illuminated page is a print, which by definition reproduces images made in other media, whether visual or verbal. In fact, only by understanding the reasonableness of Todd's proposal can one fully appreciate how radically Blake broke with conventional modes of composing and printing by not transferring texts or images.[12]

Todd's theory presupposed Blake's adaptation of the "counterproof," a method of transferring outlines that preserves the direction of the original in the print. He proposed that Blake, instead of rewriting his text in graphite on paper, rewrote it in an acid-resistant ink on leaves coated in gum arabic (otherwise the ink would enter the fibers of the paper). He rewrote text clearly and

extends the skills of writing and drawing, as Blake claims in his prospectus for the illuminated books (E 692–93). Dividing the labor of writing and execution reflects two very different ways of thinking about the text, a difference becoming increasingly blurred as we move from pens to typewriters to computers with numerous fonts and page-making programs.

I wonder if Rossetti would have made as many alterations if he was the one resetting type. In theory, letterpress printing has the potential of being part of a writer's composing process, a potential typically thwarted by economically grounded practice. But most authors, from poet to historian, pamphleteer to scientist, would no doubt correct proofs against manuscript and not vice versa because they thought in terms of writing and not in terms of typesetting and printing. (A fascinating exception to this rule is Laurence Sterne's *Life and Opinions of Tristram Shandy*, which unites bibliographical and linguistic codes for mutual support, as is brilliantly demonstrated by Essick's "Representation, Anxiety, and the Bibliographic Sublime.") The difference between letterpress and illuminated printing can be framed in terms of a medium's propensity versus what can be forced on or from it. That propensity is shaped by tools and the physical acts these media require, as well as by tradition and convention. The pen, brushes, and ink (albeit acid-resistant) of illuminated printing are the tools of writing and drawing, and writing and drawing are the paradigms that enabled Blake to use his new graphic medium as part of the composing process.

12. The theory of transferred texts was developed by Ruthven Todd with Stanley Hayter in 1948 ("The Techniques of William Blake's Illuminated Printing," *Print Collector's Quarterly* 29 [1948]: 25–36). It was not seriously challenged until 1980, when Robert N. Essick, in *William Blake: Printmaker* (Princeton, N.J., 1980) argued for the likelihood that Blake wrote his texts directly on the plates, backward (pp. 89–91). Even after this, the theory of transferred text (especially the assumptions upon which it is predicated) was still widely accepted, which is why in *Blake and the Idea of the Book* I undertook to show that it was not only aesthetically clumsy but also technically impossible in light of actual composition and illuminated-book production (as opposed to that of individual plates). Below I summarize chapters 1–4 from that book.

legibly, exactly as he wished it to appear on plates, on leaves cut specifically to fit their designated plates—or within the outline of the plates drawn on the leaves—for the plates of an illuminated book are not uniform in size or shape. He would then carefully register each leaf or page face down onto its designated plate, pass leaf and plate through the press, and soak the pair in water to facilitate the transference of the text—which would then appear backward ("counterproofed") on the plate and be left standing in relief after the plate was etched. Furthermore, the leaves, taken together, would have constituted a fair copy, but they would have been destroyed in the process of transference (this, Todd believed, explained the absence of manuscripts for the illuminated books).[13] Producing the leaves in advance in this manner necessarily divided the manuscript into pages that corresponded exactly to plates. Hence, Blake would have been able to cast off copy—and thus execute plates out of order. And, in advance of production, he would have known which pages were to be illustrated and the size and position of the illustrations. He would thus have known ahead the proportion between text and image per page, even if he had not yet determined the illustrations, and have had general mock-ups of pages. What is produced in metal would be, as Gilchrist mistakenly assumed, an "imitation of the original drawing," that is, a "facsimile" of what had been invented on paper.[14]

Todd's theory breaks down quickly when examined historically and technically. Conventional methods of transferring texts in etching and engraving do not work in relief etching, which is why Todd imagined Blake radically adapting one. The method he and Hayter describe, however, is strikingly similar to the one invented in 1798 by Alois Senefelder (an actor who did not know reverse writing) for use in lithography. In Blake's time, moreover, all engravers were trained in reverse writing. The evidence shows that Blake drew his illustrations on plates directly, without the assistance of transfers; and when he had sketched an illustration beforehand, he merely redrew it on the plate to fit. The vignette of Nebuchadnezzar in the second state of *Marriage* plate 24 (see figure 3) is a case in point: When the plate was first printed, for *Marriage* copy K, the vignette had not yet been drawn on it (figure 1), which meant that Blake had to mask the plate's unetched bottom half during printing (see n. 22 below). Only after printing plate 24, with the three accompanying plates, did Blake decide to continue designing it, at which point he added the vignette of Nebuchadnezzar from his Notebook (figure 2). Because Blake redrew this image freehand on the plate, the printed image is the reverse of the drawing (figure 3).

13. Todd, "Illuminated Printing," 34.
14. Gilchrist, *Life of William Blake,* 1:69.

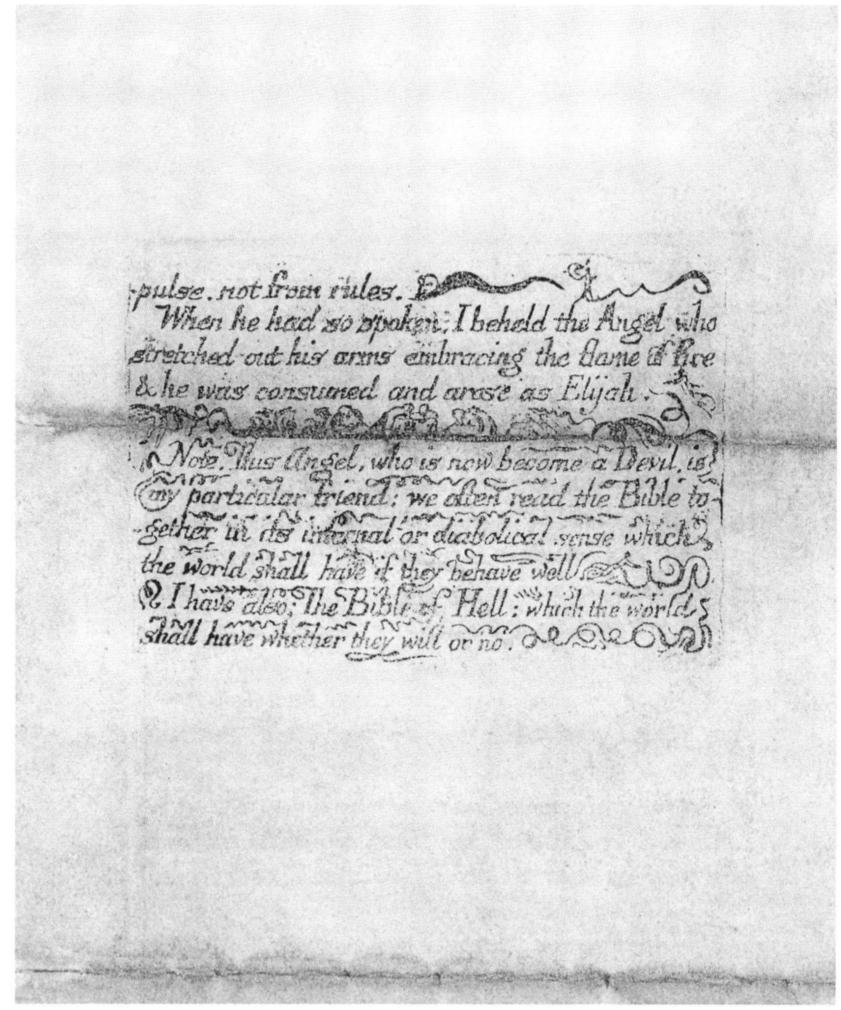

Figure 1. *The Marriage of Heaven and Hell,* copy K, plate 24, first state (Fitzwilliam Museum).

The Notebook drawing has no indication of text and appears not to have been drawn as part of an illuminated-page design. It may have been drawn as part of an emblem series that Blake began circa 1789–90 and thus before the writing and execution of plates 21–24. In any event, Nebuchadnezzar was not chosen randomly; Swedenborg points specifically to Nebuchadnezzar's dream in Daniel 2:44 as foretelling the New Church as the last and eternal church, a passage reprinted in the *Minutes* (p. 130) of the first General Conference, which, as I have noted, was attended by Blake. Whether Swedenborg reminded Blake of an earlier drawing of his or generated a new one, Blake continued to invent plate 24 and deepen the meaning of his text by responding creatively to his own first prints. If, on the other hand, he was merely reproducing a preexistent design, then plate 24

Let a Man who has made a Drawing go on & on & he will produce a Picture or Painting but if he chooses to leave it before he has spoild it he will do a Better Thing

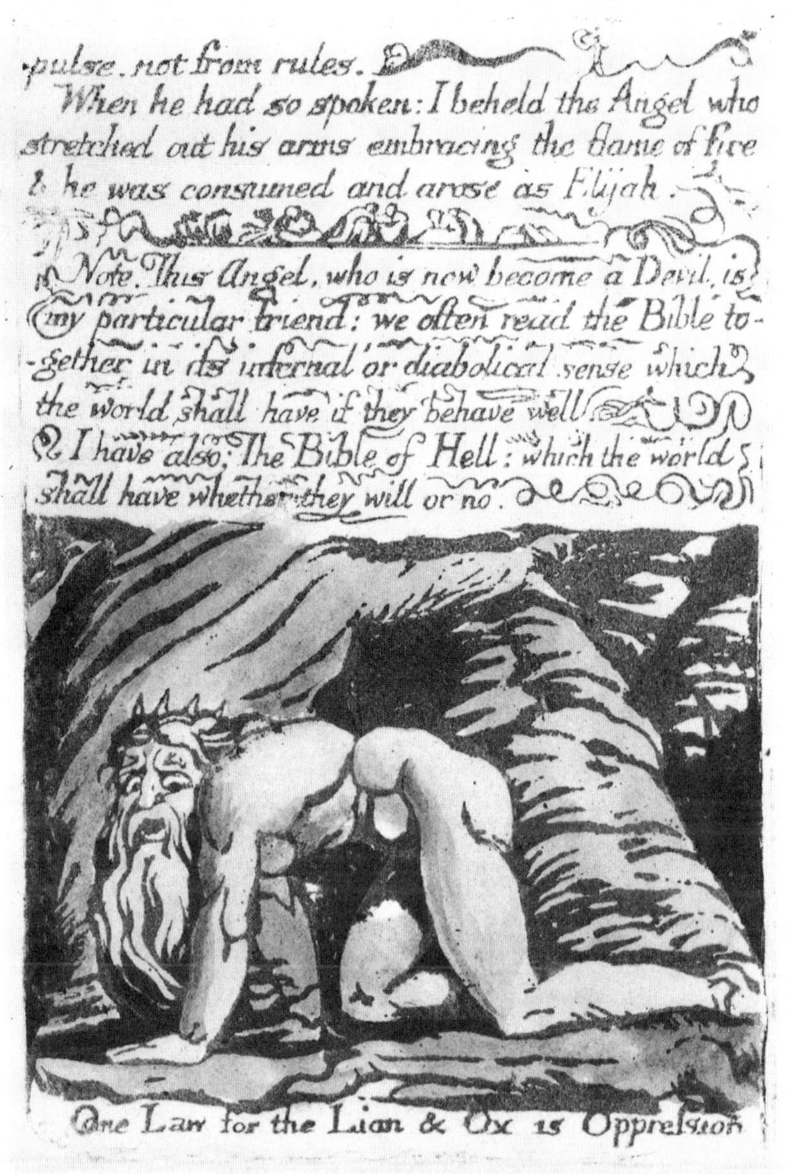

Figure 2. (opposite) Vignette used for plate 24 of *The Marriage of Heaven and Hell*, Notebook, page 44 (British Library, MS. Add. 49460).

Figure 3. (above) *The Marriage of Heaven and Hell*, copy C, plate 24, second state (Pierpont Morgan Library, PML 17559).

as first printed would probably have included its vignette, and/or the vignette in the Notebook would probably have had text, or some indication of its placement in the design. Instead of transferring or copying the appearance of a page already designed, Blake designed his page *while executing it,* combining his raw materials—text and image—for the first time on the plate itself instead of on paper.

To assume, then, that Blake counterproofed texts—which preserves the direction of the original—while drawing illustrations directly on the plate—which reverses the original—is to assume not only that he could not write backward but also that he was completely indifferent to the relation of text and illustration that he supposedly had designed on paper and was attempting so fastidiously to reproduce in metal. Rather than complicating the composing process with anachronisms and contradictions, we should assume that Blake treated his texts as he did his illustrations. He did not need to prepare a fair copy for a compositor any more than he needed to prepare a detailed drawing or page design for himself. He merely needed to rewrite his texts—however they were first prepared and in whatever condition—legibly (albeit backward) on the plates, placing word and image at the same time, using the same brushes and pens, the tools of "the Painter and the Poet" (E 692). Thus, Blake probably never had what he did not need, a fair copy of an illuminated book, let alone a manuscript divided according to its final form on plates; he did not know—or need to know—the length of any of his illuminated books when he began to etch their plates. In the case of the *Marriage,* where the bibliographical evidence indicates that units were executed at different times (see below), Blake presumably ended up with an assortment of texts written at different times, probably on various sizes and kinds of paper, but never a fair copy of a completed manuscript. As with his other illuminated books, Blake did not know the number of plates the *Marriage* would require until after it was executed.

Blake's technique and tools allowed him to combine the raw materials of text and image on the plate to produce original page designs, as opposed to reproducing or facsimilizing preexistent designs. The amount of text written on a plate, the line breaks, letter size, line spacing, and the size and place of illustrations were not predetermined by a mock-up of that page; they were aesthetic decisions made during production, which ensured the marriage of invention and execution.[15] The tech-

15. Such decisions included where text would be positioned on the plate. When space was not a problem, Blake would begin the first plate of a section or unit with a vignette and, if space permitted, he also ended with one. He would also begin texts that he knew would run short with vignettes (e.g., *Marriage* plate 3). But when the fit looked tight, he would begin writing at the top of the plate (e.g., plates 12–13). Blake may have given the text for plates 21–24 four plates to keep it from being cramped, but this also may be a sign that Blake intended a four-page pamphlet, that is, intended to print on a conjunct sheet of paper that could be folded into a pamphlet. The first printing of plates 21–24 was in fact in this format (see below).

nique also allowed Blake to begin etching plates as soon as he had completed writing a section or chapter—that is, upon completing an autonomous textual unit, or one that he thought was auto-nomous at the time—should he want to. This unprecedented interplay between graphic execution and textual composition is easily seen in the structure of *Songs of Innocence, Milton,* and *Jerusalem.* The first work consists of independent texts whose various lettering styles indicate various plate-making sessions; the second was printed circa 1811 in two books but was dated 1804 by Blake and begins with the ambitious prediction that it will be complete "in 12 Books," indicating that production began long before the text itself was completed; and the last work, which was also dated 1804 though not completed until circa 1820, has two sets of plate numbers etched in the metal, the result of Blake's inserting plates and changing his mind about the book's organization.

Being able to execute and design plates before completing a manuscript made it technically possible for Blake to think and work outside the letterpress paradigm—if not also to conceive of producing a disjointed work like the *Marriage.* It made it possible for a text to progress through production, with sections produced at different times and out of order. However, if it is credible that plates 21–24 were the first unit of the *Marriage* written and executed, to describe the production of these plates as "out of order" seriously confuses the issue, for at the time of production there was no order to be out of. To assume that an order existed at this time is either to think in terms of a completed manuscript or to imagine Blake beginning the *Marriage* with only a vague idea of a disjointed, miscellaneous work of which these plates, numbered 21–24 only later, were to become part. Besides relegating invention to paper, or to the mind, such assumptions raise numerous problems. Why start here? Did Blake think this episode would make a good opening for the *Marriage,* only to change his mind later? Not likely; the "Note" announcing the forthcoming "Bible of Hell" at the end of plate 24 functions rhetorically as a conclusion, exactly as it does in the *Marriage* as a whole. Announcing a forthcoming work at the end of a publication is reasonable if the work carrying the announcement is completed, but it is very odd for Blake to have included such an announcement here if he had only a vague notion of wanting to compose a miscellaneous book. He would have had to know not only that this text was a section of something larger but also that it was the last unit of that still unwritten text.[16]

16. That Blake had the *Marriage* committed to memory and thus could start wherever he wished is highly unlikely. While mentally constructing and then recording text proved an effective mode of composing for Milton and Wordsworth, it seems very unlikely to have been employed by a poet whose memory was remarkable but who appeared disinclined to use it consciously for composing text: Blake spoke of writing "from immediate Dictation twelve or sometimes twenty or thirty lines at a time without

The "Note" contributes to the Swedenborgian satire, in that it calls to mind Swedenborg's announcement near the end of *True Christian Religion:* "Inasmuch as the Lord cannot manifest himself in Person . . . and yet he foretold that he should come, and establish a New Church, which is the New Jerusalem, it follows, that he will effect this by a Man, who not only can receive the Doctrines of that Church in his Understanding, but also publish them in Print."[17] Printing Swedenborg's text was the raison d'être of the Theosophical Society, founded in 1783 by Robert Hindmarsh and other Swedenborgians to promote "the Heavenly Doctrines of the New Jerusalem, by translating, printing, and publishing the Theological Writings of the Honourable Emanuel Swedenborg."[18] The Society was itself modeled after the Manchester Printing Society, which began in 1782 to print and publish Swedenborg's works in English. The Swedenborgian New Jerusalem Church emerged in January 1788 from a splinter group of the Theosophical Society led by Hindmarsh. Publishers, including Blake's friend Joseph Johnson, typically announced forthcoming books at the ends of pamphlets, but the Swedenborgian context suggests that Blake had Hindmarsh in mind.[19]

Blake's "Note" ends in the middle of the plate, but instead of starting another episode he left the space blank, printed it in that state, and then added a vignette, creating a second state of the plate (see below). He is clearly thinking of plates 21–24 as an autonomous unit, but, as will become clear, it was probably not one of several units he was then planning to write but rather the unintended model for what he was to write. Blake's "Note" ends a text that at four plates in length was nonetheless the second-longest work in illuminated printing when it was written in 1790. The longest was *The Book of Thel,* which, as we will see, appears to have consisted only of plates 2–7, with just five text plates, at that time. At four pages, then, the autonomous text attacking Swedenborg would not have seemed unusually short for Blake to print as an indepen-

---

Premeditation & even against my Will" (E 729); and of writing "when commanded by the spirits and the moment I have written I see the words fly abo[u]t the room in all directions—It is then published and the Spirits can read—My MSS [are] of no further use" (G. E. Bentley Jr., *Blake Records* [Oxford, 1969], 322). Thus he appears to acknowledge an immediacy to his composing that undermines the hypothesis that he invented lengthy texts entirely in his head before executing them.

17. Emmanuel Swedenborg, *True Christian Religion,* 3d ed. (London, 1795), n. 779.

18. See Robert Hindmarsh, *Rise and Progress of the New Jerusalem,* ed. Edward Madeley (London, 1861), 7.

19. Hindmarsh listed Swedenborg's books in translation, in Latin, and in press at the end of pamphlets and books. He began advertising *The Wisdom of Angels Concerning Divine Providence* in 1789 as "Now in Press . . . 6s. to subscribers and 7s.6d. to nonsubscribers." It was published in 1790. Unlike the other Swedenborgian books he read, Blake annotated his copy of *The Wisdom of Angels* very critically (see Viscomi, "The Lessons of Swedenborg"). He also priced the *Marriage* at 7s.6d. (E 693).

dent work. The earliest and only extant independent printing of plates 21–24, known as *Marriage* copy K, strongly supports this hypothesis.

✑ *Marriage* COPY K: PAMPHLET, PROOFS, OR INCOMPLETE *Marriage?* ✑

Plates 21–24 were printed in black ink on both sides of one conjunct half-sheet with a bottom deckled edge.[20] The sheet was folded to form a pamphlet with the following configuration: 21/22–23/24. These four monochrome prints are not proofs (a correction to the views we expressed in *Early Illuminated Books*, 115; and see Viscomi, *Blake and the Idea of the Book*, 394 n. 10), despite their ink color and uncolored condition and the presence of two first-state plates (21, 24). Plates 22 and 23 were printed together as an inside forme and were carefully registered onto the paper and aligned to one another by eye. They were printed first, with plates 24 and 21 printed as the outside forme and registered by eye to plates 23 and 22, so that the lines of text on recto and verso of the leaves roughly align. There would have been no reason for Blake to take such pains with his printing if he were merely pulling working proofs—that is, checking to see if the design is finished or stands sufficiently in relief, or if the printing pressure is correct—but it is perfectly appropriate for producing illuminated pamphlets and books.

More revealing still, the borders of all four plates were carefully wiped of ink so that they would not print, a practice Blake followed almost without exception when printing illuminated books between 1789 and 1795.[21] In preparing itaglio plates for printing, printers wiped clean the beveled edges to ensure

20. *Marriage* copy K is now bound, but whether the paper was conjunct or not must be inferred. It now appears that its plates were printed on both sides of two similarly sized leaves, but this is unlikely, since both leaves share the same bottom-deckled edge and have the same inside measurement—that is, are the same height at the fold in the binding—but have slightly different outside measurements. (The left side of the half-sheet is 24.5 cm; the middle, at the fold, is 23.85 cm; the right edge is 23.7 cm; the top is 29.2 cm; and the bottom is 28.95 cm.) It seems more likely that Blake used a slightly uneven sheet of paper cut approximately 24 by 29 cm from a much larger sheet (Viscomi, *Blake and the Idea of the Book*, 394 n. 11); when folded, it formed a neat pamphlet of four pages without needing to be professionally bound. *Marriage* copy L, which consists only of plates 25–27 ("A Song of Liberty"), provides another example of this style of printing, since it too was printed on one sheet of paper folded in half to form a pamphlet (see note 22).

21. By "plate borders" I mean the thin relief line surrounding the illuminated plate that was created where the edges of the plate were covered by strips of wax in order to "dike" the acid that was poured on the plate's surface. The portion of metal covered by the wax was protected and thus, like the acid-resistant text and design, remained in relief. Blake used the borders as part of the overall relief-line system that supported the ink dabber, preventing it from touching and thereby blemishing the shallows, which were designed to remain white, that is, unprinted.

an aesthetically pleasing platemark (the plate's embossment into the paper); wiping the borders of relief plates is an adaptation of this practice—though its effect was the erasure of the tell-tale signs of graphic reproduction—because relief plates were printed with less pressure and did not leave pronounced platemarks. This erasure transforms an otherwise overt imposition of metal onto paper into an image that looks as if it were drawn by hand on the paper, executed spontaneously like sketch and autograph. Printing relief plates to appear like manuscript pages would have been unnecessary if Blake's intent was merely to proof.

Only one other textual unit in the *Marriage* was printed with this kind of care and attention—and it too was produced as a pamphlet. "A Song of Liberty," which consists of plates 25–27, was independently printed at least twice. These printings are referred to as *Marriage* copies L and M; the latter is untraced but described in a 1918 Christie's catalogue (see Bentley, *Blake Books,* 287); the former is now in the Robert N. Essick Collection (figure 4). Copy L consists of three uncolored impressions that were printed in black ink, with wiped borders, on a conjunct sheet of laid paper folded in half, forming a four-page pamphlet: 25/26–27. (They are not proofs, but are the only extant illuminated impressions on laid paper [a correction to our statements in *Early Illuminated Books,* 115; and Viscomi, *Blake and the Idea of the Book,* 394 n. 10]). Plates 25 and 26 were carefully registered recto-verso so that their lines are aligned; facing plates 26 and 27 are equidistant from the paper's top edge and the center fold. Plate 25 is in its first state; plate 27 is in a second (and final) state.[22] Though printed separately at least twice, "Song" may not have been issued as a pamphlet—or at least, despite its potential for separate printing and issue, no such copies are extant. The extant and untraced copies both appear to have passed through John Linnell's family, which indicates that they remained with Blake until at least 1818, when he met his young patron (see Bentley, *Blake Books,* 301). Yet, while these two copies were apparently not issued, one cannot infer from the absence of other copies that the

22. The untraced *Marriage* copy M is described in the 15 March 1918 Christie's catalogue, lot 198, as missing the last eight lines on plate 27—that is, the "Chorus." This absence suggests that the plate was in its first state, with the bottom third of the plate still unetched. As in the first state of plate 24 in *Marriage* copy K, the unetched area would have remained in relief and would have had to be either wiped of ink or masked over during printing. Plate 25 in copy M is presumably in the first state. Like copy L, copy M was printed in black ink and was uncolored. It is described in the Christie's catalogue as "octavo," whereas copy L was described as "quarto." These descriptions do not refer to printing formats, and the different descriptions do not necessarily mean that copies L and M were different sizes or that the latter was not also printed as a pamphlet or on laid paper. What the Christie's cataloguer considered "octavo" is not known, nor is it known whether copy M was trimmed.

Figure 4. (opposite) *The Marriage of Heaven and Hell,* copy L, plates 26–27 (collection of Robert N. Essick).

hurl'd the new born wonder thro' the starry
night.
11. The fire, the fire, is falling!
12. Look up! look up! O citizen of London
enlarge thy countenance; O Jew, leave coun
ting gold; return to thy oil and wine; O
African! black African! (go. winged thought
widen his forehead.)
13. The fiery limbs, the flaming hair, shot
like the sinking sun into the western sea.
14. Wak'd from his eternal sleep, the hoary
element roaring fled away;
15. Down rush'd beating his wings in vain
the jealous king; his grey brow'd councel-
lors, thunderous warriors, curl'd veterans,
among helms, and shields, and chariots
horses, elephants: banners, castles, slings
and rocks,
16. Falling, rushing, ruining! buried in
the ruins, on Urthona's dens.
17. All night beneath the ruins, then
their sullen flames faded emerge round
the gloomy king,
18. With thunder and fire: leading his
starry hosts thro' the waste wilderness

he promulgates his ten commands,
glancing his beamy eyelids over the
deep in dark dismay,
19. Where the son of fire in his eastern
cloud, while the morning plumes her golden breast,
20. Spurning the clouds written with
curses, stamps the stony law to dust,
loosing the eternal horses from the dens
of night, crying Empire is no more!
and now the lion & wolf shall
cease.

Chorus

Let the Priests of the Raven of dawn,
no longer in deadly black, with hoarse note
curse the sons of joy. Nor his accepted
brethren whom, tyrant, he calls free; lay the
bound or build the roof. Nor pale religious
letchery call that virginity, that wishes
but acts not!

For every thing that lives is Holy

"Song" was never issued; by that logic, the unique copies of *The Book of Los* and *The Book of Ahania* demonstrate that those works were never issued. We can say with reasonable assurance that whatever his original intentions for the "Song," Blake attached it to the *Marriage*. These three unillustrated pages of twenty numbered statements and "Chorus" read—and look—like a coda. As we will see, "Song" was probably written after the *Marriage's* first twenty-four plates, appears to have been generated in part by the *Marriage's* theme of a new age (plate 3), and is the size of *Marriage* plates because it was executed using materials left over from the production of the *Marriage*.[23]

Textual and visual features of plates 21–24 also support the hypothesis that the plates were intended as a pamphlet. The absence of a catchword on plate 24 implies that Blake did not anticipate subsequent plates; there is also no catchword on plate 20, suggesting that plates 21–24 were also composed independently of the preceding textual unit, plates 16–20. The text is polemically coherent, with well-defined objectives: to undermine Swedenborg's credibility and to champion Blake and his positions. The former objective required Blake to refute the New Church's essential claims that it was "distinct" from the old and that it was founded on the true or "internal sense" of Scripture (resolutions 1, 12–15, 17, 29, 32; *Minutes*, 126–29). The latter required Blake to position himself as an authentic visionary and offer his own readings of the Word. The attack also belongs to a turning point in Swedenborg's English reputation, when his "news from the spiritual world" was wearily dismissed by his critics but eagerly awaited by his followers.[24] The awareness by both camps of Swedenborg's claims that he spoke directly with angels provided the requisite context for Blake's seemingly unprepared-for first sentence on plate 21: "I have always found that Angels have the vanity to speak of themselves . . ." (see Viscomi, "Lessons of Swedenborg").[25]

23. The model for "Song," at least in tone, may have been the "Song of Deborah" in Judges 4, as pointed out to me by Morton Paley. The oracular tone and mood, though, also point to Blake's *French Revolution*, which Blake was presumably writing at the time; it is dated in proofs "1791" (possibly a projected date), and printed as a sixteen-page pamphlet. Its pages were stabbed through three holes like an illuminated book.

24. *Analytical Review* 5 (1789), 382.

25. E. P. Thompson notes that "against the argument that this is not Blake's voice but a provocative voice reading Swedenborg in an 'infernal' sense . . . it should be recalled that he was to rework many of the same themes some years later and in his own voice in 'The Everlasting Gospel'" (see E. P. Thompson, *Witness against the Beast: William Blake and the Moral Law* [Cambridge, 1993], 173). I concur. While it is safe to define the various "I's" of the Marriage as narrators, personas, or speakers, and not Blake himself— in that language itself prevents it from being otherwise and the visions depicted are fictitious—I refer to the speaker of plates 21–24 as Blake because the Bible of Hell he announced as forthcoming was Blake's, as was the personal anger and disappointment with Swedenborg. The tone resembles that found in Blake's

The unit is structurally and rhetorically as well as polemically autonomous. Its three features—statement, "Memorable Fancy," and "Note"—provide the well-defined beginning, middle, and end of the rhetorically complete pamphlet. The unit begins with an entrance whose objective is to catch the audience's attention and an exposition that sets forth the facts, defines the terms, and presents the issues to be proved. The entrance is beautifully and yet confrontationally realized by Blake's "divine humanity" (figure 5); the exposition consists of distinct paragraphs forcefully explaining why Blake thinks Swedenborg is neither original nor new. The following section, in which an angel and devil debate the nature of God, functions as the confirmation, in that it sets forth through the two parties the arguments for and against Swedenborg's idea of God, the central issue dividing the two visionaries. The devil wins the debate, as is evinced by the angel's conversion. The text ends with a "Note" that teasingly promises more infernal readings if the world should "behave well," while confidently announcing Blake's future project, whether the world "will or no." As first written and printed, with Nebuchadnezzar missing, the "Note" was the entire conclusion; it restates Blake's basic premise that "infernal" is better than "internal" sense, and it leaves the reader wanting—or fearing—more. With the addition of the vignette, exposition and confirmation are framed by a visual and verbal entrance and conclusion.[26]

Moreover, the three-part structure of plates 21–24 differs from other units in the *Marriage*. In the other units with these features, the "Note" (on plates 6 and 17) was placed *before* the Memorable Fancies, thereby preventing the full closure effected by a Note. And no other unit in the *Marriage* works as autonomously or, when finished, returns the reader to its beginning. Plates 21–24 effect this kind of closure both thematically and materially. The concluding announcement on plate 24, that "I have also: The Bible of Hell," returns the reader to the "I" and the resurrected figure on plate 21. When reading the four plates on a folded, conjugate

---

private writings—particularly the satiric verses and epigrams—the Public Address, and the prefaces in *Milton* and *Jerusalem*. Blake's speaker is a mask, but it is the mask of authority that Blake wears presenting himself as critic and equal of Swedenborg; he continues to do so, I believe, in the subsequently composed episodes and Memorable Fancies, where the speaker identifies himself as a printmaker and writer who believes in the Poetic Genius and his own prophetic role. The distance between speaker and author is always a matter for critical debate; here, I consider it quite narrow, deliberately transparent—as is appropriate for a manifesto or prophetic proclamation—and playful. For the view that Blake never "speaks straight" see Harold Bloom, "Dialectic of *The Marriage of Heaven and Hell*," in Bloom, ed., *William Blake's* The Marriage of Heaven and Hell (New York, 1987); and for the view that the *Marriage* lacks an authoritative voice, see Robert F. Gleckner, *Blake and Spenser* (Baltimore and London, 1985), 71–116; and Andrew M. Cooper, *Doubt and Identity in Romantic Poetry* (New Haven, Conn., 1988). See also n. 51 below.

26. These four parts represent Aristotle's reduction of the seven parts of the classical oration; see Richard A. Lanham, *A Handlist of Rhetorical Terms* (Berkeley and Los Angeles, 1968).

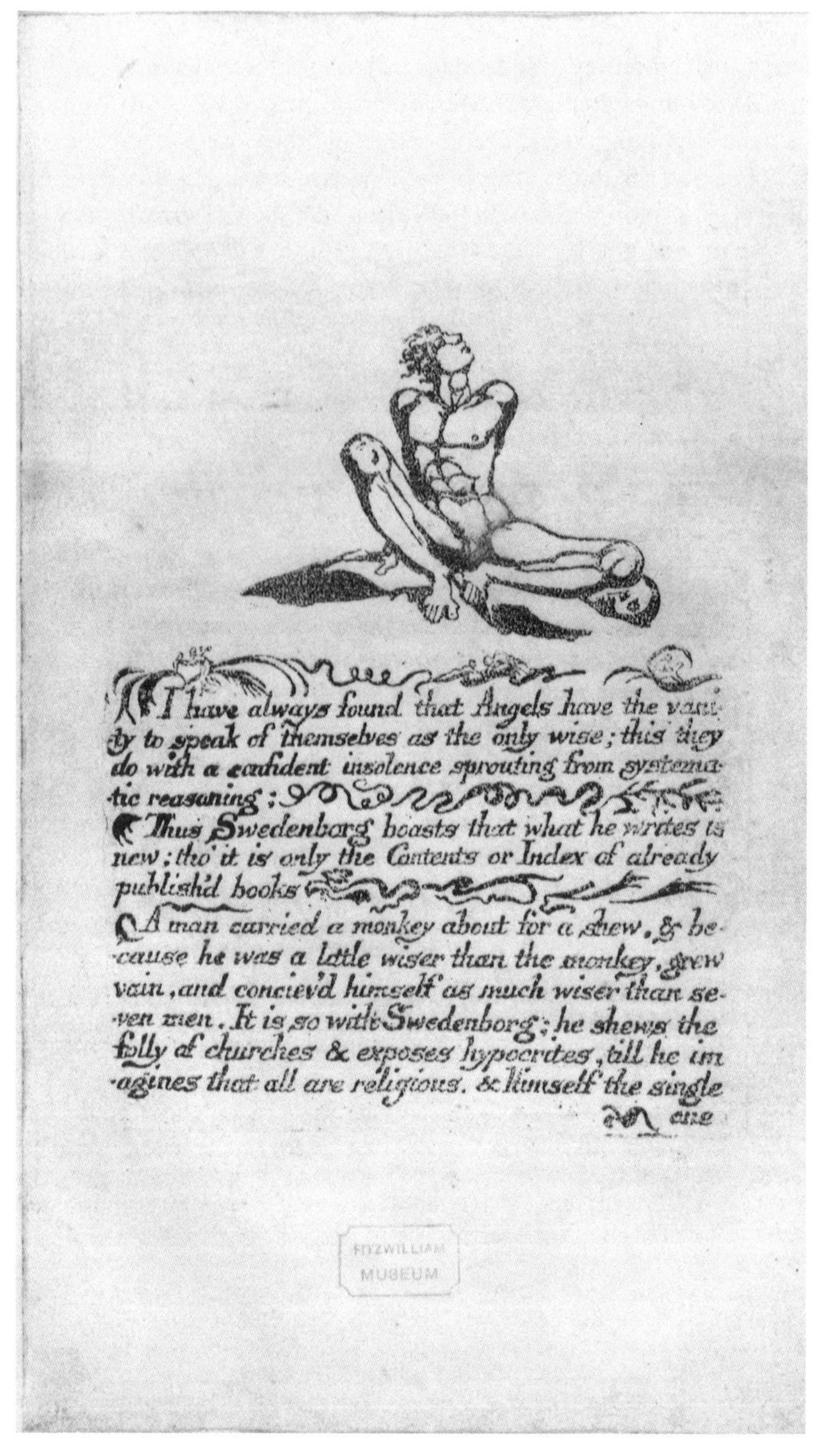

Figure 5. *The Marriage of Heaven and Hell,* copy K, plate 21, first state (Fitzwilliam Museum).

sheet—that is, as a pamphlet as in *Marriage* copy K—the reader would return physically to plate 21 after reading plate 24; flipping to the beginning moves the reader from defeated tyranny and oppression to the liberated New Man. The same movement occurs if the pamphlet is opened when one reads plate 24, in which case plate 21 would be on the right, facing 24 (see figures 5, 3).

As we can see, the claim that plates 21–24 were the *first* of the *Marriage's* twenty-seven plates written *and* executed is certainly plausible: nothing in the content of plates 21–24 refutes the possibility; and no technical facts now known about illuminated printing contradict it. The division of the *Marriage* plates according to the formation of the letter *g* into three distinct sets significantly strengthens it.

✣ THE LETTER G AND THREE SETS OF *Marriage* PLATES ✣

David Erdman was the first to notice that Blake moved the serif of his *g*s from the right to the left.[27] In Blake's first illuminated books, *All Religions are One* and *There is No Natural Religion* (both 1788), Blake used a roman script with a right-serifed *g;* in "The Argument" (plate a3), he also employed the sans-serifed, italic *g* that he used in his manuscripts, including *Island in the Moon* (c. 1784) and *Tiriel* (c. 1789). Blake used the roman right-serifed *g* in all but two of the poems in *Songs of Innocence;* he used the sans-serifed *g* in the title of "Night" and the text of "The Voice of the Ancient Bard."[28] He used the sans-serifed *g* in all *The*

---

27. David V. Erdman, "Dating Blake's Script," *Blake Newsletter* 3 (1969): 8–13 at 12; see also E 801; and Bentley's counterargument, "Blake's Sinister 'g,' from 1789–93 to ?1803," *Blake Newsletter* 3 (1969): 43–45.

28. Blake also used the right-serifed *g* for "A Divine Image" and "To Tirzah," two poems intended for the *Songs of Experience* (1794). Erdman dates the former poem circa 1790–91 because of the lettering style; I would suggest circa 1789–90, and that the origin of "A Divine Image" lies in Blake's rejection of Swedenborg. The poem's counterpart, "The Divine Image" in *Innocence,* appears to be a "simple and orthodox statement of the central doctrine of the New Church" (Kathleen Raine, "The Swedenborgian Songs," in Harvey Bellin and Darrell Ruhl, eds., *Blake and Swedenborg: Opposition Is True Friendship* [New York, 1985], 78); but it too may be anti-Swedenborgian; see Thompson, *Witness against the Beast,* 146)—a thesis supported by Erdman's hypothesis that *Innocence* was issued later than its 1789 date (E 791). If so, the poem and its *Experience* counterpart may be closer to the date of plates 21–24, in which there are clear echoes of the early 1790 issues of the *New Jerusalem Magazine* and of reviews of Swedenborg in mid-1790 issues of *Analytical Review* (see Viscomi, "Lessons of Swedenborg").

    Erdman dates "To Tirzah" post-1803 (E 800), the date he believes Blake returned to his right-serifed *g,* while Bentley dates it 1797 (*Blake Books,* 414–17). If the lettering styles indicate dating parameters and do not overlap, then both of these dates are incorrect. The poem appears in copies of *Songs* printed circa 1795 (Viscomi, *Blake and the Idea of the Book,* chap. 29) and was most likely written around the time of "A Divine Image." Both poems express anti-Swedenborgian sentiments (see Thompson, *Witness against the Beast,* 149) and could have been written as early as circa 1789–90. Both were executed on the versos

Book of Thel plates except 1 and 8, which is to say, on plates 2–7, the core of the narrative. (The first and last plates of *Thel* have long been recognized as additions to the core narrative [E 790], but I have argued that they were added sooner than has been proposed; see Viscomi, *Blake and the Idea of the Book,* chap. 25, and below). *Thel* plate 8 has both sans-serifed *g* and the new left-serifed *g;* the sans-serifed *g* was occasionally used with a serifed *g*—right and left—in the *Marriage* as well (for example, plates 21 and 26 [see figures 5, 4]), but no plate in *Thel* and only plate 7 of the *Marriage* has both kinds of serifed *g.* The leftward *g* replaced the rightward *g* during the production of the *Marriage,* and the sans-serifed *g* dropped out altogether in the next illuminated books executed, *Visions of the Daughters of Albion* and *America, a Prophecy* (both 1793). The right-serifed *g* reappeared for the major epics, *Milton* and *Jerusalem,* begun in 1804, long after all the early illuminated books were executed.

Why the rightward *g* reappeared is not known. The reasons for abandoning it in favor of a leftward *g,* however, and using the latter consistently for years, seem easier to determine. Erdman does not propose a reason, but it seems evident that the change ensured aesthetic consistency in the script, for the serifs (when present) on other letters, such as *b, d, h, l, k, p,* and *t,* lean leftward. They do so because Blake began the letter with a pen stroke moving to the letter's stem, which is to say, moving in the same direction that the hand moves while writing (this is true whether writing forward or backward). A rightward serif on the *g,* however, requires a backward/downward stroke if the *g,* like the other letters, was to be written without lifting the pen; or it required an upward stroke moving in the direction of the hand but added to the letter last, requiring a two-step gesture. The leftward serif, then, allowed Blake to start his *g* at the serif and to write it, like the other letters, in one continuous act (stroke/serif, top loop, stem, bottom loop). Once adopted, the new *g* was consistently used because it was easier and more efficient to make and, equally important, its style and execution were continuously reinforced by the style and execution of the other letters.

Erdman believes that Blake changed his *g* in early 1791, while working on the *Marriage.* Consequently, because *Thel* plates 1 and 8 have this new *g,* he believes that *Thel* was not finished until 1791 (E 790). Erdman is correct that work on the two books overlapped (see below), but the overlap probably took place in 1790. As

---

of *Innocence* poems: "To Tirzah" is on the verso of "A Cradle Song" plate 1, and "A Divine Image" is on the verso of "Infant Joy." Bentley recognized the first pair but recorded "The Sick Rose" as being on the verso of "Infant Joy" (*Blake Books,* 382). A close examination of the shapes of the plates, however, reveals that this is impossible and that "A Divine Image" is on the verso.

previously argued, the evidence for extending the period of the *Marriage*'s production beyond 1790 is weak. Erdman also proposes that the *Marriage* plates can be divided into sets according to the style of their *g;* again, he is correct, but he incorrectly identifies the sets and misinterprets their meaning.

Erdman discerns two sets of plates in the *Marriage:* plates 2, 3, 5, 6, 11, 12, 13, 21, 22, 23, 24; and plates 4, 7, 8, 9, 10, 14, 15, 16, 17, 18, 19, 20, 25, 26, 27 (E 801). But in this scheme, the plates with the earlier type of *g* are not sequential, nor are they the first eleven plates of the book. Why, then, do they share the same *g?* According to Erdman, "after Blake had a complete version of *The Marriage* (probably minus the 'Song') on copper, he began thinking of improvements and amplifications . . . and made them by inserting new plates, onto which old and new matter were inscribed (at a time when he had changed his g)."[29] Erdman proposes, in other words, that Blake completed writing and executing the *Marriage* plates before or by early 1791, when he believes that Blake introduced his new *g,* and that Blake continued to make changes for the next few years that required remaking—and thus rewriting—entire plates.[30] The plates sharing the early *g* are from the original "complete version," those that were not replaced. What was on the plates that were replaced is impossible to determine, because no impressions are extant. Hence, Erdman can argue that Blake worked on the *Marriage* for three years—though during most of that time he may have been merely fine-tuning the text—and at the same time make no attempt to trace the text's evolution. Plates with leftward *g*s simply replaced plates whose texts may have been either mostly the same as the replacement's or completely different.

Although this hypothesis does not address the issue of plate chronology, it does subtly suggest that the *Marriage*'s final form was affected by execution, by the remaking of plates—a suggestion possibly meant to account not only for the change in lettering style but also for the *Marriage*'s disjointed structure. Nevertheless, the hypothesis proposes a composing process so impractical and costly— with Blake replacing over 50 percent of his earlier work—that it is surely mistaken on economic grounds alone. Mostly, though, it misreads the bibliographical evidence because it fails to recognize the flexibility built into illuminated printing. Blake could execute plates as soon as text became available. In this light, text with the earlier lettering style reflects the first parts of the *Marriage* written and etched, and text with the latter style reflects portions written and

29. Erdman, "Dating Blake's Script," 12.
30. Erdman also states that *Thel* plate 8 is probably a replacement for "an earlier version" (E 790); it is also clear here that he thinks that the composing and etching of illuminated books are sequential (and presumably causal) events.

etched later. Lettering style, combined with narrative integrity, can be used to identify sets of plates and the textual units within those sets, which is the first step in tracing the evolution of the *Marriage*. Inspected in this manner, the plates form three sets, instead of two, that can be sequenced (sets A, B, and C).

Set A consists of plates 2, 3, 11, 12, 13, 21, 22, 23, and 24. Plates 2, 3, and 11 are self-contained units, meaning that their texts do not carry over to other plates. Plates 12 and 13 constitute "A Memorable Fancy" as a self-contained unit. Plates 21–24 are an autonomous unit that includes another Memorable Fancy. Plate 12 has a catchword, and this indicates that its text continues and ends on plate 13; plates 21, 22, and 23 have catchwords, indicating that they are part of a larger narrative, which ends on plate 24. Plates 13 and 24 do not have catchwords, nor do plates 2, 3, or 11; they neither acknowledge nor anticipate subsequent plates—which is to say, the plates that now follow these may or may not have been extant when these were produced, and may or may not have been produced immediately after them. The first set of plates, then, appears to consist of five autonomous units (2; 3; 11; 12–13; 21–24).

Set B consists of plates 5, 6, 7, 8, 9, and 10, which form three interconnected and continuous textual units, with catchwords on all but the third and last plates. The three sections include "infernal" readings of *Paradise Lost* and the *Book of Job* (plates 5–6), the narrator's trip to hell (plates 6–7), and the Proverbs of Hell (plates 7–10). These six plates form a set that can be sequenced after set A: the text carries over to plate 6 and from plate 7; and plate 7 (figure 6) has in its first line the rightward *g* used on plates 5 and 6—which, however, is immediately followed by the leftward *g* used on plates 8–10. Plate 7, integral to this group of plates, is thus a transitional plate, making the entire set transitional as well.[31]

Set C consists of plates 16, 17, 18, 19, and 20, which, like plates 21–24, constitute one autonomous unit, with "A Memorable Fancy" written and situated as an integral part of the text. Catchwords appear on all but plate 20. These plates have the leftward *g* exclusively and form a narrative unit, including Blake's and the angel's trips to the leviathan's abyss and the cannibalizing monkey house.

Sets A, B, and C are not difficult to identify, and the sets so constituted indicate that plates 21–24 were among the first *Marriage* plates written and executed. But the constitution of the three sets also raises new questions: where do plates 1, 4, 14, 15, 25, 26, and 27 belong? Plate 1 is the title plate and has no lowercase *g*; plates 4, 14, and 15 have the leftward *g* and are autonomous textual units, although each has some direct thematic tie to hell and/or the devil (see below). And plates 25–27 also have the leftward *g* and form the autonomous textual unit

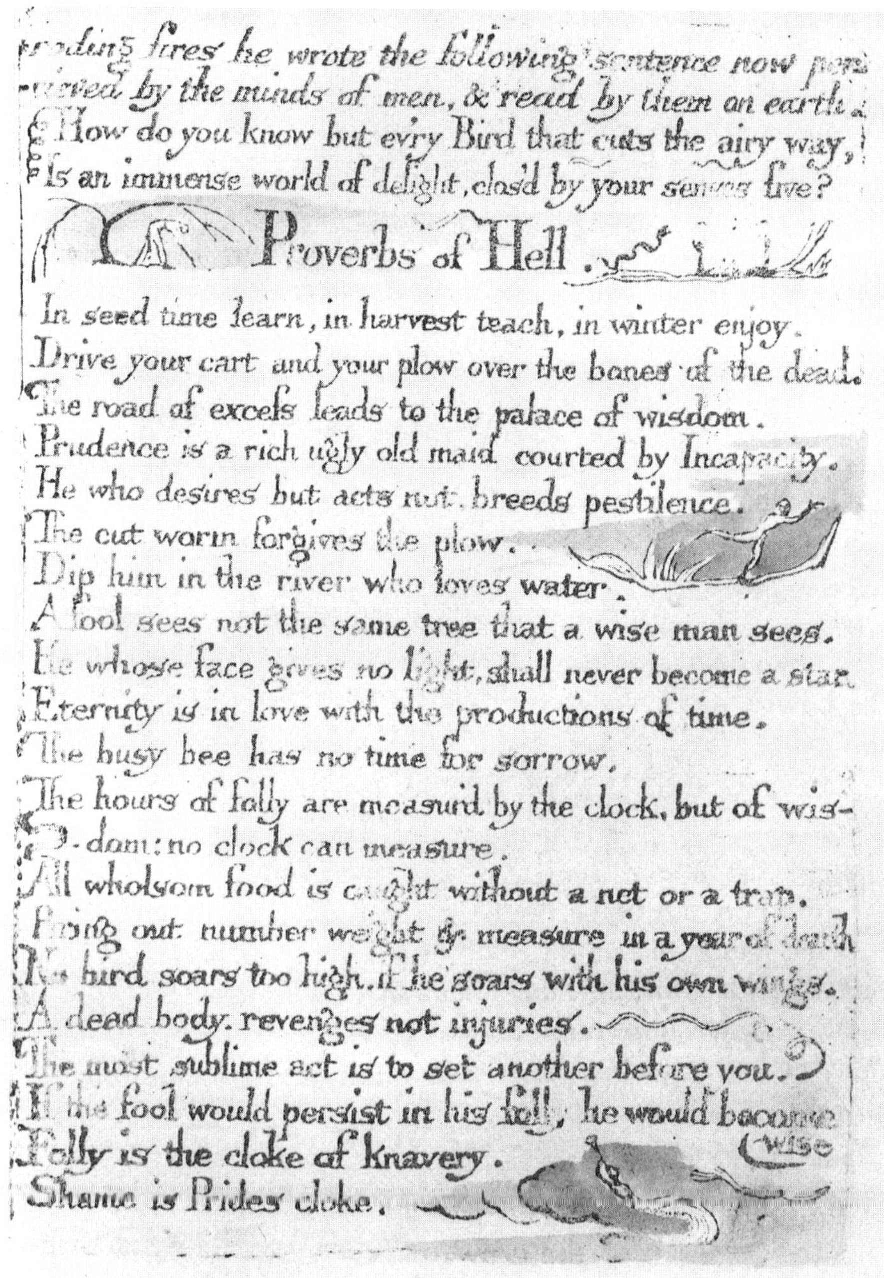

Figure 6. *The Marriage of Heaven and Hell,* copy C, plate 7
(Pierpont Morgan Library, PML 17559).

31. Plate 7 is the only plate within a textual unit without a catchword. It is an odd omission in an otherwise consistent pattern, but the omission does not support Erdman's argument that the plate was a replacement—he calls the first rightward *g* a mistake ("Dating Blake's Script," 12; cf. Bentley, "Sinister 'g,'" 44)—because a replacement would have been able to include the first word of the subsequent plate.

known as "A Song of Liberty." Were these plates produced along with the set B or set C plates? After plate 10 but before plate 16? Or after plate 20? Or were plates 1, 4, 14, and/or 15 produced after plates 25–27?

We can now begin to determine where these plates belong and, more importantly, to recover the production chronology of all the plates. This may seem like a tall order indeed, but these objectives are realizable if we examine fully the bibliographical and technical evidence.

Reconstructing the Sheets of Copper Used in the *Marriage*

The style of script provides a material basis for classifying *Marriage* plates and establishing the roughest kind of production sequence. The copper on which the script lies provides even more information.

Most illuminated plates were etched on both sides. That Blake used both sides of his plates can be inferred from the presence of platemaker's marks, which were stamped into the verso of the sheets, visible in impressions from *Experience, Urizen, Europe,* and elsewhere. The versos of the *Innocence* plates, for example, were used for *Experience;* the versos of the *Marriage* plates were used for *Urizen;* the versos of *America* were used for *Europe.* The plates that are recto-verso can be identified by shared measurements (see Bentley, *Blake Books,* 145, 167, 382, on the likely pairing of plates). In intaglio graphics, etching the versos of plates still in use was extremely unusual, because designing, etching, or printing the verso places the recto on the workbench, brazier, or press bed, where it can be scratched. Scratches on intaglio plates, like all incised lines, hold ink and thus print as blemishes. When the design is in relief, however, lines slightly incised across it usually fill with ink and do not show; if they do show, it is as fine white lines that can be filled with pen and ink or covered over with watercolors. For aesthetic reasons, then, etching both sides of an intaglio plate is highly unorthodox, but these considerations do not apply to relief etchings, and thus Blake could take full economic advantage of this practice.

Blake also saved money on materials by etching over old designs—that is, over discarded etchings or engravings—which he presumably purchased from platemakers at a reduced price. *Jerusalem* plate 47 (figure 7), for example, was drawn and written over an etching; it is important to note that Blake did not erase the intaglio line system but simply drew over it, using it as a patterned ground, knowing that the white lines of the previous design would not interfere with the bold relief outline and that alterations could be made if necessary when coloring the impression. And it is equally important to note that he did erase the incised lines in the area he used for text, a decision probably more practical than aesthetic, since the text was written with a pen, which requires a smoother ground than the brush used for the illustration. Removing the underlying line system makes it easier to write with a pen and easier for the small letters to be read. Blake did not try to erase the entire design, but only those areas required by his new page design. The erasure was presumably accomplished by burnishing the incised lines and then possibly hammering up that area from the back (a technique called *repousage*)—assuming its verso was not to be used.[32]

Perhaps Blake's most astute economic decision—and presumably one open to other printmakers as well—was to cut his small plates from larger sheets of copper himself. The *Innocence* plates, for example, are quarters of larger sheets (see Viscomi, *Blake and the Idea of the Book,* chap. 5). Blake cut plates out of sheets using relatively simple methods, such as deeply scoring the hand-hammered sheet of copper with a needle and burin and then snapping it between two plates or boards; or cutting the sheet in half with a hammer and chisel on an anvil.[33]

The *Marriage* plates are quarters of sheets the size of *The Approach of Doom* (approximately 30 by 21 cm). *Doom* (figure 8), in fact, was quartered, and these were used for *Marriage* plates 12, 13, 20, and 27. We know this because on the versos of these plates are *The Book of Urizen* plates 27, 5, 14, and 16. The white lines from *Doom* can still be seen in *Urizen* plates 27 (figure 9) and 14, revealing that the plates are the top- and bottom-left quarters of *Doom* respectively. When flipped upside down, plate 16 fits neatly into the top-right quarter, and very faint traces of the earlier design are visible in some impressions. The only *Urizen* plate that fits the bottom right quarter is plate 5, a surprise at first, because this means that its text was written over relief lines and shallows (the white areas of the figures' robes). But *Doom* was probably etched very shallowly, for nothing more is required of plates whose relief lines are dense or closely arranged, and, as noted with *Jerusalem* plate 47, Blake could plane textured ground to accept text. Moreover, the impression of plate 5 in *Urizen* copy D shows slight traces of the earlier design. In the other impressions, these traces are obscured by color printing and/or washes added to the print. Also, when reconstructed, the bottom-right corner matches that of *Doom;* corners of sheets were usually rounded (from slightly, as here, to markedly, as in most of the *Job* plates) by the commercial platemaker.

---

32.   Other illuminated plates engraved over erased designs include *Jerusalem* plate 96, engraved over the advertisement for "Moore & Co."; see David V. Erdman, "The Suppressed and Altered Passages in Blake's *Jerusalem,*" *Studies in Bibliography* 17 (1964): 1–54 at 36–37. *On Homers Poetry* appears also to have been etched over a used plate (Bentley, *Blake Books,* 335), as were two of the *Job* plates (G. E. Bentley Jr., "Blake's *Job* Copperplates," *Library* 26 [1971]: 234–41).

33.   Ernest Lumsden, *The Art of Etching* (London, 1925), 28.

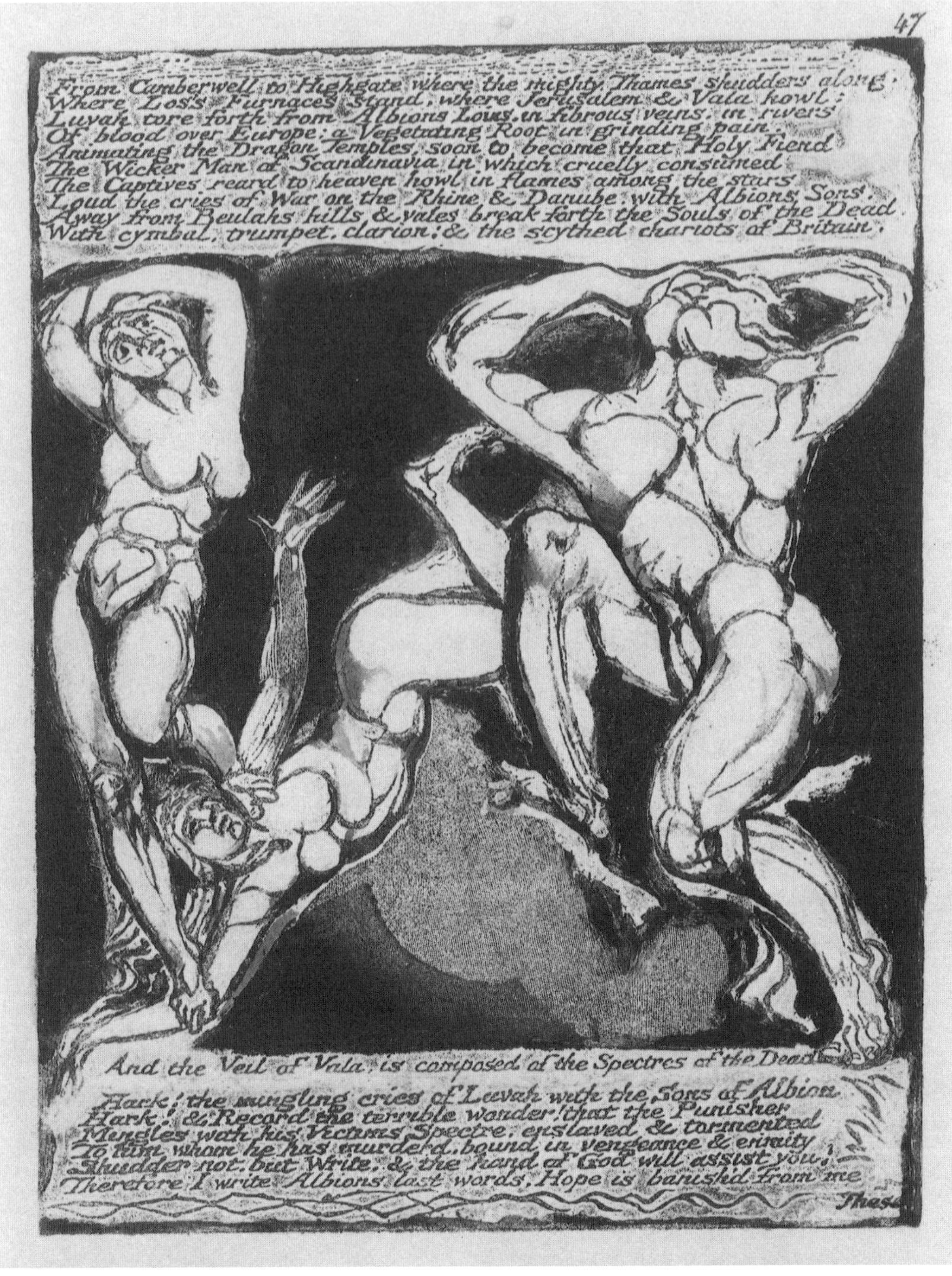

Figure 7. *Jerusalem,* copy F, plate 47 (Pierpont Morgan Library, PML 953).

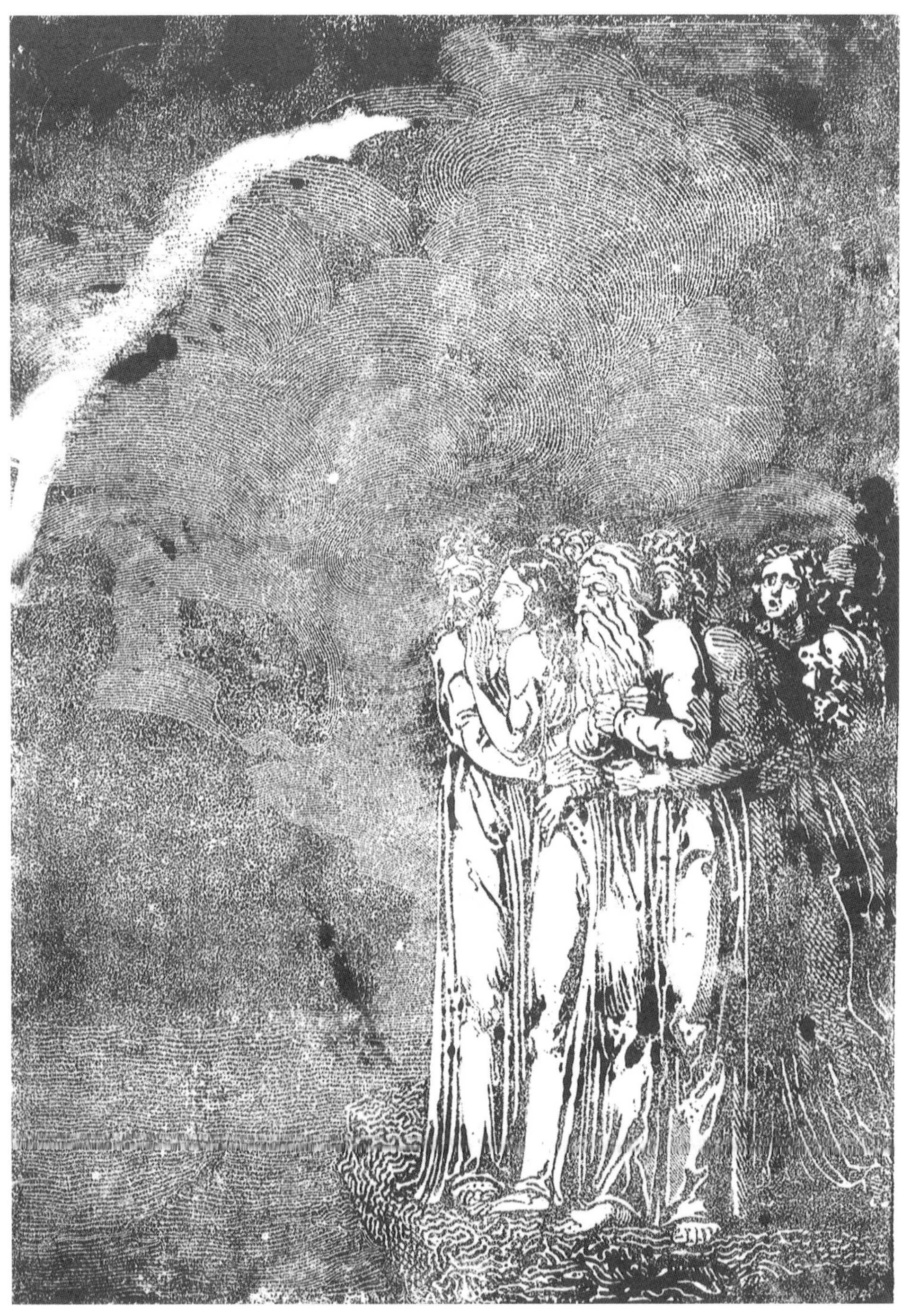

Figure 8. *The Approach of Doom* (British Museum Print Room).

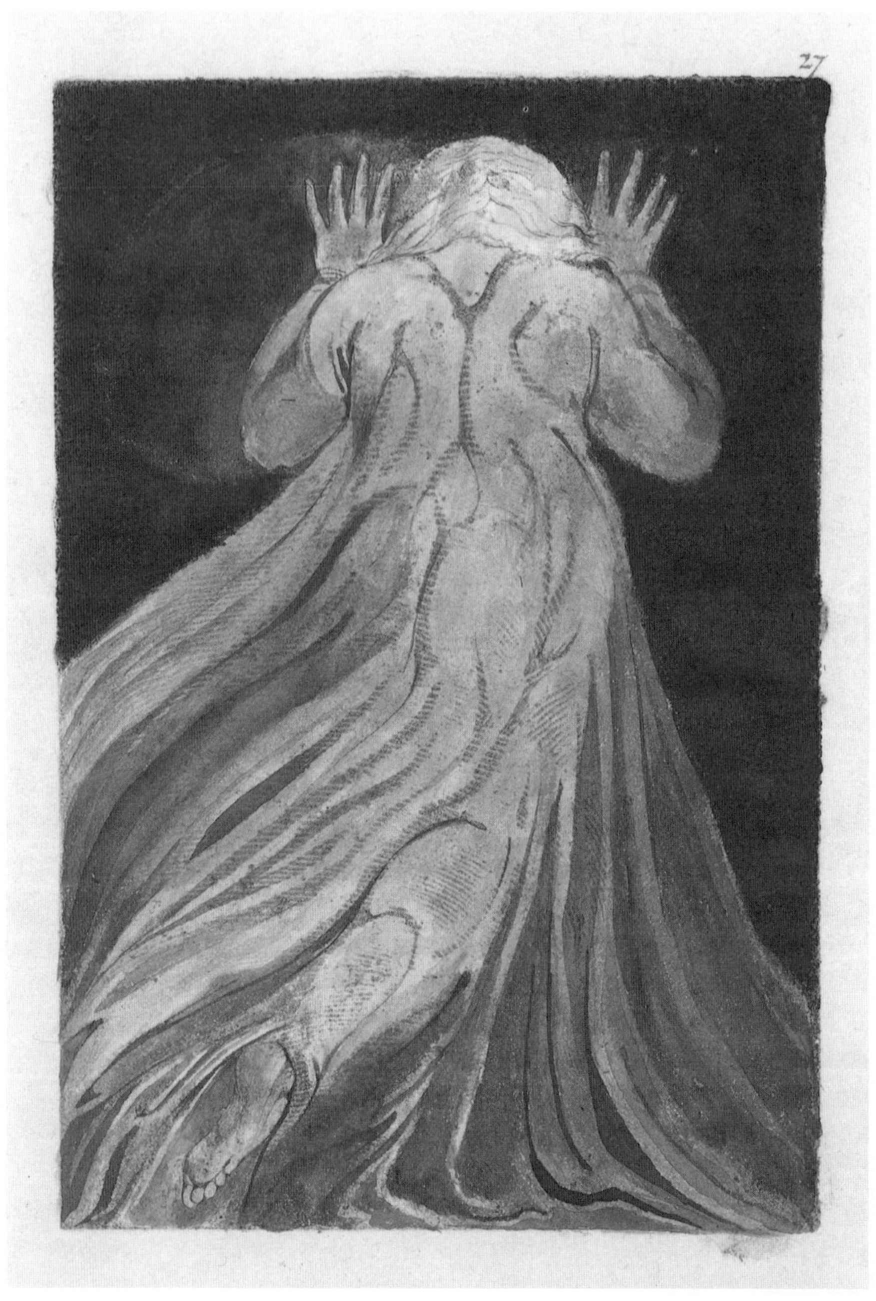

Figure 9. *The Book of Urizen,* copy B, plate 27 (Pierpont Morgan Library, PML 63139).

The quartering of *Doom* provides crucial information about how Blake cut his sheets into plates and about the kind of variants we can expect when trying to reconstruct those sheets. *Doom* is recorded as being 29.7 by 21 cm (Bentley, *Blake Books,* 167 n. 1). These measurements are close but not exact and actually give the wrong idea of the plate's shape. They imply that the sides are the same length and the top and bottom are the same width, and they hide the slight bowing out across the plate's middle. But the plate was not a perfect rectangle, as the four measurements for *Doom* reveal: 21.25 cm (top); 21.02 cm (bottom); 29.80 cm (right); 29.95 cm (left). The sheet was first cut in half vertically, and then its two vertical halves were cut in half (see below, and the appendix, diagram 1). All four quarters are different sizes and, like the parent sheet, imperfect rectangles, from which we can infer that the three cut-lines were estimated by eye rather than measured with a ruler. These variations from perfect rectangles allow us to reconstruct the parent sheet and determine which quarter was used for each *Marriage* plate.

From reconstructing *Doom*, we learn that correctly reconfigured quarters form the same shape as the parent sheet, with a variation of only a few millimeters. The variation in size is minimal, to be sure, especially given the crude method of cutting sheets into plates and the loss of metal due to cutting. Variation also exists among impressions pulled from the same plate. Indeed, plate sizes are inferred from the plate's slight embossment into paper—that is, from impressions—and impressions from the same plate may vary slightly in size because different printing papers absorb more or less dampness and shrink differently.[34] By measuring the plates of seven copies of the *Marriage* and six copies of *Urizen*, I discovered that plate measurements could vary from impression to impression as much as 3 mm, but the shape of the plate (and hence the fit of the quarters) almost always remained the same because the paper shrank evenly. For example, if the top of the plate was wider than the bottom, that relation remained, despite variation in the measurements between different impressions.[35]

34. *The Approach of Doom* exists as a unique impression, had various impressions been pulled from this plate as from the *Urizen* plates, they would no doubt vary, and one of them may have been even closer in size and shape to the four combined *Urizen* plates.

35. The quartering of *Doom* also reveals that Blake did not bevel his relief plates or carefully round their corners. In intaglio graphics, because of the great pressure required to transfer an incised design to paper, rough and unbeveled edges and sharp corners could easily rip the paper (at worst) or produce an aesthetically distracting platemark (at best). Because printing pressure in relief graphics is minimal, Blake did not need to worry about pronounced platemarks or ripping his paper. Hence, he cut his plates and left them as cut, presumably removing any remaining burr but not beveling the sides. Leaving the edges of plates rough, a feature that now assists in reconstructing the sheets, saved time and labor and thus made practical sense. But

We learn from the quartering of *Doom* that sheets could be cut either verti-cally to produce two long halves that were then cut in half, or horizontally into two wide halves that were then cut in half. The two plates cut from one *vertical* half will share the same *width* (bottom and top of the two resulting plates) but rarely the same length; together, though, they will be the same length (or within 1 mm of it, depending on the variance of the impressions measured for the recon-struction) as the combined length of their paired vertical half. Likewise, the two plates cut from a *horizontal* half will share the same *length* (right and left margins of the resulting plates) but rarely the same width; together, though, they will share the same width (or within less than 1 mm) as the combined width of the sheet's other horizontal half. Because of these proportional relations, the quarter plates cannot be arranged into sheets arbitrarily; a plate must share its width or length with another plate, and then those two plates together must share their combined width or length with another pair of plates. The probability, then, that four plates forming a sheet are the plates originally cut from that sheet is quite high.

We also learn that the sheets of copper Blake started out with were often ir-regular, and combined with his method of cutting plates from sheets and esti-mating the cut-lines by eye, this irregularity explains why illuminated plates are slightly uneven—not perfectly rectangular, and never uniform within a book. Consequently, four measurements must be made to describe accurately the shape

Blake behaved the same way with some of his intaglio plates, like those in *The Book of Ahania* and *The Book of Los.*

Bentley states that the versos of the *Ahania* plates were used for the *Los* plates (*Blake Books,* 113), and I had concurred, adding that the six *Ahania* plates came from the recto of one sheet of copper (*Blake and the Idea of the Book,* 414 n. 26). Upon closer examination of *Ahania* and *Los,* however, I realize that Bentley and I were mistaken. The six plates constituting *Ahania* came from one beveled sheet of copper quartered, with plates 1 and 2 (title and frontispiece) on the versos of plates 6 and 3 respectively. The five plates of *Los* are quarters from a beveled sheet the same size, with plate 1 (title) on the verso of plate 4. This configuration makes much more sense than the one I first proposed, because the designs executed on the versos of plates are without text and were heavily color printed, which would hide any scratches picked up during production, whereas text plates would have their white background jeopardized. The sheets used for *Ahania* and *Los* had four rounded corners and can be reconstructed because each of their quarters has one round corner. What is so surprising is that Blake, contrary to graphic conventions, did not proceed to round the three other corners of each intaglio plate. He left them sharp, or cut off (or pounded down) their points, but made no effort to file them round or to bevel the edges. It is this cava-lier attitude toward his printing that earned him Muir's dubious compliment, that he was a printmaker who displayed "skilled carelessness" (G. E. Bentley Jr., "'Blake Had No . . . Quaritch': The Sale of William Muir's Blake Facsimiles," *Blake: An Illustrated Quarterly* 27 [summer 1993]: 4–13 at 6).

of an illuminated plate.[36] By closely measuring all four sides of the *Marriage* plates, and noting the shape and any distinguishing marks in the platemarks—a convex or concave edge, a slight nick or swelling inward or outward, or corners that are round, pointed, dull, or cut—I began to piece together the quarters and reconstruct the original sheets, much as one would a jigsaw puzzle.[37] Most of *Urizen's* plates are on the versos of the *Marriage* plates, and knowing the measurements and distinguishing marks of the former helped me to verify the latter's plate configurations.[38]

On the next page is a table of reconfigured sheets based on minute examination of *Marriage* copies A, C, D, E, F, G, and I, and *Urizen* copies A, B, C, D, F, and G. In addition to measuring all four sides of the plates, I also traced in most cases the right and left margins and used the tracings to find and verify the plate's pair in the half-sheet and each plate's position in the sheet. (For the measurements

36. The plate sizes recorded by Bentley (*Blake Books,* 67–70) and David Bindman (*The Complete Graphic Works of William Blake* [London, 1978]) differ from one another because different books were measured and because papers shrink differently. But neither set of measurements can be used to reconstruct sheets because each set includes measurements for the top and right margins only; this yields an accurate sense of the plate's size but not a record of its shape.

37. This information, along with the variation among impressions, is also used to identify the pairs of plates etched recto-verso. The plates were flipped over either vertically or horizontally. To verify pairs, I traced a platemark of one plate, flipped the tracing over vertically or horizontally, and laid it on the platemark of the second plate. If the two plates were etched recto-verso, the platemarks match. (My list of paired *Marriage* and *Urizen* plates differs only slightly from Bentley's; see note 38.) What is not reliable is the shape of the corners. They help in reconstructing the sheet, but because plates are three-dimensional objects, a plate's corner can be pounded down so that it prints roundish, while the same corner from the verso will print square, thereby producing a difference that does not necessarily prove different plates.

38. *Marriage* plates 1, 3, 4, 11, and 23 appear not to have been used for *Urizen. Blake Books* adds *Marriage* plate 19 to this list, but plate 19, according to its shape and tracings (see note 37), was more likely paired with *Urizen* plate 21, which Bentley lists as being paired with *Marriage* plate 16 (pp. 166–67). *Urizen* plate 2, which Bentley lists as having no pair, is probably on the verso of *Marriage* plate 16. Bentley also suggests that *Urizen* plates 12 and 22 and plates 17 and 26 are recto-verso. This is possible, but these paired plates may also have been halves of a sheet, which is especially likely for the latter pair, since their width across the middle differs by 2 mm. From a printing perspective, it makes more sense to have two separate plates to ink than one that has to be turned over during the printing session. Only *Urizen* plates 6 and 19 have no match whatever; the latter has a platemaker's mark (in the rock to the left of the woman's leg), which Blake designed around and gouged out. Apparently, plate 19 is on the verso of a used plate. As will be shown, the *Marriage* plates not used for *Urizen* came from three different sheets; they may have been unused because of irregularities in the copper or because they contained deeply stamped platemaker's marks, or marks less advantageously placed. (On Blake's ability to conceal or incorporate such platemaker's marks in his *Europe* designs, see Michael Tolley, "The Auckland Blakes," *Biblionews and Australian Notes and Queries* 25, no. 2 [1967]: 6–16.)

of the *Marriage* plates, see the appendix.) The plates are repositioned as quarters: an upside down *A* next to a plate indicates that the plate fits upside down; an arrow between the vertical or horizontal halves indicates that sheet was first cut vertically or horizontally, respectively. The second column shows the probable *Urizen* plates that are on the versos of the *Marriage* plates reconstructed into sheets. The *Marriage* sheets are identified as I–VII and are sequenced according to the A (rightward *g*), B (rightward *g* and leftward *g*), and C (leftward *g*) sets discussed earlier. Lowercase *x* refers to a blank quarter; uppercase *X* refers to a quarter that had already been cut and used; lowercase *o* refers to a quarter whose identity is indeterminate.

From this evidence, we can conclude that Blake used seven sheets of copper to produce the *Marriage*. Had all of them been cut into plates at the same time— as his sheets of paper were when he printed his illuminated books in small editions—then the resulting twenty-eight plates, each one a quarter of a sheet,

		Marriage	*Urizen*	
A	**I**	22 ǀ 24 ∀ ←	15 ǀ 10	
		∀ 23 ǀ 21	x ǀ 11	
A	**II**	↓ 12 ǀ x verso	27 ǀ x	
		x ǀ 13 verso	x ǀ 5	
A	**III**	↓ ∀ 2 ǀ 3	28 ǀ x	
A B		1 ǀ 5	x ǀ 18	
B	**IV**	6 ǀ 7 ←	20 ǀ 24	
B A		∀ 8 ǀ 11	7 ǀ x	*Urizen* plate 7 has etched lines = used plate
B	**V**	↓ 15 ǀ 9	23 ǀ 8	
		14 ǀ 10 ∀	3 ǀ 4	*Urizen* plate 4 has etched lines = used plate
C	**VI**	17 ǀ 16 ←	13 ǀ 2	
		19 ǀ 18 ∀	21 ǀ 25	
C	**II**	↓ X ǀ x	X ǀ x	
		20 ǀ X verso	14 ǀ X	
	II	↓ X ǀ 27 ∀ verso	X ǀ 16	
		X ǀ X	X ǀ X	
	VII	25 ǀ 26	9 ǀ 1	
		o ǀ o	o ǀ o	

would almost certainly have been stored as a group. The plates forming multiplate units, such as plates 21–24, or 5–10, or 16–20, would have been chosen from that large group and would not consistently come from the same or sequential sheets of copper. But because the plates forming multiplate and contiguous units do indeed form sheets, the sheets were most likely cut in preparation for those units—that is, cut as needed rather than cut in advance for a long, let alone twenty-seven-page, manuscript. That plates 21–24 form one sheet substantially verifies the hypothesis that these plates were written and executed as an autonomous unit (see appendix, diagram 2); to support the hypothesis that this autonomous unit preceded the others as an independent, anti-Swedenborgian pamphlet, it is necessary to prove that its sheet was the first one cut, which is the objective of the following section.

In reconstructing the seven sheets, I found just one anomaly: plate 11 is among the set B plates. I expected to find it cut from sheet III, which yielded plates 1, 2, and 3—the other set A plates. Instead, plate 11 was cut from sheet IV, along with plates 6, 7, and 8. It does not belong to their unit, which contains the Proverbs and their introductory material, but like plate 6, plate 11 has the right-serifed *g*, whereas plates 7 and 8 have the left-serifed *g*. From its place in the sheet sequence, plate 11 appears to have been executed between plates 6 and 7, after the story of usurpation and Milton that begins on plate 5 and continues to the middle of plate 6; but before the Memorable Fancy that starts in the middle of plate 6 and continues with four lines on plate 7—that is, the transitional plate with both rightward and leftward *g*s. The production sequence appears to have been 5–6, 11, 6–10. Are we seeing traces of a moment of inspiration? Did Blake momentarily stop committing the Proverbs and their introductory material to copper to write and execute plate 11? Or had he brought that text to the printshop along with the texts for plates 1, 2, 3, and 5–10? These nine plates seem to have been executed in the same session (see below).[39]

39. In "The Caves of Heaven and Hell," I suggest that plate 11 appears to have been inspired by four topics: Adam's return to Paradise, Reason's usurpation of desire, heaven's derivation from the "Abyss," and misreadings of Milton's poetry (plates 3, 5–6). It appears also to have been influenced by the narrator's trip into the fires of creativity and the devil's message about "immense worlds of delight" possibly "clos'd by your senses five" (plates 6–7). All of these ideas figure into Blake's version of a much discussed subject, the origin of organized religion. Blake locates the origin in systematic misreadings of the ancient "poetic tales" by the "Priesthood," whose misreading resulted in the usurpation of our original and creative powers of perception.

◔ Sequencing Seven Sheets of Copper ◕

Reconfiguring the *Marriage* plates into their seven original sheets and sequencing them according to sets A, B, and C provides a rough idea of the work's evolution. Clearly, if we are to understand the genesis of the *Marriage* in greater detail, we need to sequence the individual set A plates and determine which of these plates or units was produced first. The reconfigured sheets suggest four possibilities for the first position: 1) plates 21–24; 2) plates 12–13; 3) plates 2 and 3; and 4) all or some combination of these set A plates, produced together. Of these possibilities, the first is by far the most likely. It is strongly supported by the way in which the quarters from *The Approach of Doom* were and were not used at the beginning of production, and by a process of elimination that takes bibliographical as well as linguistic codes into account.

The Approach of Doom (c. 1788), possibly Blake's first experiment in relief etching (Viscomi, *Blake and the Idea of the Book,* chap. 20), predates the *Marriage.* It was thus on a sheet of copper already on hand when Blake wrote the set A plates, but it is very unlikely to have been the first sheet cut, because only two set A plates—the textual unit consisting of plates 12–13—were cut from it. This means that two quarters were left untouched at this time, raising troubling questions: If Blake cut *Doom* for the set A plates, why did he not use all four quarters immediately? If it were cut first, why aren't two of the plates from the unit 21–24, or plates 2 and 3, on those remaining two quarters? These two unused quarters indicate that *Doom* was most likely cut after the sheet yielding plates 21–24; they also indicate that *Doom* was cut before the sheet yielding plates 1–3, and 5.

That plate 5 was executed on the fourth quarter of the sheet that yielded plates 1–3 suggests that these plates were executed near in time; that the text of plate 5 continues on a plate cut from a new sheet suggests that Blake knew the text did not end with that one plate but required more. That this new sheet (IV) yielded plates 6, 7, 8, and 11—plates with both rightward and leftward *g*s—and not any of the plates in the textual units of plates 12–13 and 21–24, indicates that sheet IV was transitional and that its four plates—and plates 1, 2, 3, and 5 from sheet III and plates 9 and 10 from sheet V—are related and were all executed after the six plates from sheets I and II.

To assume that Blake began the *Marriage* with the plates of sheet III (1, 2, 3, and 5) makes no sense technically, because it also requires that after quartering sheet III and executing plates 1–3, Blake skipped plate 5 and proceeded to quarter sheets I and II, whose plates (21–24, 12–13) also have the rightward *g* of plates 2–3. A plate sequence of 1–3, 21–24, 12–13, 5–10 means a sheet sequence of III, I, II, III, IV, V, which raises this question: why was the fourth quarter of sheet III used for plate 5 and not for one of the "subsequent" plates, that is, 21–24, or 12–13? Even if we assume that plates 5–6 were not part of the larger unit as identified here, we are faced with the same question. For example, if plates 5–6 followed plates 12–13, then why were they not written on the two remaining quarters from sheet II (*Doom*)? Why would Blake go back to sheet III for plate 5 and acquire sheet IV for plate 6? If plates 5–6 followed plates 1–3 for a plate sequence of 1–3, 5–6, 21–24, 12–13, 7–10 and a sheet sequence of III, IV, I, II, IV, V, then why weren't the three quarters from sheet IV used for the subsequent plates?

Blake is highly unlikely to have executed plates 11, 12, and 13 together as one unit, even though plate 11—about "ancient Poets" and their distorted derivative, "Priesthood"—now introduces the visionary episode about prophets, an episode that exemplifies ideas raised on plate 11. It is unlikely because, as mentioned, plate 11—along with plates 6, 7, and 8, which continue the text begun on plate 5—came from sheet IV; and plates 12 and 13 came from sheet II. Had they been written and executed together, one would expect that plate 11 would have appeared on one of the quarters from sheet II (*Doom*), or at least on a quarter from a contiguous sheet (e.g., III)—like *all* other related plates in the *Marriage*.[40]

There is a logic to using and not using materials, as is evinced by the pattern of plates that form units also forming sheets. *Doom*'s unused quarters imply a hiatus in production between sheets II (*Doom*) and III. The hiatus suggests that Blake executed the plates of sheets I and II before those of sheet III; and that when he returned to the studio to execute the next group of plates for what was now evolving into a book, he brought with him three sheets (III, IV, and V) and the texts and ideas for plates 1–3 and 5–10—and possibly for plate 11, although this may have been written and produced while Blake was executing plate 6; and he may have brought plates 14 and 15 as well. Blake either forgot he had the two *Doom* quarters or, because he knew he needed many more plates than two, began

---

40. The plate order of *Marriage* copy G, printed circa 1818, differs from all other copies. It is 1–11, 15, 14, 12, 13, 16–27. Copy G still retains the statement-narrative (or introduction, followed by Memorable Fancy) structure, but plate 11 introduces the Memorable Fancy found on plate 15, and plate 14 introduces the Memorable Fancy found on plates 12–13. This shift in the position of plates 12–13 is consistent with the hypothesis that they were not originally conceived with plate 11.

using the plates quartered from the sheets specifically acquired for his new texts.[41] Thus, the process of elimination yields the same chronology of plate production for the set A and B plates that is suggested by the reconfigured sheets of copper: 21–24, 12–13; 1–3, 5–6, 11, 6–10, followed by plates 14 and 15.

The linguistic code does not falsify this sequence; in fact, it independently suggests the same. It suggests that plate 3, with its perfunctory mention of Swedenborg, was written after plates 21–24; and moreover, that Blake almost certainly did not start with plates 12 and 13. These plates form "A Memorable Fancy," which retells the narrator's dinner with Isaiah and Ezekiel. But what is "A Memorable Fancy" and why is the narrator telling us about this visionary encounter? Three of the five Memorable Fancies in the *Marriage* are on set B and set C plates, which means that they were not yet executed. And yet the parodic intentions of plates 12–13 seem to require some preparation or context, nicely provided by plates 21–24, where Swedenborg is attacked by name; and his Memorable Relations parodied as "A Memorable Fancy."[42]

The episode on plates 12–13, in which Isaiah states that his "senses discover'd the infinite in every thing," may have been inspired by the contrary vision exemplified by Nebuchadnezzar, whose animal-like posture resembles that of the figure on plate b11 of *There is No Natural Religion* (see also the reproduction of *Nebuchadnezzar,* color plate XVI). Together, the prophets and Nebuchadnezzar—the latter symbolizing both Swedenborg and the mad King George III—dramatize the theme of plate b11: "He who sees the infinite in all things sees God He who sees the Ratio only sees himself only" (E 3). Moreover, Isaiah and Ezekiel, two prophets whom Swedenborg quotes extensively, are exactly the right witnesses to prove Blake's claims that Swedenborg's readings of Scripture are old and weak and that his ideas of Christ and the Ten Commandments are ordinary and orthodox (plates 21–23). Swedenborg says that he, like the prophets, sees angels. He also claims that

> I have been informed how the Lord spoke with the prophets
> through whom the Word was given. He did not speak with them
> as with the ancients, by an influx into their interiors, but through

---

41. Two of the three sheets of copper were old, as is indicated by traces of earlier etchings in the *Urizen* plates (4 and 7) that are on the versos of the *Marriage* plates (10 and 8).

42. Memorable Relations "contain particular Accounts of what had been seen and heard by the Author in the spiritual World, and have in general some Reference to the Subjects of the Chapters preceding them" (translator's note, in Swedenborg's *True Christian Religion*).

spirits who were sent to them, whom He filled with His look,
and thus inspired with words which they dictated to the
prophets; so that it was not influx but dictation. And because the
words came forth immediately from the Lord, they are each filled
with the Divine, and contain within an internal sense, which is
such that angels of heaven perceive them in a heavenly and spiritual sense, when men perceive them in a natural sense.[43]

He clarifies this in *Apocalypse Revealed*, where he states that the prophets distinguished between vision and dictation, being in the spiritual state for the former and in the body for the latter: "when they spoke the Word, they were then
not in the spirit, but in the body, and heard from Jehovah Himself, that is, the
Lord, the words which they wrote."[44] Blake's prophets, however, identify themselves as "poets," affirm an internal voice, refute external instruction, and make
no distinction between vision and writing, or between spirit and sensual body.
In the *Marriage,* Isaiah says:

> I saw no God. nor heard any. in a finite organical perception:
> but my senses discover'd the infinite in every thing, and as I was
> then perswaded. & remain confirm'd; that the voice of honest
> indignation is the voice of God. I cared not for consequences
> but wrote. (Plate 12)

Isaiah ironically echoes Swedenborg's description of Adam and the ancients:

> So with the man of the Most Ancient church; whatever he saw
> with his eyes was heavenly to him; and thus all things and every-
> thing with him were as if living. From this it may be seen what his
> Divine worship was, that it was internal and not at all external.[45]

---

43. Swedenborg, *A Treatise Concerning Heaven and Hell* (1778; 2d ed., London, 1784), n. 76 and n. 254.

44. *Apocalypse Revealed,* in *Swedenborg's Works,* Rotch Edition, 32 vols. (Boston and New York, 1907),
     vol. 28, n. 945. He appears to contradict this statement in *Arcana Coelestia,* n. 6212 (vol. 11 in
     Swedenborg's Works): "It is known from the Word that there was an influx from the world of spirits and
     from heaven into the Prophets, partly by dreams, partly by visions, and partly by speech; . . . and into
     their very gestures, thus into those things which are of the body; and that then they did not speak from
     themselves nor act from themselves, but from the spirits which then occupied their body. Some at such
     times conducted themselves like insane persons, as did Saul when he lay naked." See I Kings 19:24; and
     compare Isaiah's going "naked and barefoot three years" (*Marriage* plate 13).

45. *Arcana Coelestia,* in *Swedenborg's Works,* vol. 2, n. 920.

Blake will advocate a return to this visionary state on plates 3 and 11, with the return of Adam to Paradise and the mythopoeic perception of the "ancient Poets."

Writing as "poets" without fear of consequences contrasts starkly with the "systematic reasoning" of angels (plate 21); the first alternative also alludes to the poet Blake writing this prophetic prose as well as his other works, and to Christ, whom the devil defines as acting "from impulse; not from rules" (plates 23–24): behavior characteristic of the artist. The devil's and angel's debate over whether God is internal or external echoes a debate recurring in Swedenborg's writings about whether salvation depends on "faith [in Christ] alone, without the works of the law—which faith is mean by the dragon"—or in Christ as well as the law (*Apocalypse Revealed,* n. 539). The debate is reconfigured on plates 12–13, where the connection of art and Christ is made explicit when the prophets state that "in ages of imagination this firm perswasion removed mountains." Christ states, "If ye have faith . . . ye shall say unto this mountain, Remove hence to yonder place; and it shall remove; and nothing shall be impossible unto you" (Matthew 17:20). By appropriating poets, prophets, and Christ for the devil's party, Blake has further defined the dialectic that unfolds on plates 21–24 between angels and devils in terms of religion and art. More to the point, he has strengthened the devil's refutation of the angel's claim that Christ sanctioned the Ten Commandments (plate 23) and strengthened his own claim that the New Church is anything but "new" and "distinct" (plates 21–22). Indeed, Blake again implies that Swedenborg misreads the Word and its prophets and thereby subjects people to false ideas, exactly like the Church he criticizes. Ezekiel states: "from [his and Isaiah's] opinions the vulgar came to think that all nations would at last be subject to the jews . . . [which] is come to pass, for all nations believe the jews code and worship the jews god, and what greater subjection can be[?]" (plate 13). The "code" refers to the "law of ten commandments" advocated by the angel and New Church but "broken" by Christ (plates 23–24). Swedenborg's worship of this code and God, then, reveals that he oppresses Christ. What Swedenborg worships confirms Blake's accusation that despite his showing "the folly of churches & expos[ing] hypocrites," he still "has written all the old falshoods" (plates 21–22). By tying Swedenborg to the very "code" the impulsive Christ rejects, Blake again refutes both of Swedenborg's claims—that the New Church is distinct from the old and that he recognizes the true Christ—and again affirms the message of plates 21–24, that the problem lies not in the Word but how it is read. Is it read diabolically or systematically, infernally or internally?

Swedenborg's God, if perceived "infernally," is revealed to be the dominating external God of the "jewish code" and as such "merely derivative," having, like "all Gods," "originate[d] in" "the Poetic Genius" (plates 12–13; see also *All Religions are One* plate 9). While Blake does not mention "poetic genius" and "origin" on plates 21–24, he implies both. The "poetic genius" is implied through the hierarchy of writings, with the "sublime" of "Shakespeare" and "Dante" representing the truly inspired works of "masters," and Swedenborg's "recapitulations" of "superficial opinions" representing mere memory and the perpetuation by followers of "all the old falshoods." The ideas of origin and originality are implied in Blake's claim that Swedenborg is a copyist and is so because he fails to consult devils who, as the origin of Blake's "The Bible of Hell," represent the "poetic genius." The idea that the poetic genius is the origin or "first principle" of perception and creativity is proposed on plates 12–13, while creativity's symbolic connection with hell will be made explicit later, on plate 6, by the narrator's trip to hell, where "fires" are "the enjoyments of Genius."

Blake started the text of plates 12 and 13 on new plates, as opposed to starting it *on* a plate as a continuation of the preceding and contextualizing text or narrative; the Memorable Fancies on plates 22, 6, and 17 begin midplate. This is consistent with the hypothesis that plates 12–13 were written and executed independently of the plates and narratives that now precede them, and were composed in light of a previously executed text that now follows them. As an autonomous textual unit, plates 12–13 seem to develop or extend contraries and themes propounded in plates 21–24, including originality and imitation, impulse and law, inspiration and memory, liberation and subjection, reading and misreading. The thematic relation between plates 21–24 and plates 12–13 places the former unit first, verifying the bibliographic code and significantly strengthening the hypothesis that plates 21–24 were not only executed first but also originally intended as an anti-Swedenborgian pamphlet. It seems reasonable to speculate that after Blake wrote and executed plates 21–24, where the Memorable Fancy is thoroughly contextualized and of a piece with the text, he began to imagine more visionary episodes in this satiric vein.

It also seems reasonable to suppose that "The Bible of Hell," which is announced *before* the *Marriage* was composed, might be referring to the *Marriage* itself, as it was anticipated at the time of Blake's anti-Swedenborgian text. Or, as I argue in "Lessons of Swedenborg," it may refer either to the Proverbs of Hell, intended as an ironic inversion of Proverbs—one of the books of the Bible that Swedenborg excluded from his list of thirty-three books of Holy Writ for "not having the Internal Sense" (proposition 12, *Circular Letter*, 122)—or to a series of illuminated works written from the infernal perspective that was to include Blake's Proverbs as the first book or volume.[46] If so, then their inclusion into the *Marriage* reflects Blake changing his mind, perhaps first planning a separate volume or pamphlet in a projected series of illuminated works but then deciding to include the Proverbs as a section of his new book. From available bibliographical and thematic evidence, then, the *Marriage* appears to have originated in two separate projects, an anti-Swedenborgian text, presumably meant as an independent work, and "The Bible of Hell," cobbled together with introductory material and a few more Memorable Fancies.

If so, that sheet I was the same size as *Doom* begins to make practical sense. The size, approximately 30 by 21 cm, was probably a common one, selected because Blake wanted the plate size it yields when quartered. He probably did not start by cutting *Doom,* because he was unwilling at the time to destroy that design. On the other hand, without a manuscript divided into pages, Blake did not know how many plates his anti-Swedenborgian text would require, given such variables as letter size, line spacing, and illustrations. He may have purchased a sheet the size of *Doom* as insurance, in case the text went long and required a fifth or sixth plate. He could then quarter *Doom* to finish it rather than purchase a second new sheet. Or he may have cut both sheets at the same time, using the plates from the new sheet first and expecting to use the plates from the old sheet for his next project, "The Bible of Hell" announced at the end of plate 24. I suggest that the temptation to broaden his satirical attack beyond Swedenborg through parodying his Memorable Relations inspired Blake to write the dinner-with-prophets episode. At this point in the action, we see a break in production, apparently followed by the writing of new texts (that is, plates 1–3, 5–11) and the eventual purchase of three more sheets.

46. According to W. M. Rossetti, Blake wrote on the verso of an undated drawing "in title-page form, 'The Bible of Hell, in Nocturnal Visions collected. Vol. I. Lambeth'" (Gilchrist, *Life of William Blake,* 2:240.2). Blake moved to Lambeth in "late summer" or "autumn 1790" (Bentley, *Blake Records,* 559, 560). Untraced since 1876 (see Martin Butlin, *The Paintings and Drawings of William Blake,* 2 vols. [New Haven, Conn., and London, 1981], 221v). This apparent sketch for a title page confirms that Blake intended "The Bible" to be a separate work, as announced in the *Marriage.* No such work is extant, but the phrase "visions collected" calls to mind "I collected some of their Proverbs" (plate 6), raising the possibility that Hell's Bible was its proverbs, that is, a collection of infernal truths or words to live by, or perhaps that it included the proverbs as part of its collection of sacred texts.

ᴥ *Marriage* PLATES LOST AND FOUND, AND *"The voice of the Devil"* ᴥ

As we have seen, the *Marriage* plates can be roughly grouped by lettering style to reveal the basic chronology of plate production, although where in this scheme plates 1, 4, 14, 15, 25, 26, and 27 belong is less easily determined. By reconstructing the sheets from which the *Marriage* plates were cut, we have exposed a deeper layer of the *Marriage's* evolution and have located where all the plates fit into the chronology. All, that is, but plate 4, "The voice of the Devil."

The first stage, in which plates 21–24 were produced, was soon followed by a second stage in which plates 12–13 were written and executed. The third stage produced plates 1–3, 5–6, 11, 6–10, including plate 1, the title page. It was cut from sheet III, which also yielded plates 2, 3, and 5, plates with the early *g*. Thus Blake etched the title page of his new work after executing at least six of its plates. This is particularly telling, given that a title page for the nonexistent "Bible of Hell" may have been designed (see note 46) and that the work had been announced on plate 24 of the *Marriage*. The position of the *Marriage* title page in the chronology of production is consistent with the theory that the work it names was not yet conceived at the time plates 21–24 were produced. Indeed, the conception of a satire of miscellaneous episodes appears to have followed the completion of the anti-Swedenborgian text and to lie in Blake's decision to combine it with his anticipated Proverbs (possibly "The Bible of Hell" or one of its volumes). Plates 12–13, the second Memorable Fancy written, appear to have been the first step in realizing this conception. The second step consisted of writing introductory texts (plates 2, 3) to the newly conceived work and texts to introduce and contextualize the Proverbs (plates 5–6). Plate 11 was executed in the same lettering style as these plates but appears to have been composed and executed after the text on plates 5–6 and before the Memorable Fancy and the Proverbs it introduces—which is to say, during this third stage of plate production.

We have found plates 14 and 15 in the chronology of plate production; both have the leftward *g* and are independent though thematically related units, filled with "information from hell," printmaking allusions, and cave imagery. Together they function as a two-plate unit of introduction and Memorable Fancy, a structure that had by this point in the composing process established itself. They were cut from the same sheet that yielded plates 9 and 10, the last two plates of the Proverbs of Hell. They were executed after plates 1–3, 5–11, but they may belong to the same stage of production, which would suggest that their texts were written along with or even during the execution of these plates. They may also, however, have been written and executed afterward, in response to previously executed texts and images, as suggested by the narrator's trip to hell, his picturing himself writing the devil's proverbs, the animated island of the ancient poets, and the cave in which the island is placed (plates 6, 10, and 11).[47] If this is the case, plates 14 and 15 would constitute a fourth stage in the evolution of the *Marriage*.

Plates 16–20 constitute the next textual unit executed. The text for this unit, he probably anticipated, required at least one sheet's worth of plates. Blake seems unlikely to have acquired sheet VI with sheets III, IV, and V, the three used previously, because at approximately 31 by 20.5 cm it was noticeably larger than these others, yielding the four tallest plates in the *Marriage*. It probably was purchased specially for this section, suggesting that the text was written after those executed on sheets III–V. The text went nineteen lines long, requiring a fifth plate (plate 20). Instead of buying a new sheet of copper, Blake returned to the third quarter of *Doom* and used it for plate 20, which is much smaller than plates 16–19—a fact (like poor registration of plate to paper) that did not seem to bother Blake (see note 35). This autonomous unit constitutes either the fourth or fifth stage of production. Blake appears to end it with a wink and a nod toward Swedenborg. Whereas the image of Nebuchadnezzar and the axiom "One Law for the Lion & Ox is Oppression" end plates 21–24, expressing Blake's anger at church and state, plates 16–20 end less aggressively: "Opposition is True Friendship." Through the course of his composition—and, one could argue, by venting his wrath—Blake appears to move from the conviction that Swedenborg symbolizes religious and political oppression to something more like gratitude for his adversary's role in generating the *Marriage,* and thus in revealing or clarifying Blake's views in his own mind. Blake sees what he has accomplished, and sees the creative import of passionate response. In the *Marriage* he not only expresses opposition but at the same time engages in the intellectual combat—or "Mental Fight" (*Milton* 2:13)—that he believed essential.

On that note, Blake apparently ended his composition. The *Marriage* now consisted of twenty-three plates, which appear to have been executed in the following order: 21–24, 12–13, 1–3, 5–6, 11, 6–10, 14, 15, 16–20.

The fourth quarter of *Doom* was used for the next, and last, textual unit, "A Song of Liberty" (plates 25–27). Because only one of its plates (plate 27) came from *Doom,* "Song" almost certainly followed plates 16–20; and because only one

---

47. The cave on plate 11 shows up in *Marriage* copies G and I, the last two copies printed, but the design was actually drawn on the copper plates and erased during printing. The same is true of the cave forms on plates 10, 15, and 20 (*Early Illuminated Books,* 135). I discuss these forms in "The Caves of Heaven and Hell."

plate remained from *Doom* at this point, the subsequent two plates (25 and 26) had to come from a different sheet. A sheet (or half-sheet) was chosen that produced plates similar in size to the last quarter of *Doom*. The size of the "Song" plates, then, may have been a matter of economic convenience and efficiency—Blake using metal on hand—or deliberately chosen so "Song" would match the *Marriage* in size as a supplementary text. As mentioned, "Song" appears to have been designed originally as an independent pamphlet, as is evinced by its two early printings (*Marriage* copies L and M). If so, then it does not really represent a fifth or sixth stage in the production of the *Marriage*—unless Blake originally intended "Song" to have a dual life, as independent text and as unit concluding the *Marriage*. It seems equally likely, though, that Blake decided to use "Song" as a "coda" soon after the production of both works.[48] The diversity of the *Marriage* could accommodate one, or many, more sections, even one with slightly larger script, new mythic characters, and numbered poetic prose, perhaps as an example of the mythopoeic prose of the "ancient Poets." Though more oracular in tone and overtly political, the "Song" fits the *Marriage* thematically. It too attacks priestcraft, kingship, the "stony law," and "ten commands," and it connects their defeat with the return to Paradise: "Empire is no more! and now the lion and wolf shall cease" (plate 27).

We have now located all of the plates in the chronology of plate production, including those missing from sets A, B, and C, except plate 4. This plate was not cut from any of the seven sheets yielding *Marriage* plates. It is the smallest *Marriage* plate (13.6 by 10.1 cm), almost 2 cm shorter on average than all the others. The exclusively leftward *g* (a correction to *Early Illuminated Books,* 114) suggests set B or set C. The plate's four sharp corners reveal that it is not a quarter sheet, which would have one dull or slightly round corner, and suggest that it was cut from the center of a sheet. But what sheet is this, and when was the plate composed? Plate 4 appears to have been executed around the time of, if not actually with, *Thel* plates 1 and 8—Thel's Motto and the concluding plate. Answering our question requires taking a brief detour through the final stages of *Thel*'s production.

Like *Marriage* plate 4, *Thel* plates 1 and 8 appear to be orphans, unconnected to the sheets that supplied plates for the larger works. By applying the methods used to reconstruct the *Marriage* sheets, we can reconfigure *Thel* plates

---

48. *Marriage* copies B and H appear to have been the first copies of *Marriage* printed (Viscomi, *Blake and the Idea of the Book,* 259–61). Both have plates 25–27 in their final states, but in both copies these plates were printed 25/26, 27, and thus are not materially connected to the preceding plates. They could have been added afterward or printed with the plates as a supplementary text that became part of the *Marriage* when the larger work was collated and stabbed.

2–7 back into their original sheet. Together, they form a roughly square sheet approximately 30.7 by 32.5 cm, in the following configuration:

$$\forall\, 4, \quad 5, \quad 6\,\forall$$
$$3, \quad 2\forall, \quad 7$$

These six plates form the core of *Thel,* and they employ the sans-serifed *g* of Blake's italic script exclusively. But a sheet that would be square rather than rectangular, and the absence of round corners on plates 6 and 7 despite their position in the sheet, raise red flags. A closer examination reveals that the six plates were probably cut from two-thirds of a 30.7 by 46.65 cm rectangle, with the missing third, 30.7 by 14.15 cm, yielding *Thel* plate 8—which is 14.15 cm long—and *Thel* plate 1 and *Marriage* plate 4, whose lengths, added to the width of plate 8, total 30.7 cm. Moreover, plate 1 has a round top-right corner and plate 8 has a round bottom-left corner, which become the sheet's top- and bottom-right corners; and the bottom of plate 4 appears to fit neatly on the right side of *Thel* plate 8 (see diagram 3 in the appendix).[49]

Plate 1 has the leftward *g* exclusively, and plate 8 has it and the sans-serifed *g,* as well as the only interlinear decorations in *Thel* (line 15)—a feature present throughout the *Marriage.* These two *Thel* plates were certainly written after the core text, but how long after is unknown. Plates 2–7 are divided into three parts, with plates 3 and 6 having catchwords and plate 5 having a catch-number, indicating only that the text continued on the next plate. Like plate 5, plate 7 ends with the catch-number IV, which merely indicates that there will be a Part IV; there is no catchword to indicate that it had been written. Apparently, Blake planned to conclude his tale with Thel entering the "house" of the "matron Clay," which he mentions on plate 7 (E 6); but if *Thel* copy a, a proof copy printed in black ink and missing plates 1 and 8, is evidence of production, then Blake had not yet written—or at least had not yet executed—the ending when he executed and proofed the core plates. While we can only guess how much time transpired

49. The versos of the *Thel* plates were not used for any other known work. The original sheet may have been a used itaglio plate, with *Thel* on its verso. If so, the strip of copper approximately 4.05 by 19.7 cm left from cutting the sheet as proposed may have contained a platemaker's mark that Blake could not work around. On the other hand, despite the excess copper, the configuration makes practical sense and reveals a consistent pattern of cutting wholes into one-third and two-thirds parts. In the first cut, two-thirds of the large sheet was cut off; this section (30.7 by 32.5 cm) was cut into six plates, which may have been all that Blake expected his narrative to require. The remaining third of the sheet (30.7 by 14.15 cm) was also cut into two pieces, a one-third piece (14.15 by 11.0 cm), which was used for *Thel* plate 8, and a two-thirds piece (19.7 by 14.15 cm). The latter piece was trimmed of 4 cm in its width, slightly less than a third, leaving a section (19.7 by 10.1 cm) that was cut into one-third (6.1 by 10.1 cm) and two-thirds pieces (13.60 by 10.1 cm). These are the sizes of *Thel* plate 1 and *Marriage* plate 4.

between *Thel* plates 7 and 8, we can be reasonably sure that *Thel* plate 8 was executed after the first and second stages and possibly after or during the third stage of the *Marriage's* evolution.

Among the *Marriage* plates that *Thel* plate 8 followed are plates 6 and 7, which record the narrator's infernal descent and the devil's message. In *Thel* plate 8, Thel too descends into the netherworld and sits besides her grave listening to the voice therein. She goes below the surface, as it were, a metaphor possibly suggested not only by the narrator's infernal visit but also by the tour he and the angel took "down the winding cavern" to "the infinite Abyss" inhabited by the Leviathan (plates 17–18). The idea that we perceive superficially—see the surface and not what lies below it—is visually expressed by the *Marriage* title page itself, where two-thirds of the design, including the words "Heaven" and "Hell," occur just below the surface, a space defined and hidden by a thin line, which, if "melted" away, would reveal "the infinite which was hid" (plate 14). Any one or all of these *Marriage* plates may have influenced Blake's depiction of Thel's descent, but it is the way her perception affects experience that seems especially close to the *Marriage*.

Like angels who see the "fires of hell" as "torment and insanity" instead of the "enjoyment of Genius" (plate 6), or see the "leviathan" instead of "a harper" singing by "a pleasant bank beside a river by moonlight" (plate 19), Thel sees the world of sexual experience as death, a netherworld filled with lamenting sounds. The angel's perception of the "fires down below," be they creative energy or sexual desire, is refuted by the narrator's leisurely stroll through hell and by the harper. Thel's perception is also disproved; like the angel witnessing the leviathan, Thel flees the scene, but the image and gestures of the tailpiece—three naked children playfully riding a very phallic, leviathan-like serpent—challenge the idea that Thel should fear her sexual desires, revealed as the true source of her restlessness in the last two questions spoken from her grave: "Why a tender curb upon the youthful burning boy?" and "Why a little curtain of flesh on the bed of our desire?" The interrogative form challenges preconceptions, and, before executing *Thel* plate 8, Blake used it to that end on *Marriage* plate 7, where a "mighty Devil" writes/etches: "How do you know but ev'ry Bird that cuts the airy way, / Is an immense world of delight, clos'd by your senses five[?]"

Thel plates 1 and 8 appear to have been written and composed at the same time and presumably came from the same sheet of copper. I think *Marriage* plate 4 was probably composed and executed with them; its top margin shares the bottom measurement (10.1 cm) of *Thel* plate 1, a strong indicator that they shared margins and were cut from the same sheet; and the bottom of plate 4 fits along the side of *Thel* plate 8 (see diagram 3, appendix). If so, then it is reasonable to assume that, just as *Marriage* plate 6 (the trip to hell) may have influenced the netherworld location of *Thel* plate 8, the idea of Thel's voice revealing the truth from the "pit" may have influenced "The voice of the Devil" of *Marriage* plate 4—or vice versa. Both plates have leftward *g*s, and in both, the "voice" knows what is hidden and symbolically represents the deep recesses of the mind.

I suspect that *Thel* plates 1 and 8 and *Marriage* plate 4 were from the same sheet of copper, a third of the sheet originally cut for *Thel* plates 2–7, but I do not know with certainty where plate 4 fits into the composition of the *Marriage*. It responds to plate 3 thematically by inverting its rhetorical structure. On plate 3, the vignettes depict the joyous copulation and laborless birth characteristic of our prefallen state ("Now is . . . the return of Adam into Paradise"), and the opening lines express Blake's optimistic anticipation of a new age, but the "religious" are given the last and seemingly authoritative word: "Good is Heaven. Evil is Hell." Plate 4 inverts this pattern, giving the religious the opening lines and vignette and the devil the last word. The vignette depicts a woman and child fleeing a man in flames, presumably the "fires of hell" as perceived by the "religious." But what the woman and child flee is no more frightening than Thel's sexually charged serpent, as the devil's voice makes clear: "Energy is Eternal Delight."[50]

Plate 4 visually echoes the relation between perception and experience as expressed on plates 5, 6, 7, 14, 16, and 20, but it explicitly corrects the last lines of plate 3: "From these contraries spring what the religious call Good & Evil. Good is the passive that obeys Reason Evil is the active springing from Energy. Good is Heaven. Evil is Hell." After plate 3, though, Blake appears to have gone on to plate 5, which attacks the idea of passivity. Its first lines state: "Those who restrain desire, do so because theirs is weak enough to be restrained . . . and being restraind it by degrees becomes passive till it is only the shadow of desire." The rest of plate 5's text and the textual unit to which it belongs (the trip to hell and the Proverbs collected there) set out to prove the "religious" wrong. By this time in the composi-

---

50. In most impressions of plate 4, a chain was added to the man's ankle, which either echoes or anticipates the chaining of the Giants on plate 16. Perhaps the chain's absence on the copper plate signifies that the plate was executed before plate 16. Its addition to later impressions of plate 4 transforms an ironic image of a devilish father-figure welcoming or releasing a child—and/or a mother-figure catching or preventing her child from flying (as in the *Experience* frontispiece)—into the struggle angels perceive between "Good" and "Evil," "Soul" and "Body," and "Restraint" and "Energy." It is also, for the reader, the struggle between Swedenborg and Blake, and the requisite oppression and demonization of the liberator. The watercolor and color-printed versions of the design, produced circa 1791 and 1795, respectively, have the chained ankle.

tion, Blake has profiled Christ, Isaiah, Ezekiel, Milton, Dante, Shakespeare, and the narrator as unrestrained figures, as active members of the devil's party. Surely, their actions and membership challenge the validity of passivity and the moral categories imposed by the "religious." Thematically, plate 4 seems unnecessary, almost ad hoc, like the Motto in *Thel*—or "A Song of Liberty" in the *Marriage*. Perhaps Blake thought his critique of the linguistic origin of what the religious call moral categories was too subtly ironic, or he simply wished to make explicit the relation between creative and procreative forces, between energy and desire.

Plate 4 continues the satire on Swedenborg by numbering the angels' and devils' particulars of faith, recalling the opening of *True Christian Religion,* where the New Church's "five particulars of faith" are presented without contraries. Plate 4 clearly responds to the "particulars" of plate 3, but a closer look reveals a relationship to other plates as well. The first error, "That Man has two real existing principles Viz: a Body & a Soul," is acknowledged on plate 14 as "the notion that man has a body distinct from his soul." The second error, "That Energy *calld Evil.* is alone from the Body. & that Reason. *calld Good.* is alone from the Soul," fuses "soul" and "body" to "Good" and "Evil," in response to plate 3's "what the religious *call Good & Evil.* Good is the passive that obeys Reason Evil is the active springing from Energy. Good is Heaven. Evil is Hell." The third error, "That God will torment Man in Eternity for following his Energies," echoes the angels' fears, as expressed on plate 6, that "The fires of hell" are "torment and insanity." On the evidence of its lettering style, plate 4 was executed after plates 3 and 6; its thematic awareness of plate 6 suggests that it was written afterward as well. But what is its connection with plate 14? Is plate 4 or plate 14 the first to question this Cartesian dualism? The union of soul and body was implied on plate 11, which precedes both plates 4 and 14 in composition; it showed that the separation of "mental deities from their objects" resulted in "Priesthood." As I propose in "The Caves of Heaven and Hell," the union of spirit and matter was inherent in Blake's incarnational aesthetic, as stated explicitly on plate 16: "God only Acts & Is. in existing beings or Men," itself a clarification of plates 22 23's "The worship of God is. Honouring his gifts in other men each according to his genius . . . for there is no other God." Contrary to Swedenborg, who believed vision required leaving the body, Blake knew as an artist that it could occur while in the body and through the physical body of art. In short, plate 4 appears to recognize more than just plate 3.

Like the texts of plates 14 and 15, that of plate 4 is short, autonomous, and thematically it is derived from hell. On plate 15, Blake states, "I was in a Printing house in Hell & saw the method in which knowledge is transmitted from generation to generation," and then proceeds to describe the book-making process in all its visionary splendor. On plate 14, Blake notes that he "heard from Hell" when "the whole creation will be consumed [in fire] and appear infinite. and holy," and implies that he, as printmaker and publisher, partakes in this apocalyptic energy. Now, on plate 4, we, like the narrator, hear news from hell, only this time we hear it directly.

In identifying the cause of the primary "Errors" as "All Bibles or sacred codes," this news from hell appears aware that the "jews code" and "ten commandments" have already been criticized on plates 13 and 23 (and 27?). The devil's "Contraries to these" errors are "True," and thus the devil implies another set of contraries, Error and Truth, which is a variation on Imitation and Original, implicit in Blake's condemnation of Swedenborg, Priests, and the "sneaking serpent," in contrast to Christ, Prophets, the "just man," and presumably Blake (plates 21, 11, 2, 3, 12–13). The corrections are indeed "True" from the devil's perspective, but there are no third parties in the *Marriage*. Blake belongs to the devil's party, and the devil and members of his party have expressed—on plates 6, 12, 13, 14, 15, and, most important, 7 and 23—what are presumably Blake's positions. On plate 7, the "mighty Devil," like Blake, speaks by writing/etching his preconception-challenging sentences "on the sides of the rock." On plate 10, he is pictured dictating the Proverbs. On plate 23, the "Devil answer'd" the angel's assertion that Christ sanctioned "the law of ten commandments," that God is an external law-giver indifferent to man, by creatively reading Christ's acts to show that "Jesus was all virtue, and acted from impulse, not from rules." The narrator witnesses the debate, which the devil, presumably speaking for Blake, clearly wins.[51]

51. John Howard notes the same, that the angels and devils are not equals, or "moral neuters," and that Blake departed from moral neutrality once he used angels and devils for satirical purposes, with angels representing the orthodox and the object of Blake's attack ("An Audience for *The Marriage of Heaven and Hell*," *Blake Studies* 3 [1970]: 19–52 at 34). Leslie Tannenbaum agrees, arguing that Blake writes as a philosophical satirist to restore Poetic Genius to its "rightful hegemony" (see "Blake's News from Hell: *The Marriage of Heaven and Hell* and the Lucianic Tradition," *ELH* 43 [1976]: 88). Cooper, on the other hand, believes that the devil's inversion of established order reifies rather than overcomes that order (*Doubt and Identity in Romantic Poetry*, 47). Cooper, though, begins with a mistaken premise. He assumes that the devil and God are contraries, but if the devil is partisan, it is on the side of God, for Christ and Jehovah, Blake states, are of the devil's party: "the Jehovah of the Bible being no other than he who dwells in flaming fire. Know that after Christs death, he became Jehovah" (plate 6). Moreover, the "marriage," or coming together of angel and devil, on plates 22–24 results in conversion (plate 24), which renders suspect the idea that contraries are equal (see Viscomi, "The Caves of Heaven and Hell"). On Boehme's role in Blake's conception of contraries and the underlying complexities of that concept as used by Blake, see Leopold Damrosch Jr., "The Problem of Dualism," in Bloom, *William Blake's "The Marriage of Heaven and Hell"*; and Thompson, *Witness against the Beast*.

Plate 4, then, while the only plate or section designated as "The voice of the Devil," is not the only occasion on which the devil speaks. And like the other debating and writing devils, he speaks with authority and conviction—and therein lies a serious critical problem. The devil is, as most Blake scholars acknowledge, a partisan, and as such cannot represent unbiased perception. Admittedly, the metaphysical framework of contraries, which can imply theoretically the "polar nature of being" as well as a "dialectical symmetry,"and thus the idea that opposing views are equally valid, occasionally undercuts Blake's authority.[52] But to assume that this was Blake's intention is to dismiss the way in which, in practice, the satiric convention of turning the world upside down loads the dice—in Blake's and the devil's favor. When plate 4 is placed within the composing process and read in light of the many plates it in fact follows, Blake's intentions for this plate and for the devil's views throughout the *Marriage* begin to reveal themselves.

On plates 4, 14, and 15, Blake presents "information from hell," but on plate 4 he does not speak for himself, nor does he use the cave imagery present in the other two plates. The script poses difficulties. The italic scripts of plates 14 and 15 closely resemble one another but differ from that of plate 4 (figure 10). In fact, the italic of plate 4 is stiff and occasionally awkward and does not closely resemble that of any of the *Marriage* plates—or the *Thel* plates, for that matter. Plate 4 does not look as though it was written with plates 14 and 15, or 16–20, or 25–27, but how long after—or before—these plates it is impossible to tell. The appearance of one's usual writing hand will vary if the writing tools and materials vary; for example, the difference could be owing to a different pen, a thicker writing solution, a more textured writing surface, or a combination of all three.

Another troubling feature of plate 4 is that it was not one of the two quarters from *Doom* left over after plates 12–13. These unused quarters suggest that there was a hiatus in production between plates 12–13 and the plates cut from the subsequent three sheets. If Blake forgot about the *Doom* quarters after a short hiatus, then it is possible that plate 4 was written around the time of plates 14 and 15 and before 16–20. These three texts required three plates and could be executed out of order. Blake wrote the texts for plates 14 and 15 on the quarters from sheet V, but instead of buying a new sheet for plate 4, he wrote it on a plate from a sheet he was then presumably cutting for *Thel* plates 1 and 8.

<hr>

52. On the polar nature of being, see Martin K. Nurmi, "Polar Being," in Bloom, *William Blake's "The Marriage of Heaven and Hell,"* 59–71 at 59; we comment on dialectical symmetry in *Early Illuminated Books*, 121.

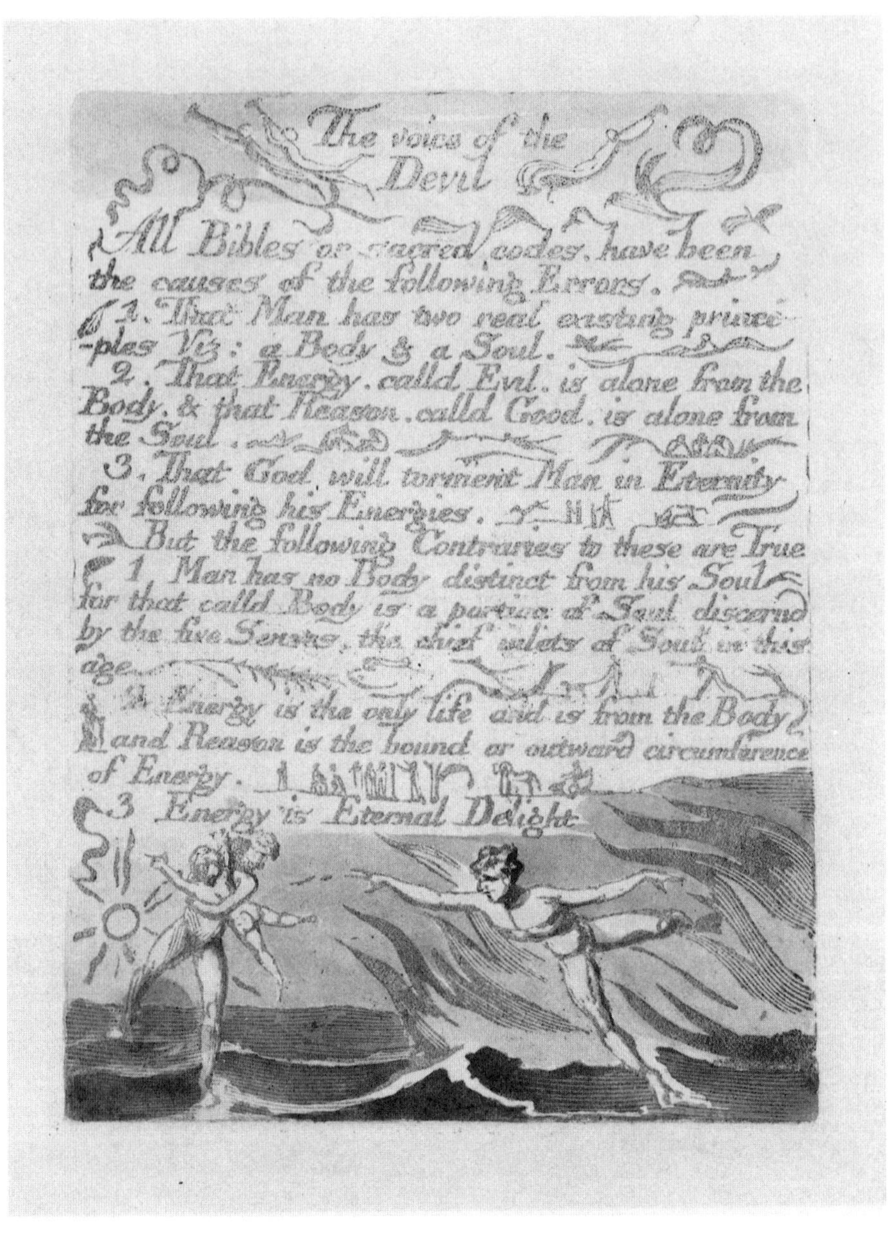

Figure 10. *The Marriage of Heaven and Hell,* copy C, plate 4 (Pierpont Morgan Library, PML 17559).

If, however, Blake remembered he had the two *Doom* quarters in stock, then plate 4 may not have been executed until after plates 16–20 *and* 25–27, for the two *Doom* quarters were used for plates 20 and 27. But this scenario suggests that plates 25 and 26 came from a sheet half the size of the others (20.8 by 14.9 cm). If the sheet had been the size of the others, there would have been two unused quarters, and one of them would presumably have been used for plate 4. Or one must imagine the half-sheet being used or cut up for other projects, none of which I have been able to identify. Unfortunately, whether plates 25 and 26 were quarters cut from a horizontal half-sheet or halves cut from a sheet half the size of the others cannot be determined.

Perhaps the most that can be said about *Marriage* plate 4 is that it was certainly not the fourth plate written or executed. Materially, it appears to have been connected with *Thel* plates 1 and 8; thematically, it appears to have been associated with *Thel* plate 8 and *Marriage* plates 14 and 15. It was introduced no earlier than two-thirds into the composition of the *Marriage*, if not added to the *Marriage* last, after "A Song of Liberty."

<h2>❧ Conclusion ❧</h2>

> "Great ends never look at means but produce them spontaneously."
> —Blake's annotations to J. C. Lavater's *Aphorisms on Man* (E 595)

The *Songs of Experience* poems were drafted in Blake's Notebook, but no separate and complete manuscript of *Experience* as a book is extant. No fair copies or even rough, partial manuscripts of any of the illuminated books are extant. There are good, legible manuscripts for *Tiriel* and much of *Vala*—works probably intended for letterpress and not illuminated printing—but not one for *The French Revolution*, which must have had a fair copy, since it was printed by Joseph Johnson. Perhaps its absence has more to do with the publisher's mishandling than Blake's. Nevertheless, one is led to wonder if the missing manuscripts of Blake's illuminated canon ever existed. Were they lost in Frederick Tatham's reputed conflagration of Blake works? Or were they the kind of manuscripts that, as Blake told Henry Crabb Robinson, were published as soon as they were written down and, once read by "the Spirits," were then "of no further use" (Bentley, *Blake Records*, 417 n. 3, and 322)?

The absence of illuminated manuscripts probably lies in reasons far less sensational or mysterious. Blake's mode of production did not require fair copies. To begin production, Blake needed text, but that text did not need to be complete.

It could consist of discrete units written at different times and on various kinds and scraps of paper, written as inspiration struck. The phrase "printed manuscript," coined by Essick to describe the illuminated book's unique conflation of print and autograph,[53] also describes the effect of illuminated printing: the printed work constitutes a completed manuscript, complete both visually and textually. This effect provides a plausible reason for the absence of the drafts and texts preceding the illuminated books. They had no authority; no one, not even Blake, "read against" them. Upon publication, they were of no further use.

The absence of drafts and manuscripts for the *Marriage*, then, is not at all unusual for an illuminated book. What is unusual is the *Marriage's* disjointed structure, its discrete textual units and diverse genres, topics, and points of view. Structurally and thematically, the work appears to have been written at different times, and in a different order from the one we have. Textual analysis, however, cannot by itself recover the chronology of plate production, without which no reasonable idea of this work's evolution is possible. When we group the *Marriage* plates according to the style of their letter *g* into three sequential sets and then reconfigure the plates back into their original sheets, the chronology of sheet and plate production begins to emerge.

The reconfigured and sequenced sheets reveal the following plate chronology: 21–24, 12–13, 1–3, 5–6, 11, 6–10, 14, 15, ?4, 16–20, and 25–27. It is at this material level that the linguistic code suggesting that plates 21–24 preceded plates 3 and 19 is verified. But the position of plates 21–24 in the chronology raises a host of questions about Blake's intentions and composing process. Why do they form one sheet? Why does that sheet seem to have been the first of seven cut? How could Blake begin the *Marriage* with these plates? Could he have thought their text was the beginning? If so, why announce forthcoming works, which has the air of a conclusion?

Had Blake a completed manuscript of the *Marriage* before he began production, it would not have been divided into pages, it is safe to say, that corresponded exactly to plates. With a continuous, undivided manuscript (that is, a manuscript or fair copy of the text but not a mock-up of the book), production would presumably have been sequential. Conversely, nonsequential production indicates that Blake began executing plates without a completed manuscript—a procedure encouraged by the exigencies of illuminated printing. Such an absence raises the possibility that what was initially produced (plates 21–24) was all that was intended at that time. The text of these plates, executed independently of the oth-

---

53. Robert N. Essick, *Blake and the Language of Adam* (Oxford, 1989), 170.

ers, is thematically and rhetorically self-contained, and its appropriateness as a pamphlet was demonstrated by their first printing, *Marriage* copy K.

Plates 21–24 preceded not only the other *Marriage* plates but possibly the idea of the *Marriage* itself. That idea appears to have originated in what were originally two separate projects, the anti-Swedenborgian pamphlet and "The Bible of Hell" announced at the end of the pamphlet. This announcement may refer to the *Marriage* as anticipated at the time of the pamphlet. Or it may refer to the seventy Proverbs of Hell, then being written, or, more likely, to a projected collection of short illuminated works written from the infernal perspective that would include the Proverbs as one of its volumes. These two projects, one finished and one presumably in progress, may have been rethought. With new introductory material, a few more Memorable Fancies, and a title that evokes Swedenborg, these became the new work Blake called *The Marriage of Heaven and Hell.* Its evolution from four-page pamphlet to a twenty-seven-page book involved four or more stages of production. Its discontinuous narrative and diverse genres, topics, and points of view resulted in part from its production history, but they may also have resulted from Blake's conceiving "The Bible of Hell" in parodic imitation of the "fragment-hypothesis of the Higher Criticism, the theory that the Old Testament is a gathering of redacted fragments" (Essick, "Representation"; see also *Language of Adam,* 142).

Arguing against the hypothesis that plates 21–24 were intended as an independent, anti-Swedenborgian pamphlet are the claim that the pamphlet was not issued and the belief that Blake had intended from the beginning to produce a grab bag of a book, one perhaps modeled on *Songs of Innocence* but consisting of various textual units, instead of individual poems, centered around a particular theme. Both objections seem to infer cause or intention from effect; the work is disjointed, hence it was meant to be so from the very beginning, with plates 21–24 part of that plan, which anticipated the ordering of discrete units at a later date. Both overlook the most obvious explanation and the most human of all traits: learning and changing one's mind, in Blake's case through material production.

Blake's original intentions for plates 21–24 cannot be inferred from the absence of issued copies or by their inclusion in the *Marriage.* The absence of copies may reflect lost or yet-to-resurface works, or it could signify a change of mind as easily as an intent not to publish. Given that "Blake was an indefatigable reviser of his pictorial works," an artist whose "creative revisionism" (Essick, *Language of Adam,* 163) is evident in nearly every printing of illuminated books, original etchings, and original engravings, and inherent to his style of drawing (Viscomi, *Blake and the Idea of the Book,* chaps. 4, 18), Blake seems more likely to have revised his idea of what plates 21–24 were than never to have intended a separate work. If we suppose that Blake had only a vague idea of wanting to write a disjointed, miscellaneous work, loosely modeled on Menippean satire, if not the theories of the Higher Criticism, it still does not solve the problem of his starting with plates 21–24, a self-contained unit with its own agenda and concluding Note. While his technique made it possible for Blake to execute plates as soon as text was available, it did not require him to do so. If he knew that there would be many more episodes to execute, why did he produce 21–24 separately?

I think that we are witnessing in the bibliographical code the material birth of an idea, the point at which the poet changed his mind, the point at which execution and invention intersect. The idea that the *Marriage* grew out of a pamphlet together with another project does not mean that the literary or biblical models do not figure into Blake's production. They possibly do, but they probably came into play *after* the pamphlet was written and executed, perhaps when Blake returned to plate 24 to add the vignette of Nebuchadnezzar, after which he wrote a second Memorable Fancy (plates 12–13). Blake appears to have changed his mind about publishing an independent pamphlet—and/or a series of individual pamphlets to constitute a Bible of Hell—deciding instead to publish a group of interrelated variations on a set of themes, nearly all of which are raised in some form or another in the original pamphlet. The *Marriage* came into being in form and content through its production, with many of its units modeled on the pamphlet's structure and its objects of satire broadened, from Swedenborg to the socioreligious system in which he belongs.

By reading *Marriage* plates and images in the sequence in which they appear to have been written, we can see that plates 21–24 played a significant role in generating the subsequent plates and units. We begin to see in detail how the images, metaphors, and themes of one plate or set of plates are refigured in later plates, and how through the accruing of plates and their arrangement the *Marriage* creates new meanings. We can begin to understand Blake's complex and very personal attitude toward Swedenborg—and toward himself for momentarily being among Swedenborg's followers. In this ongoing study, I seek to trace Swedenborg's influence in even greater detail. I also seek to show where and how Blake depicts his own life as a printmaker and his ideas about books, reading, imagination, and perception. To trace these ideas and topics through the *Marriage* as it evolved is to witness Blake's mind at work.

University of North Carolina

APPENDIX

There are nine complete copies of the *Marriage,* copies A–I. I have examined all of these copies but have complete sets of plate measurements from only five (A, C, D, F, G). These five represent four different printing methods. Copies A and C (along with copies B and H) were printed on both sides of their leaves and lightly washed, c. 1790; copy D was minimally color printed on large sheets of paper on one side of the leaves, c. 1795; copies E and F were color printed from both levels of the plates on one side of the paper, c. 1794; and copy G was printed with plate borders on one side of the leaves, c. 1818. Copy I was printed in the same style as copy G in 1827. Copy K refers to the first printing of plates 21–24; copy L refers to the second separate printing of plates 25–27.

The measurements, in centimeters, are given for all four sides (*T*op, *B*ottom, *L*eft, and *R*ight); unrecorded measurements for a side mean that the plate's embossment is too faint to be read.

The plates are reconfigured into seven sheets (I–VII) and sequenced according to sets A, B, and C:

I	II	III	IV	V
22 24∀	12 x	2 3	6 7	15 9
∀23 21	x 13∀	1 5	∀8 11	14 10∀

VI	II	VII
17 16	x 27∀	25 26
19 18∀	20 x	—

Tables of plate measurements begin on the next page; diagrams 1–3 follow the tables. The symbol ∀ indicates that a plate fits upside down.

Marriage copies

	A	C	D	F	G	K
Sheet I						
21 T	10.80	10.90	10.80	10.90	10.90	—
21 B	10.80	10.90	10.80	10.85	10.85	10.70
21 L	15.30	15.30	15.15	15.15	15.20	15.20
21 R	15.40	15.40	15.20	15.30	15.30	15.30
22 T	10.75	10.80	10.80	10.85	10.90	—
22 B	10.85	10.85	10.85	10.90	10.95	10.75?
22 L	14.95	14.95	14.75	14.90	14.90	14.70?
22 R	15.00	14.95	14.80	14.90	14.90	14.75?
23 T	10.10	10.10	10.05	10.10	10.15	10.00
23 B	10.05	10.10	9.95	10.02	10.10	10.00
23 L	15.25?	15.20	15.15	15.10	15.15	15.10
23 R	15.15	15.15?	14.95?	15.10	15.05	15.00?
24 T	10.00	10.00	9.95	10.00	10.00	9.90
24 B	9.95	9.95	9.85	9.90	9.90	9.80
24 L	14.80	14.80	14.60	14.70	14.70	14.80
24 R	14.95	14.90	14.75	14.80	14.82	14.85
Sheet II						
12 T	10.40	10.45	10.40	10.40	10.50	—
12 B	10.35	10.40	10.40	10.30	10.40	—
12 L	15.35	15.45	15.30	15.25?	15.40	—
12 R	15.45	15.55	15.30	15.25?	15.50	—
13 T	10.45	10.50	10.45	10.50	10.60	—
13 B	10.55	10.70	10.55	10.60	10.65	—
13 L	15.05	15.05	14.90?	15.00	15.00	—
13 R	15.05	15.05	14.80	15.00	14.90	—
20 T	10.30	10.35	10.30	10.30	10.35	—
20 B	10.35	10.40	10.35	10.40	10.40	—
20 L	14.50	14.55	14.40	14.50	14.50	—
20 R	14.50	14.60	14.45	14.50	14.50	—

	A	C	D	F	G	L
27 T	10.55	10.70	10.55	10.60	10.65	10.70
27 B	10.40	10.50	10.40	10.45	10.45	10.52
27 L	—	15.30	15.15	15.25	15.25	15.10
27 R	—	15.40?	15.15	15.30?	15.25	15.18
Sheet III						
1 T	10.10	10.20	10.15	10.20	10.25	—
1 B	10.40	10.40	10.40	10.40	10.45	—
1 L	15.25	15.15	10.10	15.25	—	—
1 R	15.25	15.15	15.10	15.20	—	—
2 T	10.25	10.30?	10.28	10.25	10.30	—
2 B	10.25	10.25	10.25	10.25	10.33	—
2 L	15.20	15.15	15.05	15.00	15.10	—
2 R	15.10	15.10	14.95	15.05	15.00	—
3 T	10.85	10.85	10.85	10.90	10.95	—
3 B	10.90	10.91	10.90	10.95	11.00	—
3 L	15.50	15.40	15.40	15.40	15.40	—
3 R	15.40	15.35	15.20	15.30	15.28	—
5 T	—	10.90	10.90	10.80	11.00	—
5 B	—	10.75	10.70	10.60	10.75	—
5 L	—	15.00	14.85	14.80	15.00	—
5 R	15.00	15.00	—	14.80	15.00	—
Sheet IV						
6 T	—	10.10	10.10	10.05	10.15	—
6 B	—	10.20	10.10	10.10	10.20	—
6 L		15.10	15.05	15.00	15.15	
6 R	—	15.10	15.00	15.00	15.10	—
11 T	9.90	10.00	9.90	9.90	10.10	—
11 B	—	9.95	9.90	9.90	10.05	—
11 L	—	15.00	14.90	14.90	15.05	—
11 R	—	14.95	14.80	14.80	14.95	—

	A	C	D	F	G
Sheet IV (continued)					
7 T	—	10.40	10.35	10.30	10.50
7 B	—	10.25	10.30	10.20	10.30
7 L	—	15.15	15.00	15.00	15.15
7 R	—	15.10	14.95	14.85?	15.10
8 T	10.40	10.40	10.30	10.30	10.45
8 B	10.30	10.40	10.25	10.35?	10.35
8 L	14.90	15.10	14.90	15.00	14.95
8 R	15.00	15.05	14.90	15.00	14.95
Sheet V					
9 T	10.15	10.20	—	10.20	10.30
9 B	10.10	10.15	—	10.10	10.20
9 L	15.15	15.10	—	15.10	15.15
9 R	15.15	15.20	—	15.10	15.15
10 T	10.20	10.30	10.30	10.20	10.35
10 B		10.20	10.10	10.10	10.20
10 L	14.95?	15.15	14.95	14.90	15.05
10 R	15.05	15.15	14.95	14.90	15.05
14 T	10.25	10.25	10.15	10.25	10.30
14 B	10.00?	10.10	10.00	10.10	10.10
14 L	15.00	15.00	14.80	14.90	14.95
14 R	15.10	15.10	14.85	15.00	15.05
15 T	10.25	10.30	10.25	10.30	10.35
15 B	10.25	10.35?	10.25	10.30	10.30
15 L	15.00	15.10	14.85	14.95	14.95
15 R	15.00	15.10	14.85	14.95	14.95

	A	C	D	F	G	L
Sheet VI						
16 T	—	10.30	—	10.25	—	—
16 B	—	10.30	—	10.25	—	—
16 L	—	16.80	—	16.60	—	—
16 R	—	16.65	—	16.45	—	—
17 T	—	10.35?	—	10.20	—	—
17 B	—	10.25	—	10.20	—	—
17 L	—	16.75	—	16.55	—	—
17 R	—	16.80	—	16.60	—	—
18 T	—	10.30	—	10.30	—	—
18 B	—	10.30	—	10.30	—	—
18 L	—	16.40	—	16.30	—	—
18 R	—	16.50	—	16.40	—	—
19 T	—	10.35	—	10.30	—	—
19 B	—	10.35	—	10.30	—	—
19 L	—	16.60	—	16.55	—	—
19 R	—	16.55	—	16.50	—	—
Sheet VII						
25 T	10.35	10.40	10.30	10.30	10.40	10.50
25 B	10.45	10.50	10.45	10.30	10.50	10.60
25 L	14.70	14.80	14.70	14.75?	14.80	14.52
25 R	14.70	14.90	14.70	14.70	14.80	14.60
26 T	10.45	10.50	10.45	10.45	10.50	10.52
26 B	10.45	10.45	10.40	10.40	10.45	10.50
26 L	14.85	14.90	14.70	14.80	14.85	14.56
26 R	14.85	14.90	14.65	14.80	14.85	14.52
Sheet used for *Thel*						
4 T	9.90	10.10	9.90	10.00	10.05	—
4 B	10.10	10.20	10.10	10.20	10.20	—
4 L	13.60	13.65	13.55	13.50	13.654	—
4 R	13.55	13.65	15.50	13.50	13.65	—

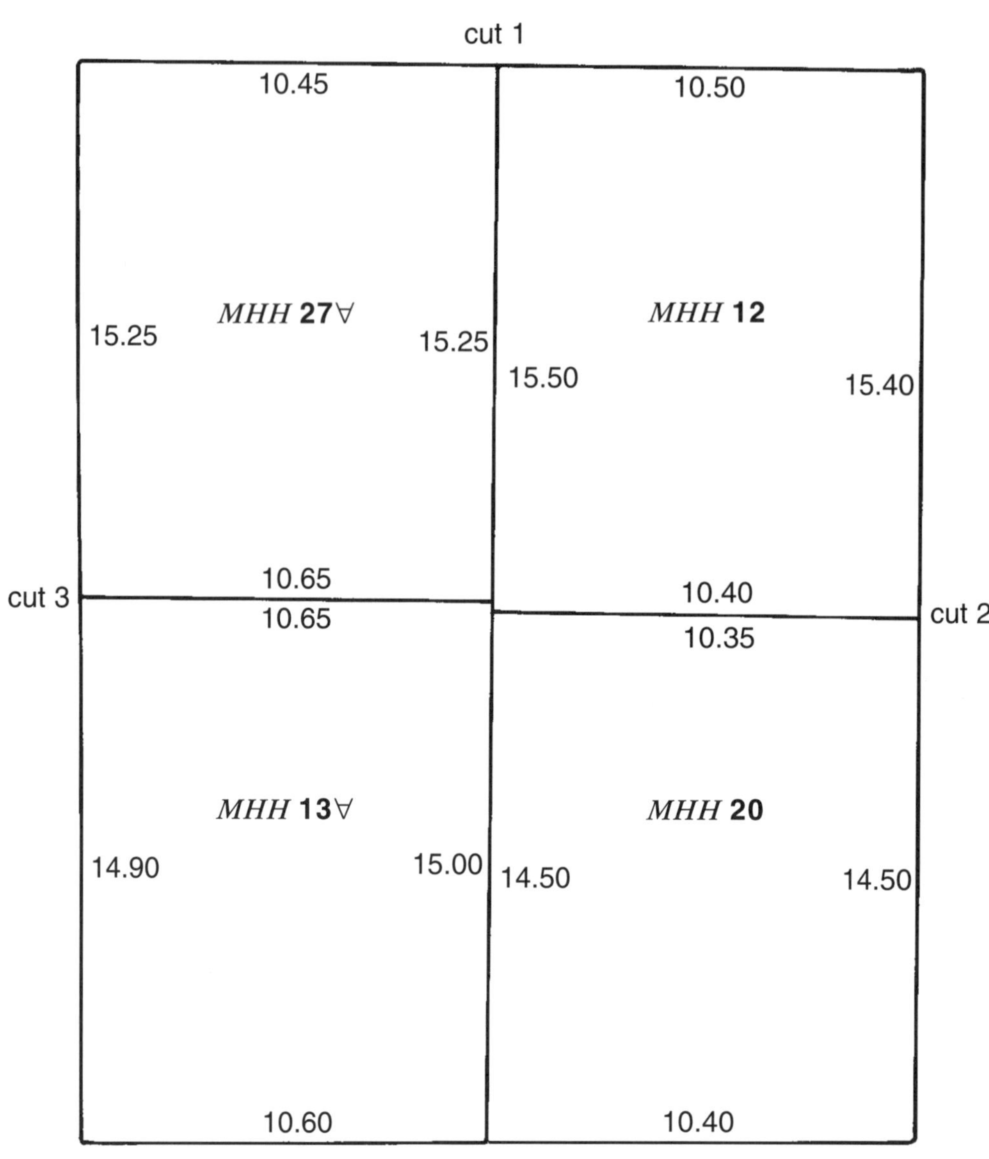

Sheet size in cm

T: 21.25   B: 21.02   R: 29.80   L: 29.95

Diagram 1. The copper plate of *The Approach of Doom,* as seen from the verso, showing the placement of *Marriage* plates 12, 13, 20, and 27. Plate measurements are from copy G. (Because this is the verso of a sheet, the plates are shown with right and left reversed.)

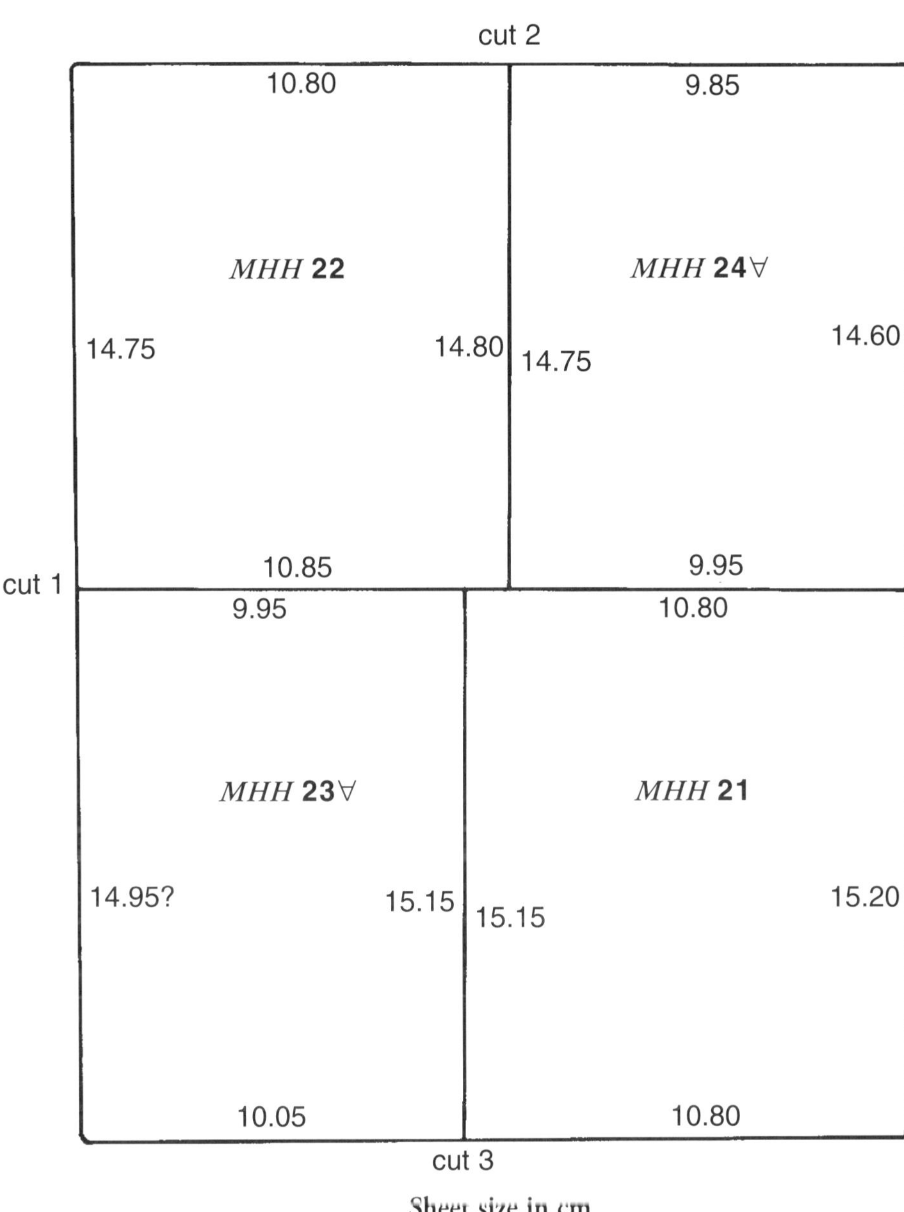

Diagram 2. *Marriage* plates 21–24, reconfigured into a sheet of copper. Measurements are from copy D.

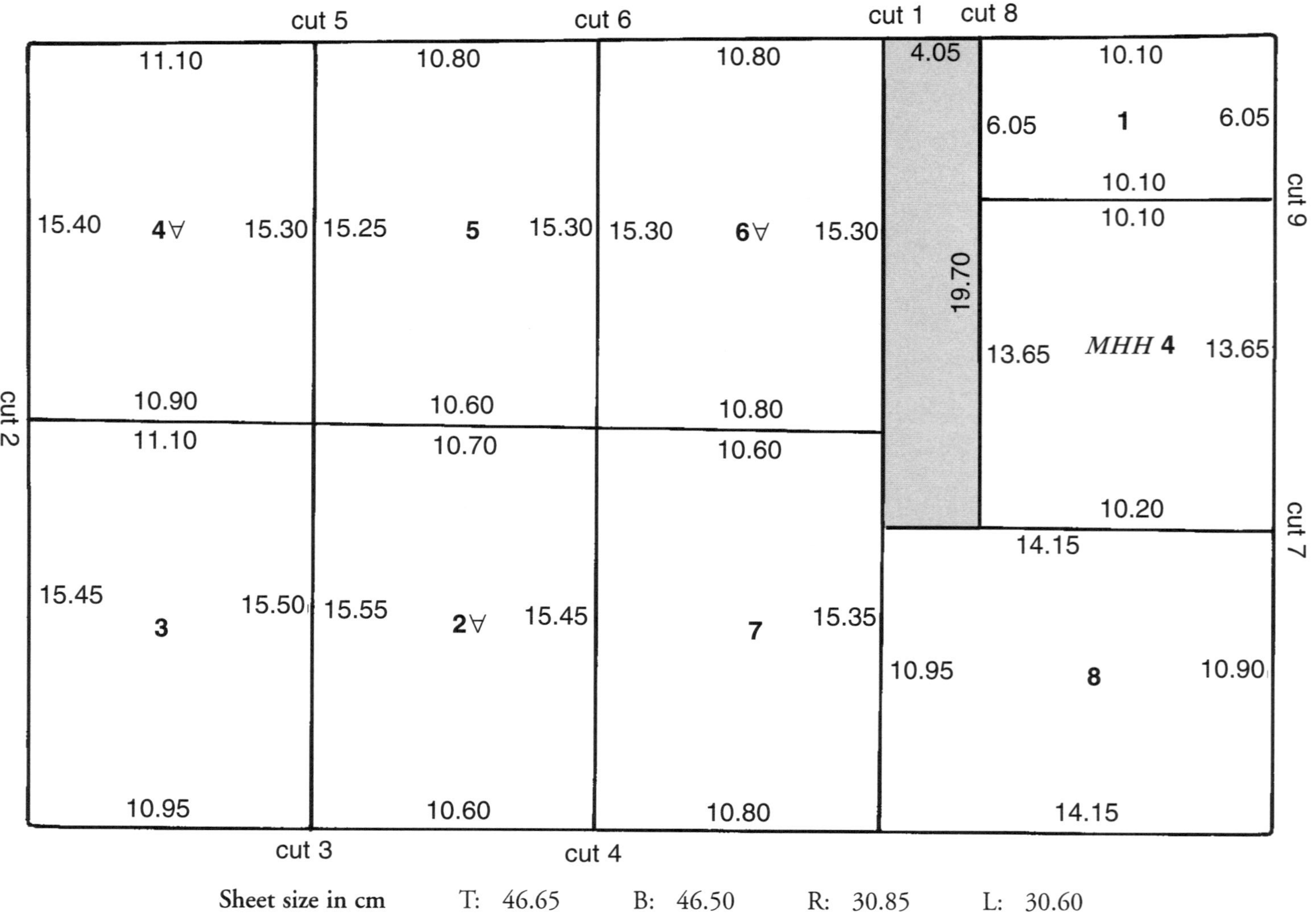

Diagram 3. *Thel* plates 1–8 and *Marriage* plate 4 reconfigured into a sheet of copper. Measurements are from *Thel* copy C and *Marriage* copy C.

Sex, Violence, and Slavery:
Blake and Wollstonecraft

A NNE K. M ELLOR

"Enslav'd, the Daughters of Albion weep" (color plate IV): when Blake in 1793 began his illuminated poem *Visions of the Daughters of Albion* with this line, he directly alluded to the fierce political debates of the 1780s and early 1790s concerning the British slave trade, the institution of slavery in the British colonies, and the abolitionist movement. Equally trenchantly, he responded to the powerful arguments for the liberation of women put forth by Mary Wollstonecraft in *A Vindication of the Rights of Woman,* published the previous year, in 1792. For it is the "daughters" and not the "sons" of England who weep in Blake's poem.

In this essay I will explore what Blake meant by "slavery" in *Visions of the Daughters of Albion* and what he considered to be the best way to "free" oneself from that condition. And I will compare Blake's "solution" to the problem of female slavery with that proposed by Wollstonecraft. Before turning to these two writers, I will briefly describe the political and social debates surrounding the British slave trade during the 1780s and 1790s.

The attempt to end the British involvement in the slave trade and to emancipate the slaves in the British crown colonies in the West Indies was perhaps second only to the French Revolution in its impact on the social consciousness of writers, in England—especially women writers—between 1780 and 1800. This attempt achieved legal standing on 14 May 1772, when William Murray, Lord Mansfield, presiding on the King's Bench, ruled in the case of James Somerset—a black slave who had been brought to England, versus his master, Mr. Stewart of Virginia—that slavery was not lawful in England. In his famous judgment, Lord Mansfield maintained that England was by nature "a soil whose air is deemed too pure for slaves to breathe in."[1] Somerset thereby gained his freedom, and England became a mecca in the eyes of slaves from the British West

---

1.   *The English Reports* 98 (King's Bench Division 27), Lofft 1 (London and Edinburgh, 1909): "Easter Term, 12 Geo. 3, 1772, K. B., Somerset *against* Stewart, May 14, 1772," 500.

Indies. Significantly, Mr. Dunning, the lawyer defending the slave owner Mr. Stewart, argued that slavery, *like marriage,* was a "municipal" rather than a "natural" relationship, and Lord Mansfield did not reject this equation. In this argument, both slavery and marriage were constructed by legal custom, like the feudal villeinage still recognized in British common law, and were not subject to "natural" law. The implied parallel between wives and slaves—and Lord Mansfield's refusal to rule against the municipal servitude of women—did not escape the attention of the women writers of the period.

The legal abolition of slavery in England itself ended neither the slave trade nor the institution of slavery in the colonies. By 1775 the "triangular" slave trade had reached its peak: typically, British merchants sent "trappers" and ships to the Gold Coast of Africa where they kidnapped or bought between thirty-eight and forty-two thousand Africans annually at a maximum of fifteen pounds per head. These Africans were then shipped to the West Indies under appalling conditions on "the Middle Passage" (figure 11). During this sea passage 13 percent typically died; another 33 percent died later, during the "seasoning" or breaking-in period at the other end. They were sold at an average of thirty-five pounds each in the

Figure 11.
Loading of a slave ship. Reproduced from the 1836 edition of *Thomas Clarkson, History of the Rise, Progress, and Accomplishment of the Abolition of the African Slave-Trade* (facing p. 236).

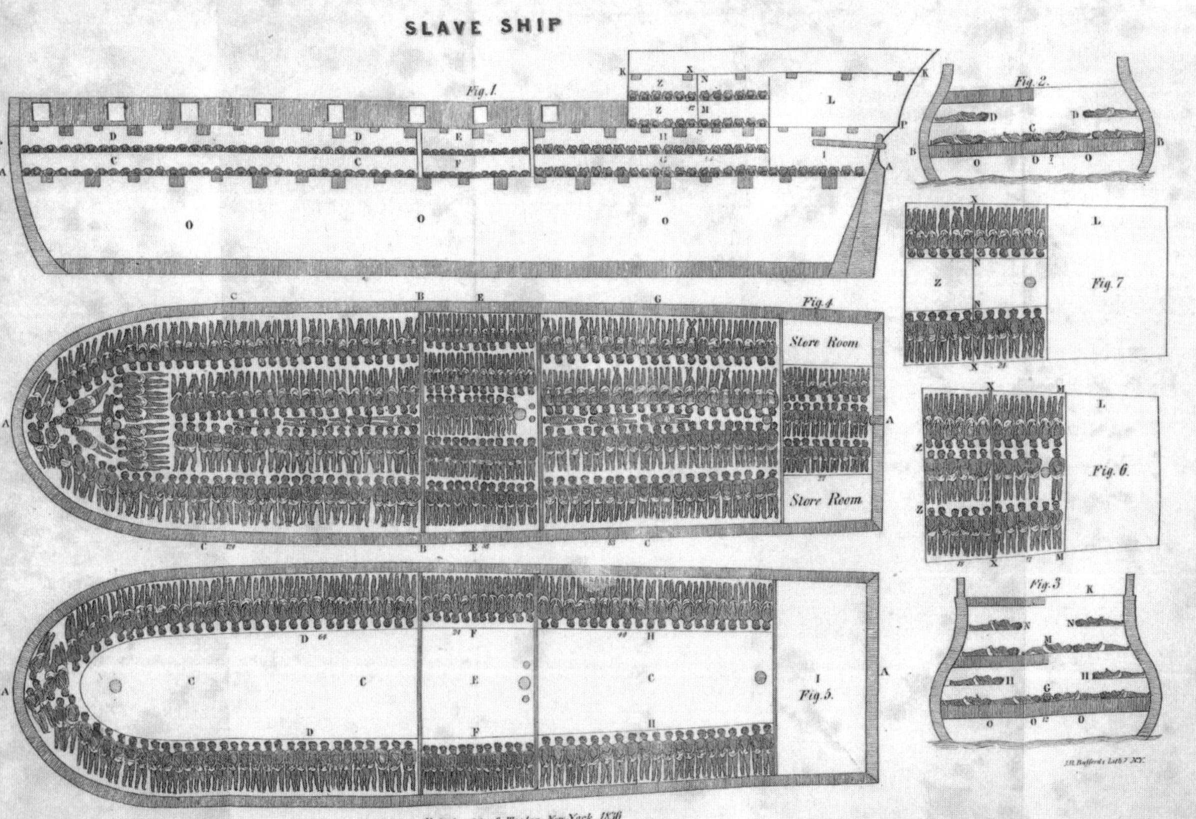

West Indies, where they worked in the tobacco and sugarcane fields. The profits from this sale were used to buy sugar and tobacco, which were then sold again, at great profit, in England and elsewhere in Europe; total profits ranged from six hundred thousand to over a million pounds annually. Bristol and Liverpool were the centers of the British slave trade, and their merchants argued persuasively in both houses of Parliament that the British economy—consumption of refined sugar and its products by this time constituted a national addiction—depended on the continuance of the slave trade. In addition, the lobby of the extremely wealthy West Indian planters—the British owners of the slave plantations, who lived either in England (as does Sir Thomas Bertram in Jane Austen's *Mansfield Park*) or abroad on their plantations (as does Mr. Vincent in Maria Edgeworth's *Belinda*)—exerted an enormous influence on British politics.

Between 1778, when Prime Minister William Pitt introduced the first legislation to regulate the slave trade, and 1807, when the slave trade was legally abolished, debate raged in England on the question. The powerful Standing Committee of Planters and Merchants urged not only that the slave trade and institution of slavery were essential to Britain's economic survival—especially because France and Holland had recently begun to make serious inroads into the slave trade—but also that the institution of slavery was morally justified. They asserted that many of the Africans had been slaves in their own countries and, further, were savages or heathens incapable of rational thought or moral feeling and hence unfit for freedom. African slaves, they insisted, should be regarded as "children" who required a benevolent master to teach them the civilizing benefits of Christian doctrine and the Protestant work ethic. Thomas Bellamy's influential play *The Benevolent Planters,* first performed at the Theatre Royal, Haymarket, in 1789, makes the pro–West Indian lobby argument in a particularly insistent form, even as Bellamy acknowledges that some slave masters abused their slaves and did not deserve their loyalty. In the final scene of Bellamy's play, the slave Oran, having been reunited with his beloved Selima by the generous slave owner Goodwin, who has purchased her for Oran, fervently concludes:

> "Lost in admiration, gratitude, and love, Oran has no words, but can only in silence own the hand of Heaven. . . . O my masters! . . . let my restored partner and myself bend to such exalted worth; while for ourselves, and for our surrounding brethren, we declare, that you have proved yourselves *The Benevolent Planters,* and that under subjection like yours, SLAVERY IS BUT A NAME."[2]

2. Thomas Bellamy, *The Benevolent Planters* (London, 1789), 13.

The abolitionists, who wished to end not only the slave trade but also the very institution of slavery in the colonies, argued in direct rebuttal that the institution of slavery itself was immoral—that it violated both the rights of man and Christian doctrine—and that the actual conditions imposed on Africans both during the middle passage and on the slave plantations were far more barbaric and uncivilized than anything they had experienced in Africa, and thus called into question the morality of England itself as a Christian nation. In 1781, the infamous legal case of the *Zong*—a slave ship whose captain, Luke Collingwood, threw 132 plague-infected Africans to the sharks in order to collect insurance on this jettisoned "cargo"—aroused widespread horror at the cruelty of the slave trade. Even fifty years later, this event was so shocking and well remembered that it inspired both J. M. W. Turner's brilliant painting *The Slave Ship* and John Ruskin's passionate moral denunciation of British imperialism in the essay "Of Water, as Painted by Turner."

The leading voices in the attempt to end the slave trade were Granville Sharp, who initiated the Somerset case, and Thomas Clarkson, the son of an Anglican headmaster and an outstanding student at Cambridge University, who found his life's work when in 1785 he wrote a prize-winning Latin essay on the assigned topic, "Is it right to make men slaves against their wills?" Although he argued the immorality of slavery in abstract terms, drawing his examples from the Quaker Anthony Benezet's powerful descriptions of the inhumane conditions of slavery in the West Indies, Clarkson soon became obsessed with the concrete evils he had discovered. On his return from collecting his prize in London, he recalled,

> all my pleasure was damped by the facts which were now continually before me. It was but one gloomy subject from morning to night. In the daytime, I was uneasy. In the night I had little rest. I sometimes never closed my eye-lids for grief. . . . I frequently tried to persuade myself in these intervals that the contents of my essay could not be true. . . . Coming in sight of Wades Mill in Hertfordshire, I sat down disconsolate on the turf. . . . Here a thought came into my mind, that if the contents of the Essay were true, it was time some person should see these calamities to their end.[3]

Pedantic, thorough, and absolutely convinced of the rectitude of his cause, Clarkson never wavered in his commitment to end slavery. In 1786 he published

---

3. Thomas Clarkson, *History of the Rise, Progress and Accomplishment of the Abolition of the African Slave-Trade, by the British Parliament* (London, 1808), 170–71.

his prize essay, *On the Slavery and Commerce of the Human Species, particularly the African,* and in 1787 joined the Quaker committee founded by Granville Sharp to abolish the slave trade. He was sent to Bristol and Liverpool by the committee to determine the actual conditions aboard the slave ships. His daring and exhaustive research, based on numerous interviews with captains, sailors, ships' surgeons, and escaped slaves, formed the backbone of the abolitionists' attacks for years to come. Armed only with pencil and paper, Clarkson crawled through the holds of ships, haunted the waterfront pubs where drunken, rowdy sailors talked most freely, and risked his life to gain access to crewmen forbidden to speak with him. He uncovered not only the appalling treatment of the Africans aboard the slave ships—where they were loaded according to either "loose" or "tight" packing (in the latter there was insufficient room for chained men, women, and children even to turn over, as illustrated in figure 11)—but also the brutal floggings, starvings, and even murder of the sailors unlucky enough to sign up for these voyages.

Clarkson's authoritative work based on this research, *History of the Rise, Progress and Accomplishment of the Abolition of the African Slave-Trade, by the British Parliament,* was not published until 1808, but he had made the results of his research available to the Privy Council committee assigned to investigate the slave trade in 1789. This committee was chaired by William Wilberforce, Member of Parliament from Hull, who headed the efforts made between 1788 and 1807 to introduce legislation in Parliament abolishing the slave trade and slavery. The largest and most sustained outcry against both the slave trade and the institution of slavery was organized by the Quakers, who established the Anti-Slavery Societies throughout England between 1780 and 1830.

Women played a major role in these societies and became the leading figures in the social protests against the slave trade. It was through their efforts that a petition demanding immediate international emancipation of slaves was submitted in 1832, with 187,000 signatures. Earlier they had organized boycotts of sugar (advocating the use of honey instead) and wrote numerous poems, novels, and tracts condemning the slave trade. Hannah More's poem "Slavery," first published in 1787 and widely circulated, is representative of works attacking the slave trade by Ann Yearsley, Helen Maria Williams, and Anna Barbauld. More insisted on the common humanity that Africans shared with Europeans— "Respect His sacred image which they bear. / . . . Let malice strip them of each other plea, / They still are men, and men should still be free."[4] At the same time

---

4. Hannah More, *Slavery, A Poem* (London, 1788), lines 135–36, 139–40, p. 10.

she denounced the "white savage" who, ruled by "lust of gold / Or lust of conquest," forfeited any claim Europe might make to being either civilized or Christian. Such attacks were reinforced by the slave narratives published in the 1780s and 1790s, most notably those by Olaudah Equiano and Ottobah Cuguano, which provided searing witness to the atrocities of slavery.

It is important to recognize that however much they advocated an end to the slave trade and the institution of slavery, all the abolitionist writers, including Equiano and Cuguano, participated in a colonial discourse that has been called "Anglo-Africanism." They shared the assumption, in Winthrop Jordan's summary, that "to be Christian was to be civilized rather than barbarous, English rather than African, white rather than black."[5] In More's revealing lines, which I quoted only in part above: "Barbarians, hold! th'opprobrious commerce spare, / Respect His sacred image which they bear, / *Though dark and savage, ignorant and blind,* / They claim the common privilege of kind; / Let malice strip them of each other plea, / They still are men, and men should still be free" (italics added).

Between the two poles of the abolitionist and pro-planter debate, many writers argued a third position, that the slave *trade* should be abolished—since Christian merchants should not deal in the buying and selling of human flesh—but that the *institution* of slavery in the West Indies should continue since it provided "better" living conditions for the Africans and greater access to Christian teaching than they could receive in their own countries. Abolishing the trade, they argued, would force planters to treat their slaves more humanely since they could no longer be easily replaced; if the slaves were simply freed, on the other hand, the planters in fairness would have to be financially compensated by the king, an enormous expense that no Chancellor of the Exchequer in this period wished to incur. This was the position endorsed in the 1780s by Bryan Edwards, the leading authority on the colonies, whose proslavery *History, Civil and Commercial, of the British Colonies in the West Indies* was published in 1793. And this was the view that prevailed in the British Parliament, which acted to abolish the slave trade legally in 1807 (although the trade continued illegally for several more years).

And this was the position endorsed by Captain John Stedman in his *Narrative of a five years expedition against the Revolted Negroes of Surinam in Guiana . . . from the year 1772 to 1777.* In 1791 and 1792 Blake engraved at least seventeen of

---

5. Winthrop D. Jordan, *White over Black: American Attitudes toward the Negro, 1550–1812* (Chapel Hill, N.C., 1968), 94. For further discussion of Anglo-Africanism in eighteenth-century British texts, see Moira Ferguson, *Subject to Others: British Women Writers and Colonial Slavery, 1670–1834* (New York and London, 1992), 5 and passim.

Stedman's watercolor drawings for the handsome folio edition with eighty engraved plates published by Joseph Johnson in 1796. Since Stedman's account had an immediate impact on Blake's attitudes toward slavery, I wish to look at it in some detail. I quote and discuss only Stedman's manuscript of the work, the version to which Blake might have had access before 1793; the published edition of 1796 was extensively rewritten and changed in significant ways by Stedman's editor, William Thomson.[6] Blake met Stedman early in 1792 and they soon became friends. Contrary to the claims of Geoffrey Keynes and David Erdman,[7] Stedman did not advocate the abolition of either the slave trade or slavery itself. His purpose was to *reform* the slave owners and thus to *improve* the institution of slavery in the West Indies.

Stedman's *Narrative* reiterates the familiar arguments of the proslavery lobby: the captured Africans were slaves in their own countries; the Africans "may live happier in the West Indies, than they ever did in the Forests of Africa" and are certainly treated no worse than the hordes of starving and abused sailors, soldiers, and prostitutes in Europe; under a fair master, slavery is but a name and the slave more accurately called a "Menial Servant"; and the slave trade, properly managed, contributes to the welfare of Europe and the colonies alike.[8] Moreover, the Africans are, in Stedman's opinion, incapable of self-government. As he concludes,

> the Grand Question that remains to be solved is—are these
> Negroes to be Slaves or a free People—to which I answer without
> hesitation—*dependent,* & under proper restrictions . . . for the
> Sake of . . . the African himself, with whose passions, debauchery
> and indolence, I am perfectly acquainted, and who like a Spirited
> Horse, when unbridled often Gallops to destruction himself,

6. For a thorough analysis of the deletions that Stedman made from his journal before submitting his *Narrative* to press and of the further changes made by William Thomson—who extensively revised Stedman's manuscript into a more proslavery and pro-Christian account—see the authoritative introduction by Richard Price and Sally Price to their edition of John Gabriel Stedman, *Narrative of a Five Years Expedition against the Revolted Negroes of Surinam, Transcribed for the First Time from the Original 1790 Manuscript* (Baltimore, 1988), xlviii–lv. See also Stanbury Thompson, *John Gabriel Stedman: A Study of His Life and Times* (Stapleford, England, 1966).
7. Geoffrey Keynes, *Times Literary Supplement,* 20 May 1965, 400; David V. Erdman, *Blake: Prophet against Empire* (1954; rev. ed., Garden City, N.Y., 1969), 230–35. Also see Erdman, "Blake's Vision of Slavery," *Journal of the Warburg and Courtauld Institutes* 15 (1952): 242–52.
8. J. Stedman, *Narrative,* ed. R. Price and S. Price, 171–73; hereafter, page references are given in the text. In this edition, slashes indicate the opening and closing of parenthetical remarks. The illustrations are reproduced from the Huntington Library's copy of the 1796 edition.

> while he tramples under his feet all that he meets with—they
> would indeed in time provide for their *imediate* Subsistance but
> would no more think . . . of amassing Wealth by industry than
> their Countrymen the *Orangoutang.* (*Narrative,* 172)

As a mercenary soldier sent to Dutch Surinam under the command of the unscrupulous Colonel Louis Henry Fourgeoud, Stedman was welcomed by the planters, shown the height of colonial courtesy, and offered the sexual services of several young black girls—all of which he eagerly accepted. After she twice saved him from death, he entered into a "Suriname marriage" with Joanna, a mulatto house slave (figure 12). In other words, Stedman paid Joanna's mother an agreed-upon sum in order to enjoy her undivided sexual and domestic services while he remained in Surinam. At the same time, he continued to have sexual relations with other black girls, most notably B---e, who on occasion joined Joanna and Stedman in their bedroom. Stedman lived with Joanna for four years and legally acknowledged their son as his own. He twice attempted to purchase her freedom but lacked the funds; finally the generous Mrs. Elizabeth Godefrooy bought Joanna and "gave" her to Stedman. But when Stedman was ordered back to Europe, Joanna refused to accompany him. As he told it, she claimed

> that dreadful as appeared the fatal separation, which she forbode
> was for the Last time never to meet again, yet she Could not but
> Prefer the Remaining in Surinam, first from a Consciousness
> that with propriety she had not the disposal of herself—&
> Secondly from pride, wishing in her Present Condition Rather to
> be one of the first amongst her own Class in America, than as she
> was well Convinced to be the last in Europe at least till such time
> as fortune should enable me to establish her above dependence.
> (*Narrative,* 603)

Stedman ends his narrative with a melancholy account of Joanna's death five years later, on 5 November 1782, and suggests that she either died of a broken heart at their long separation or was poisoned by blacks jealous of her social status. Although Stedman self-servingly conceals the fact of his marriage to a white woman ten months earlier, it is equally possible that this event led Joanna to commit suicide.

In his effort to reform the inhumane practices of slave owners, Stedman consistently equated the brutality of the planters with that of the rebel slaves who, under the command of Boni, had flogged all their white prisoners "to death for the recreation of their Wives and their Children" (*Narrative,* 189). But because

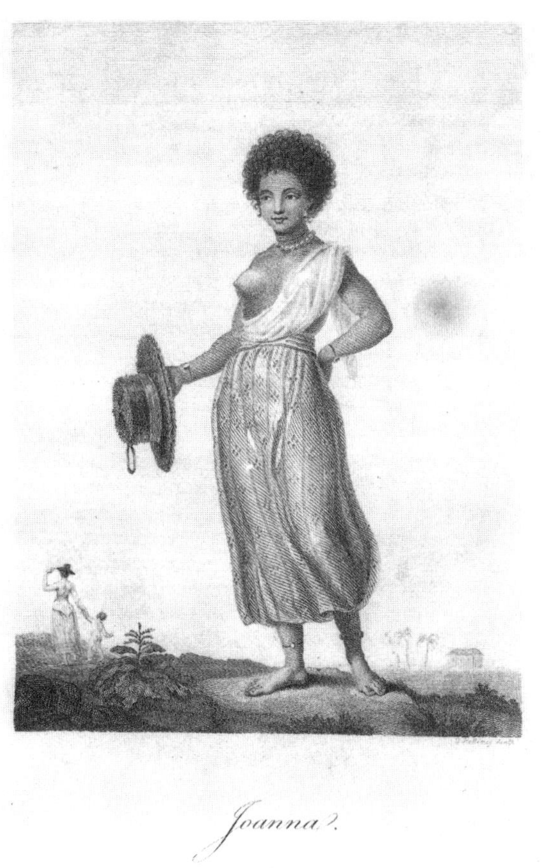

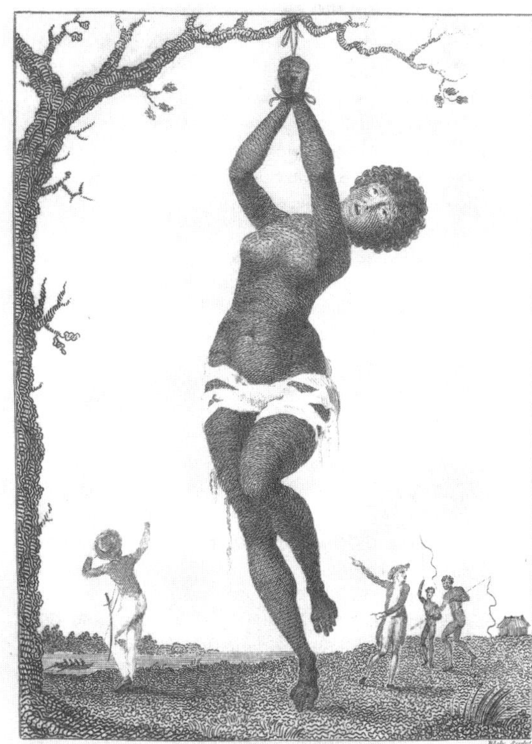

Figure 12. Vol. 1, facing p. 88.

Figure 13. Vol. 1, facing p. 326.

Stedman encounters the slave owners far more often, it is their atrocities that dominate his narrative as well as his drawings. Here I cite but three of his three dozen or more descriptions of atrocities, and include the illustrations engraved by Blake after Stedman's drawings (figures 13, 14, and 15). In the 1796 edition, although the plates occupy a full page, each is carefully placed alongside the corresponding description.

> [Figure 13] The first Object that attracted my Compassion was . . . tied up with both Arms to a tree, a truly beautiful *Samboe Girl* of about 18, as naked as she came to the World, and lacerated in such a shocking Condition by the Whips of two Negro Drivers, that she was from her neck to her Ancles literally died over with blood—It was after receiving 200 lashes that I perceived her with her head hanging downwards, a most miserable Spectacle, Thus turning to the overseer I implored that she might be untied from that moment, which seem'd to give her some Relief, but my Answer was from the humane Gentleman,

> that to prevent all Strangers from interfearing with his Govern-
> ment, he had made it an unalterable rule, in that Case always to
> redouble the Punishment, and which he instantaneously began
> to put in execution—I tried to stop him in vain, he declaring the
> delay should not alter his determination but make him take
> vengeance with Interest upon Interest—Thus I had no other
> remedy left but to leap in my boat, and leave the detestable ras-
> cal like a beast of prey to enjoy his bloody-feast til he was
> Glutted. *(Narrative, 264)*

Note the ways in which Stedman's illustration *evades* the violence of his text: the girl is not entirely naked but rather modestly draped with a loincloth; no blood is visible; the overseer is not actively lashing her, nor is Stedman's attempt to stop the overseer represented. Instead we see a classically draped female body in an erotically charged position, a female in all respects European in appearance save for a shaded skin tone.

> [Figure 14] Not long ago [a "decent looking Man" tells the new-
> comer Stedman], I saw a black man hang'd alive by the ribs,
> between which with a knife was first made an insision, and then
> clinch'd an Iron hook with a Chain—in this manner he kept liv-
> ing three days hanging with his head and feet downwards and
> catching with his tongue the drops of water /it being in the rainy
> season/ that were flowing down his bloated breast while the vul-
> tures were picking in the putred wound. (*Narrative,* 103)

Again, the violence of the text is visually evaded: the Negro is modestly draped, his chest unbloated, the suffering bystander is absent, and—a point to which I wish to return—there are no vultures feeding on his flesh.

> [Figure 15] This man being Sentenced to be brook *Alive* upon the
> Rack [the decent-looking man continues], without the benefit of
> the *Coup de Grace,* or mercy Stroke, laid himself down Deliber-
> ately on his Back upon a Strong Cross, on which with Arms &
> Legs Expanded he was Fastned by Ropes—The Executioner /also
> a Black/ having now with a Hatchet Chop'd off his Left hand,
> next took up a heavy Iron Crow or Bar, with Which Blow after
> Blow he Broke to Shivers every Bone in his Body till the Splinters
> Blood and Marrow Flew About the Field, but the Prisoner never
> Uttered a Groan, or a Sigh—the Roaps being now Unlashed I
> imagined him dead & Felt happy till the Magistrates moving to

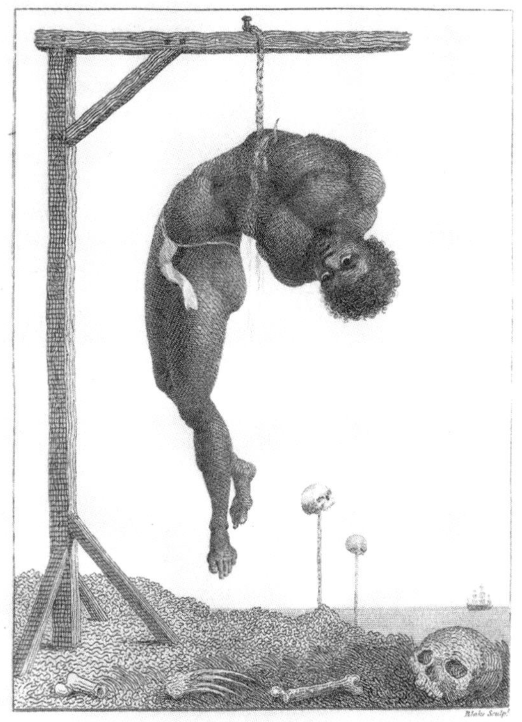

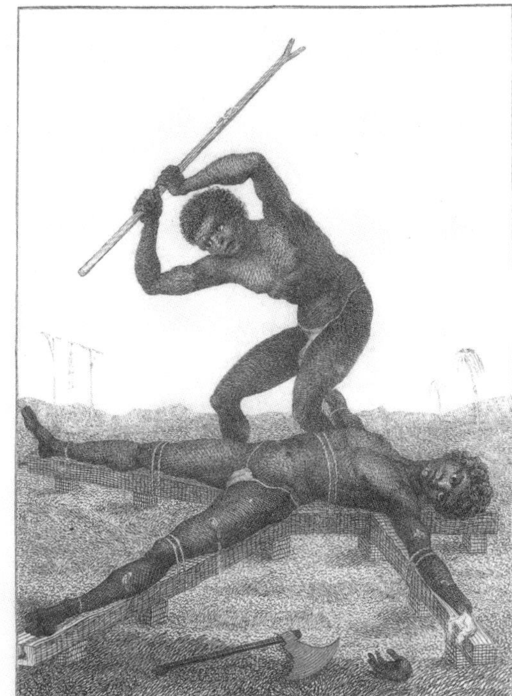

Figure 14. Vol. 1, facing p. 110.   Figure 15. Vol. 2, facing p. 296.

> Depart he Wreathed from the Cross till he Fell in the Grass, and
> Damn'd them all for a Pack of Barbarous Rascals, at the Same
> time Removing his Right hand by the help of his Teeth, he
> Rested his Head on Part of the timber and ask'd the by Standers
> for a Pipe of Tobacco Which was infamously Answered by kick-
> ing & Spitting on him, till I With some Americans thought
> Proper to Prevent it. (*Narrative*, 546–47)

Again the pattern of visual evasion recurs: the executed Negro is modestly clothed,
his body remains on the cross, his bones unsplintered, his mouth closed, his hand
at a distance. No bystanders—neither the magistrates nor the Americans—appear.
Instead, the image is that of a black Christ-figure crucified by his own kind.
Through this recurrent visual erasure of violence, Stedman subtly mitigates the
horror of the numerous atrocities his text recounts in scrupulous detail.

Offsetting this record of European barbarism, and consistent with the pattern of visual mitigation, is Stedman's insistence on the benevolence of many of
the planters—their willingness to educate and domesticate their slaves—and the
consequent happiness of the slaves whom he came to know well. As a house
slave, Joanna was permitted to establish her own home with Stedman, a cottage

he celebrates as a pastoral Eden inhabited by Milton's Eve. He devotes many pages to a detailed description of the slaves' well-being and their cheerful, healthy lives; I cite a brief excerpt, with Stedman's illustration engraved by Blake (figure 16):

> I Will introduce a Negro Family in that State of Tranquil Happiness to Which they are all entitled When they are Well treated by their Owners: they are Supposed to be of the *Loango Nation* by the marks on the man's Body, while on his Breast may also be seen the letters J. G. S. being the enitials of my name, And Supposed to be the Cypher by which each master knows his Property—he Carrys a Basket with Small Fish on his Head & a net, While a large Fish is in his Hand, All Caught by Himself; & While his Wife /Who is pregnant/ is employ'd in Carrying Different kinds of Fruit, Spinning a Thread of Cotton and Comfortably Smoking her pipe of Tobacco. . . .
>
> Under such a mild Government no Negroes work is more than a Healthy Exercise, which ends with the Setting sun, Viz at 6. O'Clock & When the Rest of the time is his Own, Which he employs in Hunting, And Fishing, Cultivating his Little Garden, or making Baskets, Fishnets &c for Sale; . . .
>
> Thus Pleasantly Situated he is Exempt from every Anxiety, And looks up to his Master as the Common Protector of him and his Family, Whom he Adores not from Fear or Flattery but from a Conviction of his being the Object of his Care and Attention— He Breathes in a Luxorious Warm Climate like his Own . . . & enjoys much more Health and Pleasure by Going naked
>
> . . . he never lives With a wife he does not Love Exchanging her for another the Moment he, or She is Tired. (*Narrative,* 534–36)

Stedman explicitly constructs the lives of these happy slaves as of his own making—the man is branded with Stedman's initials—and it is a construction that greatly appealed to his European readers.

Stedman argues throughout his *Narrative* that the institution of slavery as such is defensible, both as a necessary underpinning of the European economy and as an opportunity to improve the lives of these noble savages. He concludes that if slaves are "Properly fed, & Attended when Sick or indisposed," and if equal justice is administered to them "by a Judge & impartial Jury even partly Composed of their own Sable Countrymen," then "the *master* will with Pleasure look on his Sable Subjects as on his Children, & the Principle Source of his

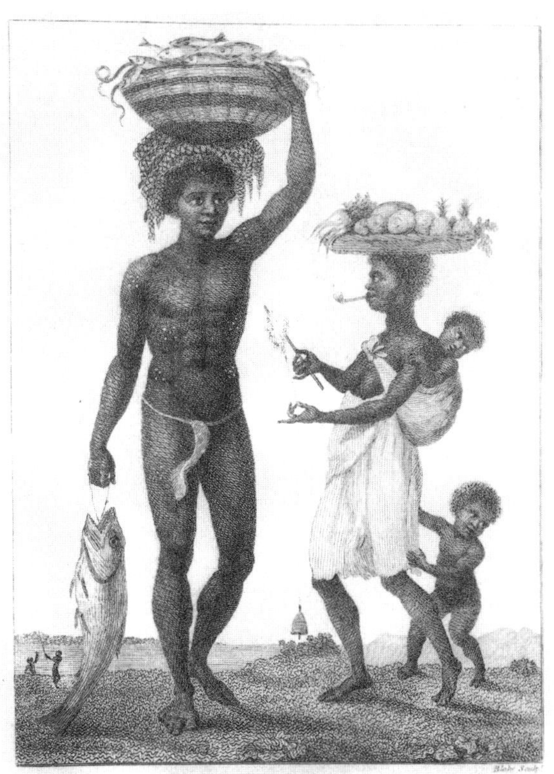
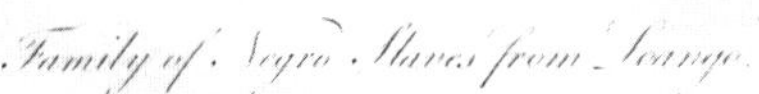

Figure 16. Vol. 2, facing p. 280.

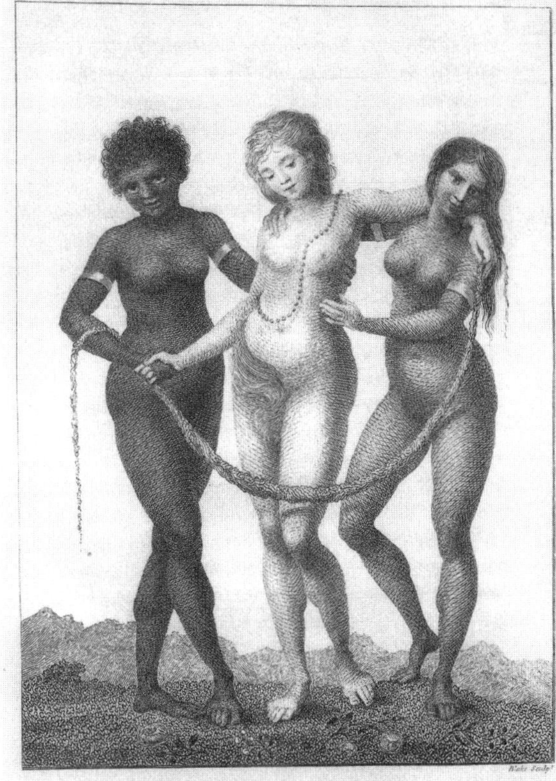

Figure 17. Vol. 2, facing p. 394.

Happiness; while the *negroes* will bless the day that their Ancestors first Set foot on American Ground" (*Narrative,* 594). Stedman visualizes this conclusion, in an image engraved by Blake (figure 17), as

> an Emblematical Picture of *Europe* Supported by *Africa* & *America* Accompanied by an Ardent Wish that in the friendly manner as they are Represented they may henceforth & to all Eternity be the Prop of each other . . . we All only differ in the Colour but we are Certainly Created by the same hand & After the same Mould thus if it has not pleas'd fortune to make us equal in Authority, let us at Least use that Superiority With Moderation & not only Profer that Happiness which we have to bestow on our Superiors & Equals, but with Cheerfulness to the very Lowest of our dependants. (*Narrative,* 618)

From our contemporary perspective, the racism and the sexism of this widely reproduced image are apparent: the women of color *support* the white woman, not vice versa. Their labor is used to shore up the central and superior European female, who wears a jeweled necklace, the overt sign of the wealth they produce, while the women of color wear arm bands reminiscent of the fetters of the slave.

More important, all three women are represented in a European body type, with the same facial features and physiognomy: all three conform to eighteenth-century neoclassical prototypes of female beauty derived from the Venus of Medici and the Three Graces. One might argue that this visual assimilation of the black female body to the classical Western white body is an attempt to "humanize" the African by insisting on her identity with the European female. Such an argument would also apply to the earlier images of Negro slaves painted by Stedman and engraved by Blake: what I have been calling an evasion of violence might instead be seen as an effort to render the African more noble and heroic. Or this "Europeanization" of the African body might simply result from Stedman's (and Blake's) neoclassical artistic training: perhaps this was the only way they were able to draw the human figure. But such arguments subtly reinforce the very point I am trying to make: that both Blake and Stedman participated in a cultural erasure of difference between races and individuals that gave priority to Western, white models. An alternative "scientific" visual style, which we would see as more documentary, was available to them: in illustrated travel books, in medical treatises, and in the studies of racial physiognomy compiled by John Caspar Lavater and Pieter Camper (these last studies noted by David Bindman in his essay in this volume). Employing such a scientific style would have enabled Stedman and Blake to portray the physiological differences between different racial and ethnic types as well as to render the cruelties of slavery in a more literal way.

Finally, Stedman's construction of entire continents—Europe, Africa, and America—as female, as the classical Three Graces, reproduces the familiar patriarchal trope of Nature as a female body designed for the aesthetic, sexual, and economic gratification of her male masters or owners. Here "Africa" is identical with the naked Joanna, still a slave with arm and ankle bands serving her white mistress (figure 12), and further defined in Stedman's text as the voluntary sexual possession of the white male military colonizer.

It is within the context of such proslavery colonialist discourse that Blake's representations of slavery must be placed. I turn first to Blake's "Little Black Boy" from *Songs of Innocence* and *Songs of Innocence and of Experience* (color plates XII–XV). Alan Richardson has recently noted the significance of the poem's construction of the black mother as a teacher of her child, thus undercutting the dominant cultural construction of the African as essentially and exclusively a "child-who-must-be-taught" and implicitly endorsing instead a program of gradual emanci-pation.[9] Richardson's point is well taken, but does not to my mind outweigh the counterargument, namely, that Blake here affirms the ideological construction of the African as one who finally benefits from Christianity. It is a child who speaks, after all, and what he has learned from his mother is a desire both to serve the white child ("I'll shade him from the heat") and to be "like" the white child and his God. Blake represents this likeness as complete assimilation: in those versions of the second plate where the black boy does not take a subservient position—and is depicted further away from that Christ who resides within as well as without in Blake's antinomian *Songs of Innocence*—he becomes entirely white, in-distinguishable from the white boy, as in some early versions (see color plates XII–XV). Had Blake given us a black Christ, for which there is historical visual precedent, he might have registered the degree to which the spectator's eye rather than his own collaborates in a Western ideological production of the white body as the superior, more "divine" body.

Blake's participation in a colonialist visual discourse is even clearer in *Visions of the Daughters of Albion*. Before turning to this poem, however, I want briefly to outline the other social discourse to which this poem directly re-sponds, a discourse of human or "natural" rights and specifically of the rights of woman. In the eyes both of her contemporaries in general and of Blake in particular, the leading exponent for the rights of woman in the early 1790s was Mary Wollstonecraft. Blake had illustrated and engraved the plates for Woll-stonecraft's *Original Stories from Real Life* (1791), illustrations that offer a pervasive criticism of Wollstonecraft's feminist doctrines. In these didactic sto-ries, which consist of conversations between the prudent, rational, and compassionate Mrs. Mason and her two young students Mary and Caroline, Wollstonecraft specifically sought to develop a radically new image of the ideal woman. Eschewing her culture's construction of the feminine gender as in-nately or essentially emotional and irrational, dominated by impulse, desire, imaginative fancy, or acute sensibility, Wollstonecraft's Mrs. Mason offers in-stead a prototype of the ideal woman as one who avoids anger, exercises compassion, loves truth, acts with prudence and modesty, and conquers the "wild pursuits of fancy."[10] She insists above all on the capacity of females to

<hr>

9.   Alan Richardson, "Colonialism, Race, and Lyric Irony in Blake's 'The Little Black Boy,'" *Papers in Language and Literature* 26 (1990): 233–48.

10.   Mary Wollstonecraft, *Original Stories from Real Life: with Conversations calculated to Regulate the Affections. and Form the Mind to Truth and Goodness* (1791; reprint, London, 1906), 154. Illustrations are repro-duced from the Huntington Library's copy of the 1791 edition.

develop virtuous habits, which she defines as the intelligent performance of acts of charity, compassion, and disinterested love. As the subtitle of her book insists, Mrs. Mason's conversations are "calculated to regulate the affections, and form the mind to truth and goodness."

That Blake is hostile to Wollstonecraft's attempt to achieve a "revolution in female manners" is apparent in the illustrations he created for her text. He initially portrays Mrs. Mason with her arms held over her charges, looking sternly down, and places them directly in front of a prison-like door (figure 18)—a setting he invoked in his design for "Nurses Song" in *Songs of Experience* to represent the oppressiveness of the female teacher (figure 19). Throughout his illustrations for *Original Stories,* Blake consistently chooses *not* to represent images of the positive rational compassion exercised by Mrs. Mason and her students. Wollstonecraft's ideal woman, Mrs. Trueman, never appears. Nor does Blake illustrate the practice of reading that Mrs. Mason constantly recommends to her students, a positive alternative to idleness that enables, in her words, "the ripenings of reason [to] regulate the imagination."[11]

As did Stedman in his drawings, Blake engages in a visual evasion of textual violence. Where Mrs. Mason consistently emphasizes the extreme hardships caused by social injustice and poverty in late-eighteenth-century England—terrible human suffering to which her charges learn to respond with intelligent charity—Blake equally consistently transforms these textual descriptions of social violence into visual images of sentimental sensibility. By so doing, he reinforces his culture's hegemonic construction of the female gender as not actively engaged in social or political reform—as instead reducing social injustice to occasions for the expression of delicate sensibility and individual compassion. A few examples will illustrate this point.

Mrs. Mason tells the story of Jack the sailor, designed to teach Mary and Caroline the pleasure of actively helping the poor. Captured by the French and thrown into prison, Jack is later released with his legs crippled and one eye blind and now scrapes out a meager existence with his family by begging; yet Blake illustrates the scene with the domestic idyll of a prosperous bourgeois family (figure 20). When Mrs. Mason tells the story of Charles Townley, whose procrastination in repaying a debt ruined his best friend and drove that friend's daughter into madness, Blake illustrates only Townley's ruined house (figure 21); neither the mad Fanny nor her dead father appears. When Mrs. Mason visits a poor Welsh family she has saved from starvation, a family

---

11. Wollstonecraft, *Original Stories,* 96.

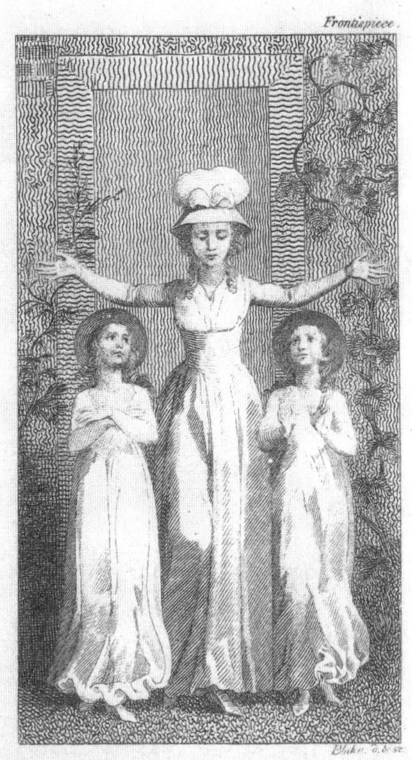

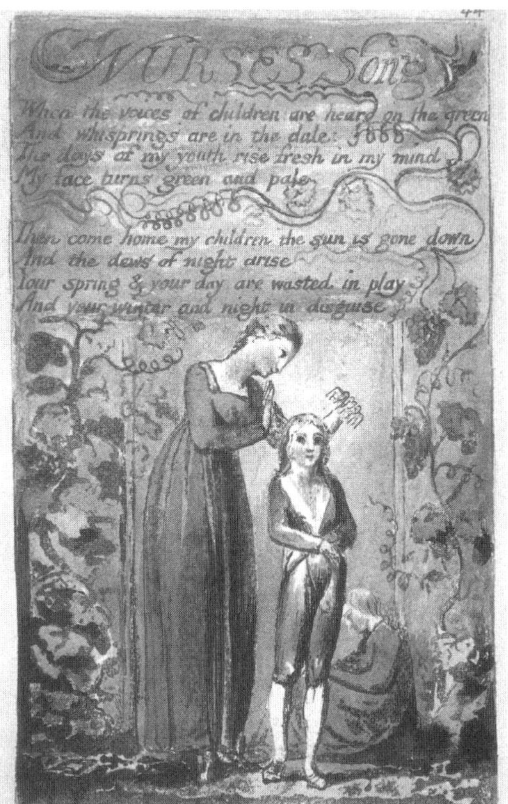

Figure 18, left. Frontispiece.
Figure 19, above. *Songs of Experience,* copy N, plate 53.
Figure 20, below left. P. 74.
Figure 21, below right. P. 94.

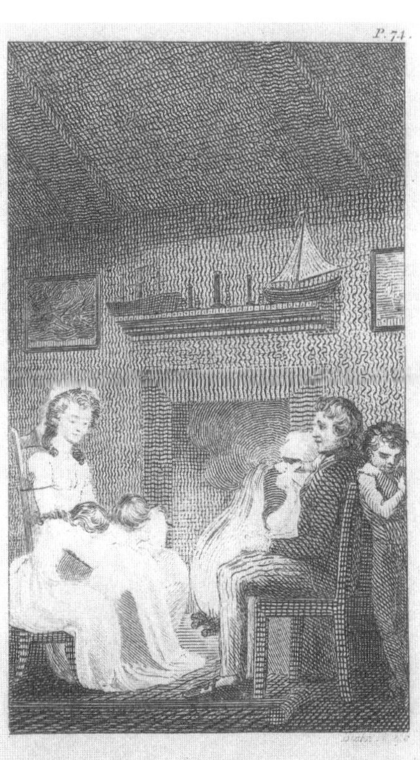

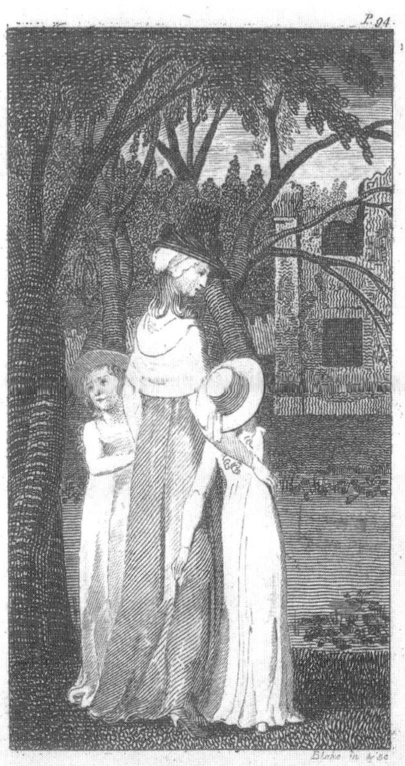

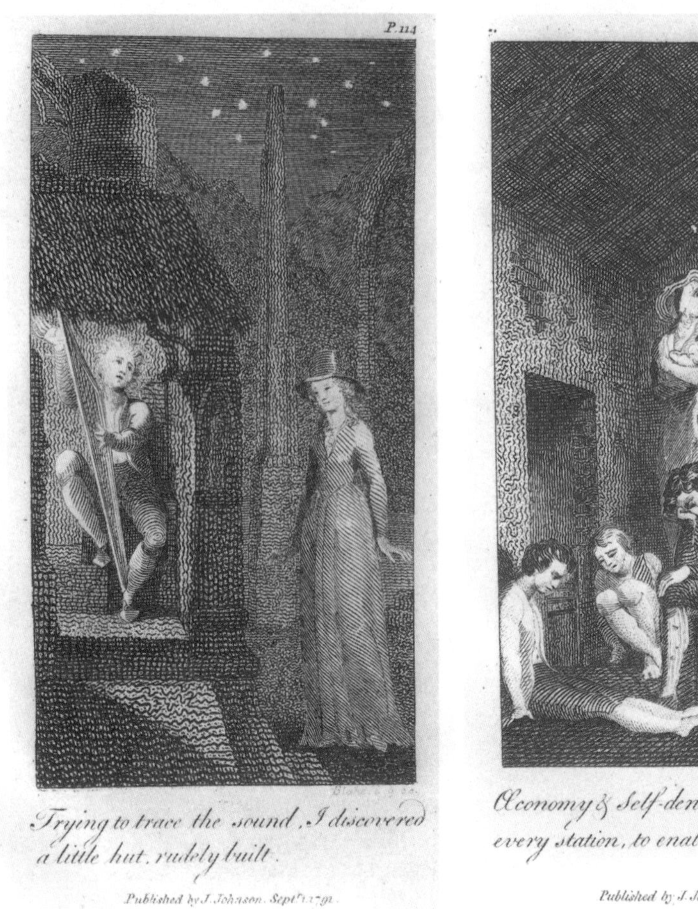

Figure 22. P. 114.   Figure 23. P. 173.

headed by an old, enfeebled Welsh harper, Blake illustrates neither her active
charity nor the harper's penury. Instead he represents the harper as young,
healthy, inspired by heavenly vision, and entirely happy (figure 22). Even when,
in his final engraving for the volume, Blake does illustrate the sufferings of an
impoverished worker and his family (figure 23), he does not show the active
gift-giving practiced in the text not only by Mrs. Mason but also by both of
her students, who have now learned to save their own resources to better help
others. Instead Blake represents Mrs. Mason and her girls as idle bystanders,
apparently indulging their feminine sensibility but without the capacity to *act*.

What I wish to emphasize here is not merely Blake's active misreading of
Wollstonecraft's text, his deliberate suppression of the life of rational charity and
social justice practiced by Mrs. Mason. I am most interested in Blake's refusal to
see Wollstonecraft's new construction of gender in *Original Stories* as a positive
female image. Instead, Blake chooses to define Mrs. Mason as a mere spectator

of suffering, and one who is gratified entirely by such passive ways of expressing pity or exercising feminine sensibility.

Blake's *Visions of the Daughters of Albion* expresses a more direct criticism of Wollstonecraft, whose *Vindication of the Rights of Woman* had been published the previous year. Wollstonecraft had pointed out that British wives were no different from slaves: "When, therefore, I call women slaves, I mean in a political and civil sense."[12] Her argument rested on both legal and psychological grounds. As we have seen, Lord Mansfield's 1772 antislavery judgment left intact the legal definition of marriage as a "municipal" relationship of the kind derived from feudal villeinage, in which the wife exists under the "coverture" of the husband. In other words, a wife is absorbed into the legal body of her husband: man and wife are "one flesh." She is not a "person" in law: she cannot own property, have custody of children, bring legal suits—although she can be held solely responsible for any crimes she commits. Wollstonecraft argued that such legal coverture produced not only an economic but also a psychological dependence of women upon their husbands or male relatives. She further insisted that this condition corrupted both partners, for women "may be convenient slaves, but slavery will have its constant effect, degrading the master and the abject dependent" (*Vindication*, 5).

Wollstonecraft assumed that females have the same souls as males and therefore the same rational capacity as men, a point implicitly acknowledged not only by the established Anglican church but even by law. For if women can be held responsible for their sins or crimes, they must have the mental ability to distinguish good from evil, right from wrong. On this foundation in logic Wollstonecraft mounted her impassioned appeal for the equal education of women and for their right to enjoy the same legal, economic, and political rights as men.[13]

In her attempt to change the construction of gender in her society—to transform women from Jean-Jacques Rousseau's submissive, coquettish child-brides, who live only to please their husbands, into rational agents—Wollstonecraft insisted on the necessity of curbing female sexual desire. In part, she wanted to break her society's identification of the female with sexuality; in the eighteenth century, "the sex" referred only to females. More immediately, she wanted to warn women against being seduced by their own sexual desire into an unhappy

---

12. Mary Wollstonecraft, *A Vindication of the Rights of Woman* (London, 1792), ed. Carol Poston (1975; reprint, New York, 1988), 167; hereafter, page references are given in the text.

13. For further discussion of Wollstonecraft's political and social theory, see Anne K. Mellor, *Romanticism and Gender* (New York and London, 1993), 31–39; and Virginia Sapiro, *A Vindication of Political Virtue: The Political Theory of Mary Wollstonecraft* (Chicago, 1992).

marriage. But Wollstonecraft's warning was fueled by an even more pressing so-cial and moral issue. Too often, the females of her day were seduced by heartless libertines who then abandoned them, dishonored and pregnant, to a life of social ostracism and prostitution. The consequences of free love, for women, were ap-parent in the streets of London, where over ten thousand prostitutes plied their trade by the end of the eighteenth century.

Therefore Wollstonecraft insisted that the ideal rational woman is also a modest woman, one who preserves her chastity and channels her sexual desire into a marriage based on mutual respect and enduring affection. Arguing that modesty is a virtue that should be acquired by men as well as by women, she as-serts that modesty "never resides in any but cultivated minds. It is something nobler than innocence, it is . . . the reserve of reason, and . . . so far from being incompatible with knowledge, it is its fairest fruit" (*Vindication*, 123). Prag-matically, however, in Wollstonecraft's view, rational modesty is essential to female social survival.

Throughout the *Vindication,* Wollstonecraft uses the term *slavery* in both a literal and a metaphorical sense. She believes that the institution of marriage in England in 1792 is legal slavery, no different in kind from that imposed on Africans in the American colonies. Commenting on the arguments of male conduct-book writers (such as John Gregory and James Fordyce) that women must be subjected to the "severe restraint" of propriety, she asks,

> Why subject her to propriety—blind propriety, if she be capable
> of acting from a nobler spring, if she be an heir of immortality?
> Is sugar always to be produced by vital blood? Is one half of the
> human species, like the poor African slaves, to be subject to prej-
> udices that brutalize them, when principles would be a surer
> guard, only to sweeten the cup of man? (*Vindication,* 144–45)

At the same time, she frequently uses *slave* or *slavery* figuratively to underline her attack on female psychological dependence. A few pages later she attacks "a slav-ish bondage to parents," for those daughters "taught slavishly to submit to their parents . . . are prepared for the slavery of marriage." But she is careful to qualify such rhetorical usages: "I do not dream of insinuating that boys or girls are always slaves, I only insist that when they are obliged to submit to authority blindly, their faculties are weakened, and their tempers rendered imperious or abject" (*Vindication,* 155).

While Wollstonecraft distinguishes between the literal and figurative construc-tion of slavery in her text, she nonetheless insists that if British women are kept in a state of ignorance or "perpetual childhood"—not educated but rather trained to be pleasing to their masters and "cunning, mean and selfish" to everyone else—they are no different in character or nature from a dependent slave. Her program for the emancipation of women is clear: the state must provide, at public expense, a comprehensive education for females that teaches them the value and practice of honesty, compassion, modesty, and useful work, an education that leads to what she would call "rational love" and an egalitarian marriage.

Blake's program for the emancipation of the "enslav'd daughters of Albion" is very different. In "The Little Black Boy," Blake had suggested that the solution to racism was the assimilation of the black body into the white, for—as the Little Black Boy insists—"my soul is white." Had Blake followed the same line of argument in *Visions of the Daughters of Albion* when addressing the issue of the enslavement of women, he might have made the same move that Wollstonecraft made, the argument that females have the same "souls" as males and hence are entitled to the same political and social rights. But instead, he translated the civil and legal slavery of British women referred to by Wollstonecraft into a specifically *sexual* slavery. Oothoon, "the soft soul of America," represents both the slave woman of the American colonies and the oppressed English woman at home. Raped by the slave owner Bromion to increase her value and then rejected by her jealous lover Theotormon, Oothoon is legally enslaved by the economic institution of slavery that entitles European men to claim, as does Bromion: "Thy soft American plains are mine, and mine thy north & south; / Stampt with my signet are the swarthy children of the sun."[14] Blake illustrates the consequences of legal slavery with an image of a black man lying on the ground (color plate V). This image seems to me to engage in an erasure of visual violence similar to that of Stedman's illustrations: no overt physical abuse appears; his pick axe lies, unused, nearby. More important, this is the only black body that appears in the designs for this poem: neither Oothoon herself nor her lover Theotormon is depicted as black, not even copper-toned.

I make this point because I wish to emphasize a pattern of displacement that governs this entire poem. Blake's primary concern in *Visions of the Daughters of Albion* is not to end the slave trade or the institution of slavery in the colonies, although he may have gone well beyond his friend Stedman in his support of abolition. His primary concern is to liberate the "daughters of Albion," *British* women, from the greater slavery they experience at home. But *that* slavery is not the civil

---

14. *The Complete Poetry and Prose of William Blake,* ed. David V. Erdman, rev. ed. (Berkeley and Los Angeles, 1982), 46; hereafter cited in the text as "E."

and legal slavery described by Wollstonecraft. It is rather, as Oothoon makes clear, the psychological slavery of "subtil modesty" (E 49)—that very rational modesty advocated by Wollstonecraft—from which Blake hoped to free both British women *and* British men.

When Oothoon plucks the bright marigold (color plate III), as Paula Bennett and Jack Goody have recently reminded us,[15] she engages in a familiar eighteenth-century language of flowers: she explicitly offers her blossomlike clitoris and her fertile womb to her lover. After she is raped and impregnated by Bromion, she insists that her body—because it is now sexually experienced—is actually more delicious: "sweetest the fruit that the worm feeds on" (E 47). Blake is here attacking the *repression* of sexual desire; the slaves whose voices Theotormon hears are "children bought with money. / That shiver in *religious* caves beneath the burning fires / Of lust, that belch incessant from the summits of the earth" (E 46; italics added). Blake condemns any theology that defines the desires of the flesh as evil, that insists that only the chaste body is lovable or marriageable, that thus produces both the public injustice of prostitution (of female children "bought with money") and the private abuse of masturbation. As Oothoon proclaims (color plate IX):

> Who taught thee modesty, subtil modesty! child of night & sleep . . .
> Then com'st thou forth a modest virgin knowing to dissemble
> With nets found under thy night pillow, to catch virgin joy,
> And brand it with the name of whore; & sell it in the night, . . .
>
> (E 49)

As Blake's image of Theotormon apparently flagellating himself suggests, the enslavement Blake attacks is largely self-imposed, a voluntary submission to a Christian belief in the necessity of chastity that makes it impossible for Theotormon to embrace the woman he desires once she has had sexual relations with another man.

Blake's solution to both Theotormon's sexual jealousy and Bromion's materialist economics—as well as Wollstonecraft's demand for women's rights—is simple. It is, as Oothoon proclaims to her oppressed sisters of Albion (color plate X), "free love"—"I cry, Love! Love! Love! happy happy Love! free as the mountain wind!"

---

15. Paula Bennett argues that all flowers carry a symbolic association with female genitalia in Western art and literature, in "Critical Clitoridectomy: Female Sexual Imagery and Feminist Psychoanalytic Theory," *Signs* 18 (1993): 235–59; while Jack Goody reminds us that the marigold was specifically associated with fertility and marriage in eighteenth-century English texts; see *The Culture of Flowers* (Cambridge, 1993).

(E 50). This is a love that defies the slave traders' economics of commodification, exchange, and consumption, a love that enables the unrestrained expression of sexual desire and its gratification. And as E. P. Thompson has recently reminded us, this is also the love promoted by the antinomian Christian sects, the Swedenborgians and Muggletonians, to which Blake adhered.[16]

But whose interest, I would ask, does such a doctrine of free love serve? To persuade her lover to accept her sexually ripened body and forswear the "frozen" marriage bed, Oothoon promises Theotormon the following:

> . . . silken nets and traps of adamant will Oothoon spread,
> And catch for thee girls of mild silver, or of furious gold;
> I'll lie beside thee on a bank & view their wanton play
> In lovely copulation bliss on bliss with Theotormon:
> Red as the rosy morning, lustful as the first born beam,
> Oothoon shall view his dear delight, nor e'er with jealous cloud
> Come in the heaven of generous love; nor selfish blightings bring.
>
> (E 50)

Wollstonecraft had argued that free love of the kind here envisioned by Oothoon is a male fantasy that serves the interests only of the male libertine. As David Erdman enthused, "The soul of America who sings passionately of 'lovely copulation' is a woman and also a continent longing for fruit in her fertile valleys. To say that she wants to be loved, not raped, is to say, economically, that she wants to be cultivated by free men, not slaves or slave-drivers; for joy, not profit."[17] Erdman's assumption that the loving and lovable woman wants to "be cultivated" —rather than to cultivate—is an assumption he shared with Blake. Perhaps Blake was thinking of Stedman's happy slave family of Loango, in which husband and wife are free to find new sexual partners when either tires of the other. Or of Stedman's own bedroom frolics with Joanna and B---e. But where Stedman recognized that the black woman as well as the man could have other partners, Swedenborg and the Muggletonians explicitly forbade this for women,[18] and Blake's Oothoon never presents this possibility to Theotormon. Nor does Blake deal with the consequences of such sexual promiscuity: who will care for the numerous children

---

16. E. P. Thompson, *Witness against the Beast: William Blake and the Moral Law* (Cambridge, 1993), 138–39.
17. Erdman, *Blake: Prophet against Empire*, 227.
18. Thompson, *Witness against the Beast,* 138.

that will be born? Note that Blake visually erases the biological fact of Oothoon's pregnancy, even though the text insists upon it—unless the back view represented (E 49; color plate VIII) is meant to suggest a pregnant female body; if so, it is a pregnancy that Blake conceals with uncharacteristic modesty.

Some readers have suggested that Blake wanted us to see Oothoon's doctrine of free love, her "silken nets and traps of adamant," as well as the nets spread by Bromion and Theotormon, as Urizenic forms of psychological enslavement.[19] Although Bromion rather than Oothoon wears the ankle fetters of the slave in the frontispiece (color plate I), this image implies that *all three* characters remain trapped within Bromion's caves. The eye of the sun looking in from behind Blake's design onto this "religious" or Platonic cave may open up the possibility of an alternative sexual economy, for, as the Motto on the title page (color plate II) asserts, "the eye sees more than the heart knows." But if the Motto urges the reader to imagine an alternative to the slavery of modesty other than free love, the poem does not suggest what that alternative could be. As the creator of this poem and its designs, Blake must take responsibility for what the work does not say as well as for what it does say.

Finally, neither the verbal nor the visual representations of sex, violence, and slavery in *Visions of the Daughters of Albion* contests the racist or sexist dimensions of the Enlightenment discourse of Anglo-Africanism Blake inherited. Blake too equates ultimate freedom with the gratification of the desires of the white European male. Insofar as the black body can be assimilated into the white body, the black man can enjoy the same "rights" as the white man. Insofar as the female body gratifies the sexual and psychological desires of the male body, she achieves her freedom. Specifically, the "freedom" visually offered to Oothoon on the left side of the title page is that of the three female Graces, now swirling in ecstatic frenzy, but still seductively displayed to the gaze of male spectatorial desire.

More troubling, Blake's designs erase the spectacle of male violence against the female body. We do not see Bromion raping Oothoon. Instead we see only their postcoital exhaustion (color plate IV). When we do see the female body ag-

19. For such readings of slavery in *Visions of the Daughters of Albion,* see Ronald Paulson, *Representations of the Revolution (1780–1820)* (New Haven, Conn., 1983), 88–95; Mark Anderson, "Oothoon, Failed Prophet," *Romanticism Past and Present* 8 (1984): 1–21; Mark Bracher, "The Metaphysical Grounds of Oppression in Blake's *Visions of the Daughters of Albion,*" *Colby Library Quarterly* 20 (1984): 164–73; and Nancy Moore Goslee, "Slavery and Sexual Character: Questioning the Master Trope in Blake's *Visions of the Daughters of Albion,*" *ELH* 57 (1990): 101–28.

gressively penetrated, it is not by a man but by a bird (color plate VI). Oothoon here becomes Prometheus, willingly mutilated by Jupiter's or her lover Theotormon's eagle for the benefit of mankind. Blake thus transforms the literal atrocities of slavery in the West Indies (recall Stedman's description of the male slave hanging from a hook, his putrifying breast eaten by vultures) into a visual *metaphor,* into a rhetorical figure of heroic Promethean suffering. Blake thereby distances us from the physical tortures of slavery and at the same time subtly suggests that the female slave welcomes her painful sexual servicing of male desire.

At the level of sexual politics, this poem—like Stedman's *Narrative* before it—must finally be seen as condoning the continuation of female slavery under a benevolent master. Does not this idealized image of a female eagerly offering her flesh to her lover's beak support Bromion's claim that the daughters of the sun "resist not, they . . . worship terrors and obey the violent" (E 45)? From this feminist perspective, one visual source for Blake's design for the Argument (color plate III), Joseph-Marie Vien's *The Selling of Cupids* (identified by Erdman),[20] reverberates with brutal irony, for *Visions of the Daughters of Albion* finally *endorses* Vien's representation of the female as a *procurer* of love and sexual gratification, no longer for upper-class ladies, as in Vien's image, but for men only.

I would like to close on a less tendentious and more theoretical note. From our perspective it is easy to see the problems inherent in the Enlightenment attempt to assimilate the black body into the white body; the same problems confront Wollstonecraft's attempt to assimilate the female body into the male body. Her doctrine of sexual equality, now institutionalized in the American legal system,[21] takes the male body as the norm and insists on women's sameness with that body. Clearly, Wollstonecraft's liberal feminism fails to give an adequate account of female difference, specifically of the difference in sexual reproduction. Blake's alternative solution to the problem of sexual difference, free love, is equally problematic. But our society has not yet developed a viable theoretical alternative to these accounts. We still need a political and legal system that can resist the Blakean or Hegelian temptation of a dialectic in which one contrary finally

20. Erdman, *Blake: Prophet against Empire,* 240–41.
21. The failure to acknowledge such difference was vividly demonstrated a few years ago by a legal case involving California Federal Savings, in which pregnancy was legally defined as a "disability" to guarantee the sexes equal health benefits—an extremely odd way to define the fundamental process of creating human life.

takes precedence over or is drawn into synthesis with the other. For Blake, it is "maleness" that, at the most fundamental level, takes priority over "femaleness," as Marc Kaplan has documented in his recent analysis of Blake and gender.[22] We still need a political and legal system that can construct racial, cultural, and sexual difference rather than assimilation as the highest social value.

University of California, Los Angeles

22. Marc Kaplan, "Weeping Woman/Weaving Woman: Gender Roles in Blake's Mythology" (Ph.D. diss., UCLA, 1993). Chapter 5 of this dissertation appeared as "Blake's *Milton:* The Metaphysics of Gender," in *Nineteenth-Century Contexts* 19 (1995): 151–78.

Color Plates

I–XI. *Visions of the Daughters of Albion,* copy E (etched and printed 1793). Huntington Library.

I.	17.1 x 11.9 cm		VII.	17 x 11.5 cm
II.	16.3 x 12.9 cm		VIII.	17.2 x 11.7 cm
III.	14.2 x 11.2 cm		IX.	15.9 x 11.7 cm
IV.	17 x 11.7 cm		X.	16.9 x 12 cm
V.	17.1 x 11.7 cm		XI.	16.9 x 11.8 cm
VI.	16.8 x 11.6 cm			

XII. "The Little Black Boy" (first plate), *Songs of Innocence,* copy G (etched and printed 1789), plate 29. Yale Center for British Art, Paul Mellon Collection. 11.1 x 6.9 cm.

XIII. "The Little Black Boy" (second plate), *Songs of Innocence,* copy G (etched and printed 1789), plate 30. Yale Center for British Art, Paul Mellon Collection. 11.1 x 6.7 cm.

XIV. "The Little Black Boy" (second plate), *Songs of Innocence and of Experience,* copy F (etched and printed 1789), plate 6. Yale Center for British Art, Paul Mellon Collection. 11.1 x 6.7 cm.

XV. "The Little Black Boy" (second plate), *Songs of Innocence and of Experience,* copy E (etched and printed 1789; coloring touched up at a later date), plate 11. Huntington Library. 11.1 x 6.7 cm.

XVI. *Nebuchadnezzar* (designed 1795; perhaps printed c. 1805). Minneapolis Institute of Arts. 43 x 60.3 cm.

XVII. *Newton* (designed 1795; printed c. 1805). Tate Gallery / Art Resource, New York. 46 x 60 cm.

XVIII. "The red limbd angel . . . ," *Europe: A Prophecy,* copy G (etched and printed 1794). Pierpont Morgan Library, PML 77235. 23.3 x 16.9 cm.

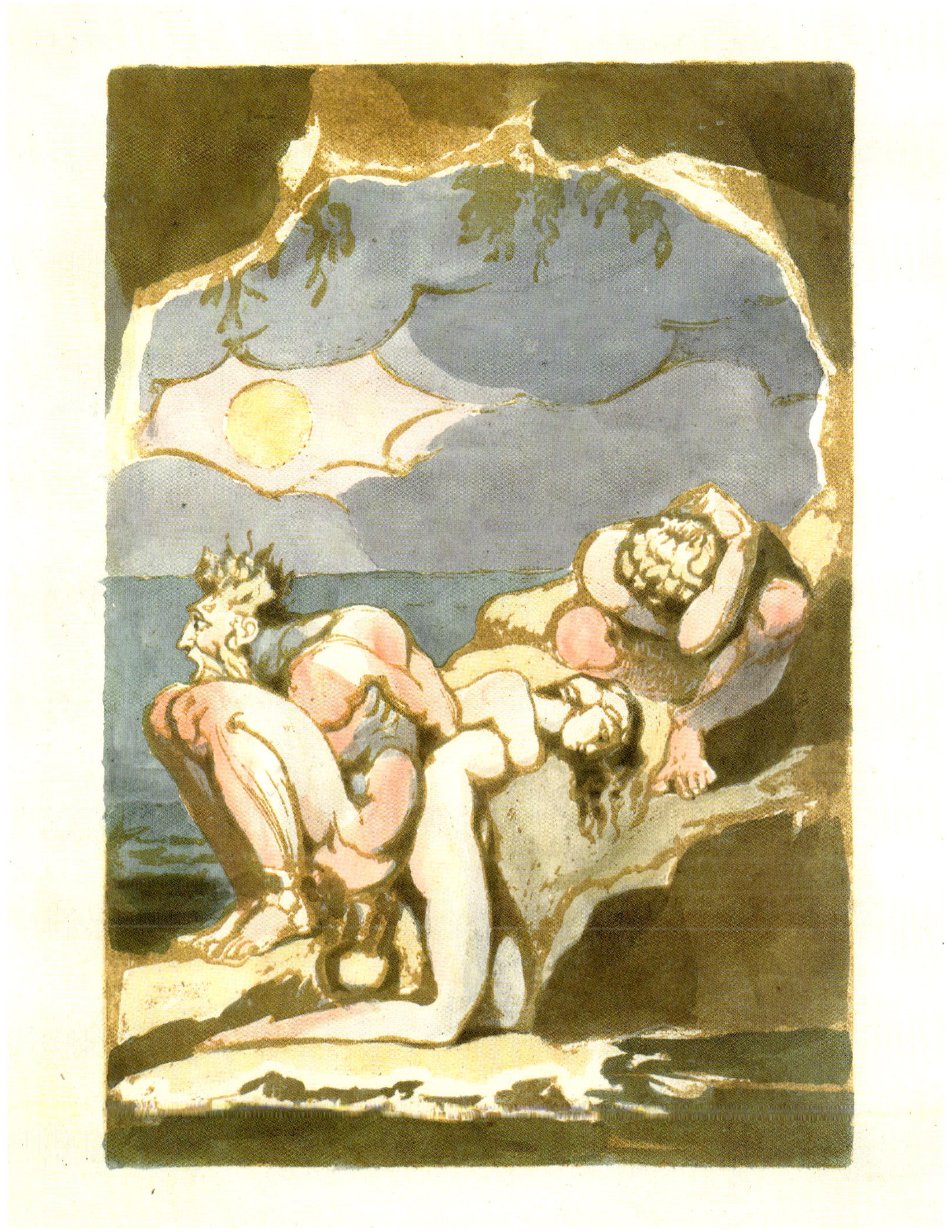

I

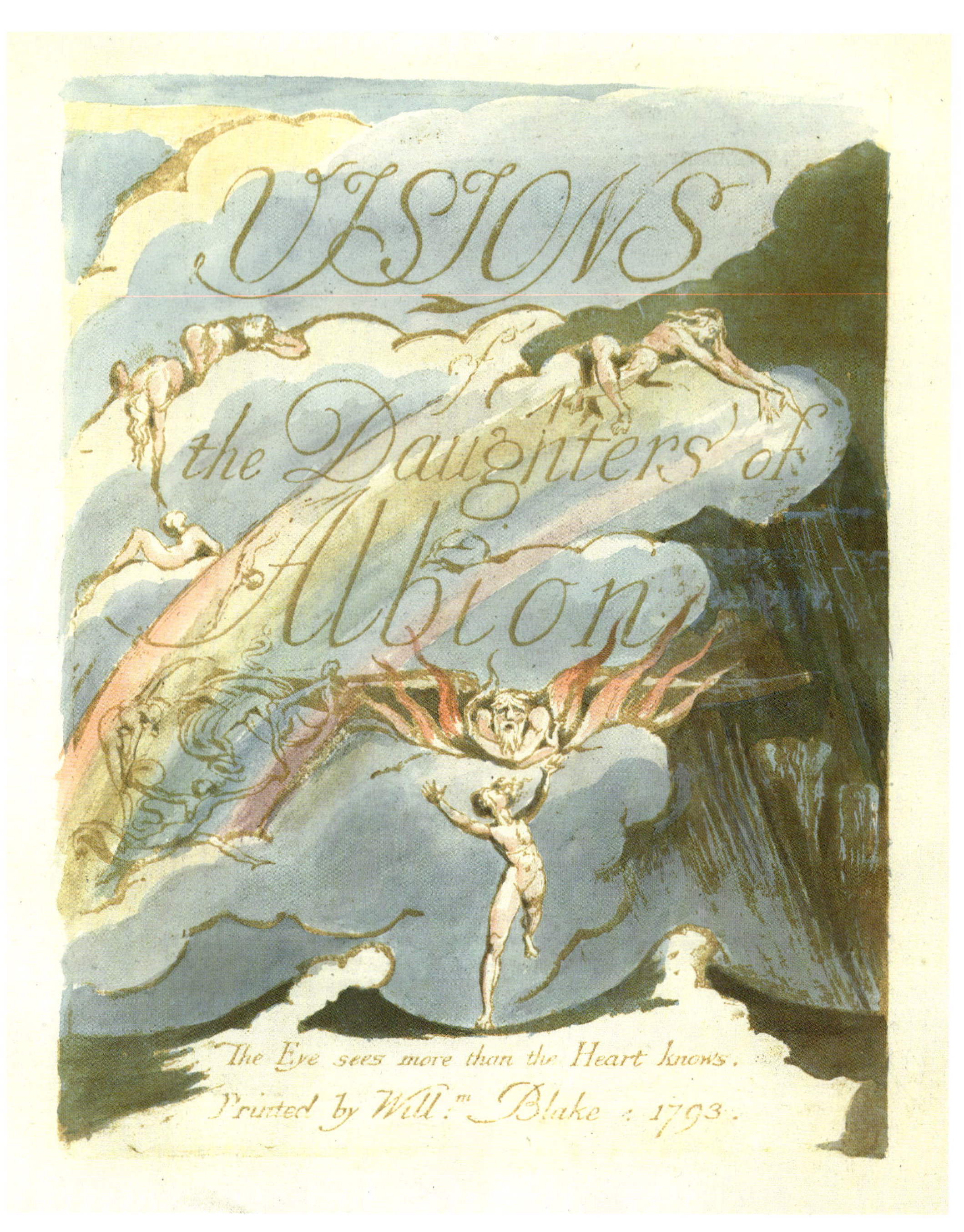

VISIONS
of
the Daughters of
Albion
The Eye sees more than the Heart knows.
Printed by Will.ᵐ Blake : 1793.

II

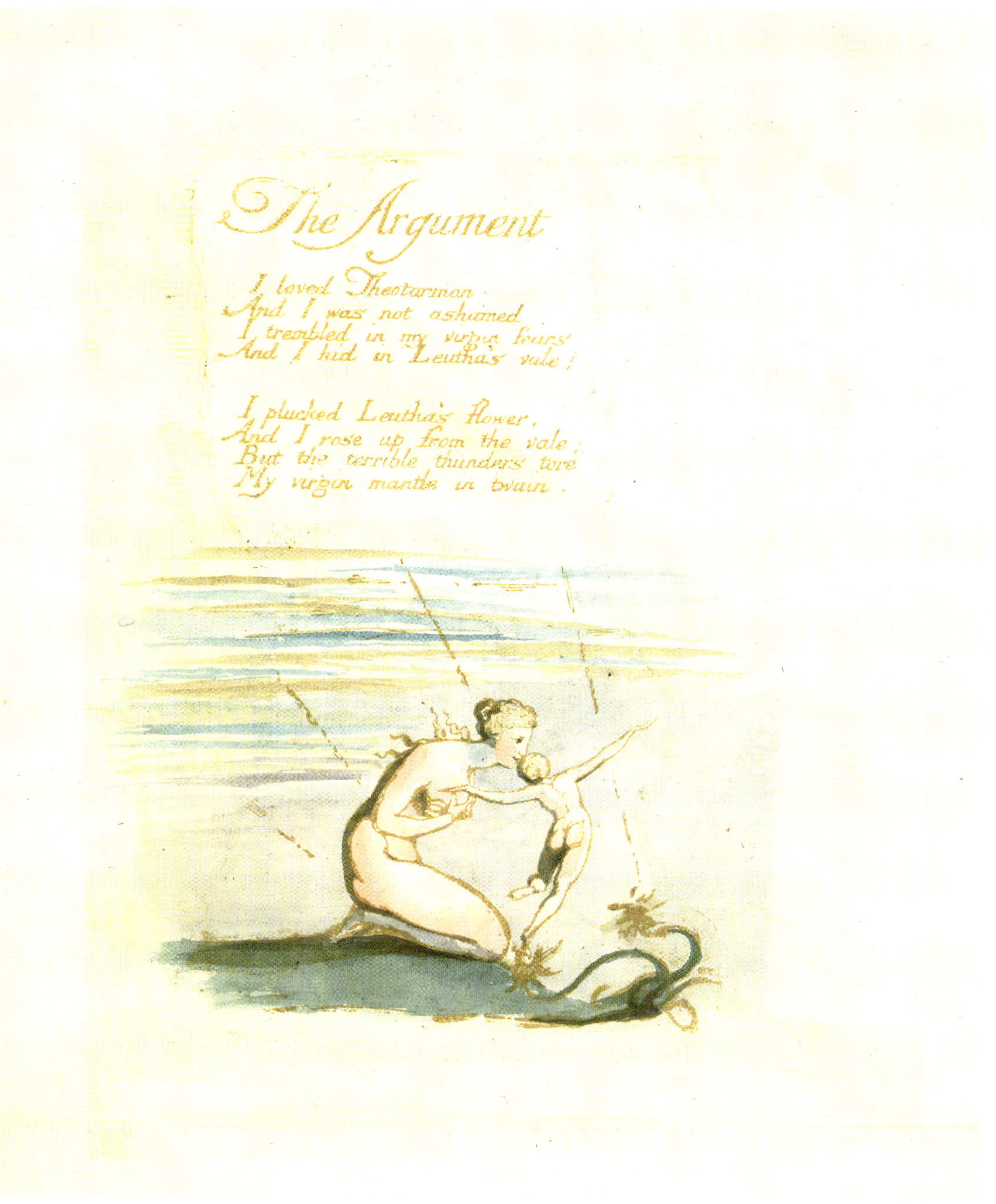

The Argument

I loved Theotormon
And I was not ashamed
I trembled in my virgin fears
And I hid in Leutha's vale!

I plucked Leutha's flower,
And I rose up from the vale;
But the terrible thunders tore
My virgin mantle in twain.

III

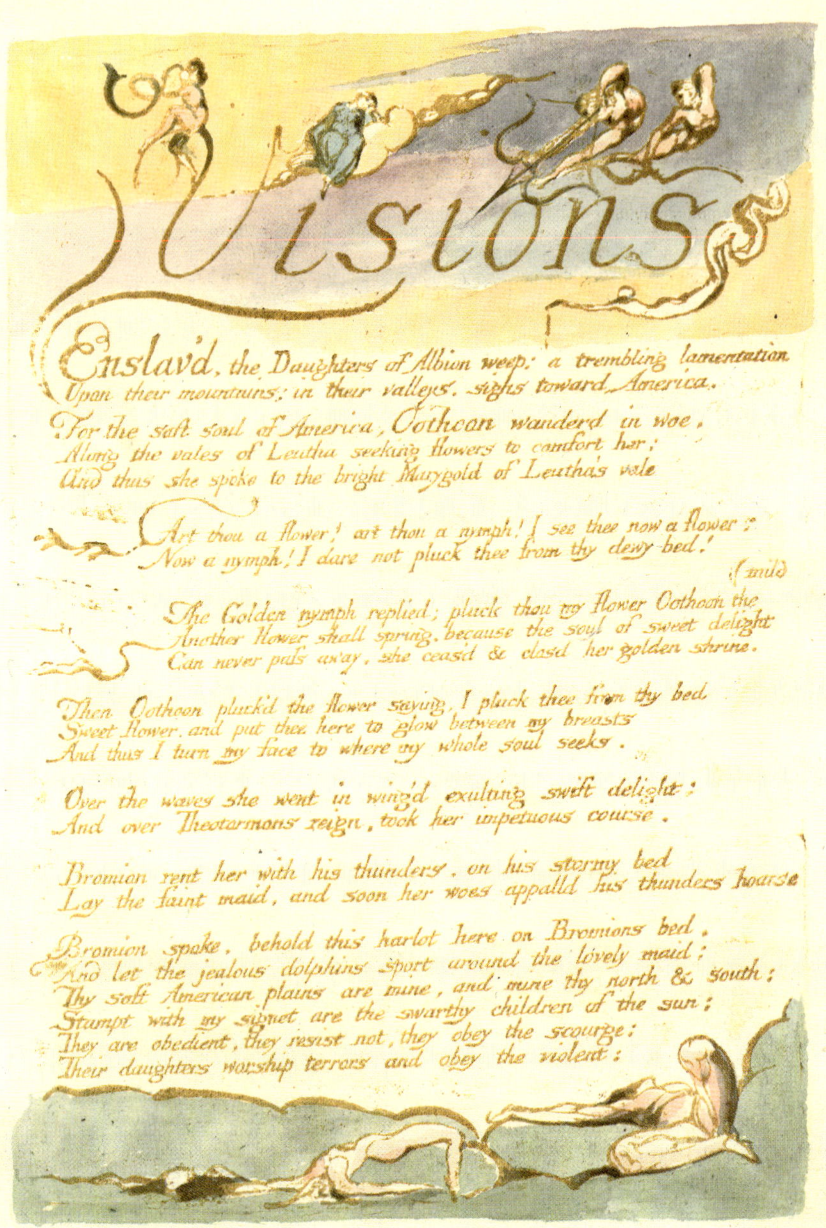

Visions

Enslav'd, the Daughters of Albion weep: a trembling lamentation
Upon their mountains: in their valleys. sighs toward America.

For the soft soul of America, Oothoon wanderd in woe.
Along the vales of Leutha seeking flowers to comfort her:
And thus she spoke to the bright Marygold of Leutha's vale

Art thou a flower! art thou a nymph! I see thee now a flower:
Now a nymph! I dare not pluck thee from thy dewy bed!

The Golden nymph replied; pluck thou my flower Oothoon the mild
Another flower shall spring. because the soul of sweet delight
Can never pass away. she ceas'd & closd her golden shrine.

Then Oothoon pluck'd the flower saying, I pluck thee from thy bed
Sweet flower. and put thee here to glow between my breasts
And thus I turn my face to where my whole soul seeks.

Over the waves she went in wing'd exulting swift delight:
And over Theotormons reign, took her impetuous course.

Bromion rent her with his thunders. on his stormy bed
Lay the faint maid, and soon her woes appalld his thunders hoarse

Bromion spoke. behold this harlot here on Bromions bed.
And let the jealous dolphins sport around the lovely maid:
Thy soft American plains are mine, and mine thy north & south:
Stampt with my signet are the swarthy children of the sun:
They are obedient, they resist not, they obey the scourge:
Their daughters worship terrors and obey the violent:

IV

Now thou maist marry Bromions harlot. and protect the child
Of Bromions rage, that Oothoon shall put forth in nine moons
time

Then storms rent Theotormons limbs; he rolld his waves around.
And folded his black jealous waters round the adulterate pair
Bound back to back in Bromions caves terror & meeknefs dwell

At entrance Theotormon sits wearing the threshold hard
With secret tears; beneath him sound like waves on a desart shore
The voice of slaves beneath the sun, and children bought with money,
That shiver in religious caves beneath the burning fires
Of lust, that belch incefsant from the summits of the earth

Oothoon weeps not. she cannot weep! her tears are locked up;
But she can howl incefsant writhing her soft snowy limbs.
And calling Theotormons Eagles to prey upon her flesh.

I call with holy voice! kings of the sounding air.
Rend away this defiled bosom that I may reflect.
The image of Theotormon on my pure transparent breast.

The Eagles at her call descend & rend their bleeding prey;
Theotormon severely smiles. her soul reflects the smile;
As the clear spring mudded with feet of beasts grows pure & smiles

The Daughters of Albion hear her woes. & eccho back her sighs.

Why does my Theotormon sit weeping upon the threshold;
And Oothoon hovers by his side, persuading him in vain;
I cry arise O Theotormon for the village dog
Barks at the breaking day. the nightingale has done lamenting.
The lark does rustle in the ripe corn, and the Eagle returns
From nightly prey. and lifts his golden beak to the pure east;
Shaking the dust from his immortal pinions to awake
The sun that sleeps too long. Arise my Theotormon I am pure.
Because the night is gone that clos'd me in its deadly black.
They told me that the night & day were all that I could see;
They told me that I had five senses to inclose me up.
And they inclos'd my infinite brain into a narrow circle.
And sunk my heart into the Abyfs. a red round globe hot burning
Till all from life I was obliterated and erased.
Instead of morn arises a bright shadow. like an eye
In the eastern cloud; instead of night a sickly charnel house;
That Theotormon hears me not! to him the night and morn
Are both alike; a night of sighs, a morning of fresh tears;

V

And none but Bromion can hear my lamentations.

With what sense is it that the chicken shuns the ravenous hawk?
With what sense does the tame pigeon measure out the expanse?
With what sense does the bee form cells? have not the mouse & frog
Eyes and ears and sense of touch? yet are their habitations.
And their pursuits, as different as their forms and as their joys:
Ask the wild ass why he refuses burdens: and the meek camel
Why he loves man: is it because of eye ear mouth or skin
Or breathing nostrils? No. for these the wolf and tyger have.
Ask the blind worm the secrets of the grave, and why her spires
Love to curl round the bones of death; and ask the ravenous snake
Where she gets poison: & the wing'd eagle why he loves the sun
And then tell me the thoughts of man, that have been hid of old.

Silent I hover all the night, and all day could be silent.
If Theotormon once would turn his loved eyes upon me;
How can I be defild when I reflect thy image pure?   (woe
Sweetest the fruit that the worm feeds on. & the soul prey'd on by
The new washd lamb ting'd with the village smoke & the bright swan
By the red earth of our immortal river: I bathe my wings,
And I am white and pure to hover round Theotormons breast.

Then Theotormon broke his silence. and he answered.

Tell me what is the night or day to one o'erflowd with woe?
Tell me what is a thought? & of what substance is it made?
Tell me what is a joy? & in what gardens do joys grow?
And in what rivers swim the sorrows? and upon what mountains

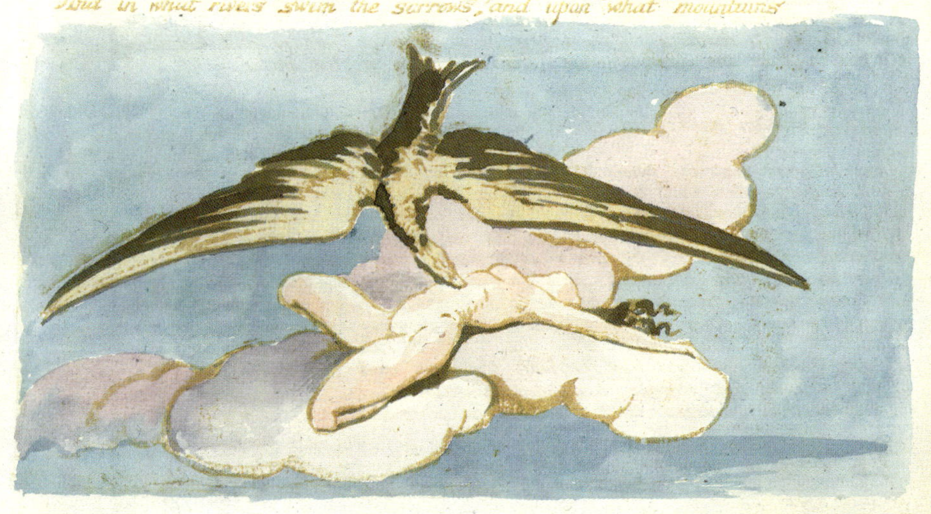

VI

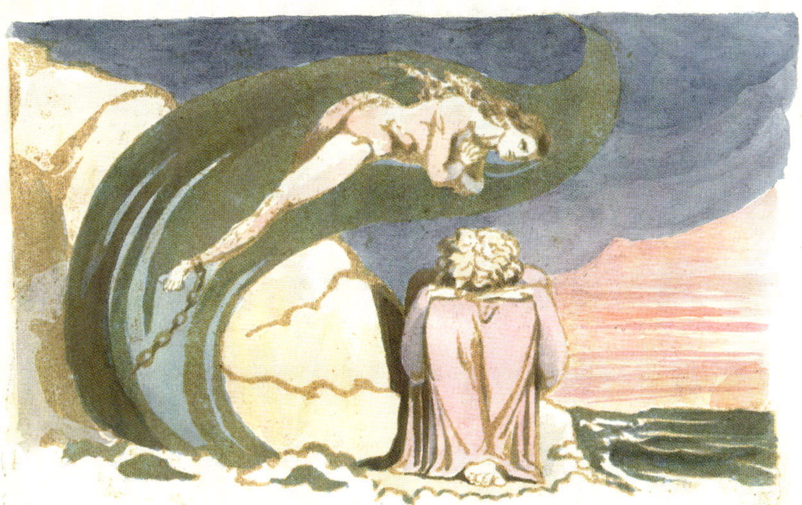

Wave shadows of discontent? and in what houses dwell the wretched
Drunken with woe forgotten. and shut up from cold despair.

Tell me where dwell the thoughts forgotten till thou call them forth
Tell me where dwell the joys of old! & where the ancient loves?
And when will they renew again & the night of oblivion past?
That I might traverse times & spaces far remote and bring
Comforts into a present sorrow and a night of pain
Where goest thou O thought! to what remote land is thy flight?
If thou returnest to the present moment of affliction
Wilt thou bring comforts on thy wings. and dews and honey and balm;
Or poison from the desart wilds, from the eyes of the envier.

Then Bromion said: and shook the cavern with his lamentation

Thou knowest that the ancient trees seen by thine eyes have fruit;
But knowest thou that trees and fruits flourish upon the earth
To gratify senses unknown? trees beasts and birds unknown:
Unknown, not unpercievd, spread in the infinite microscope,
In places yet unvisited by the voyager. and in worlds
Over another kind of seas, and in atmospheres unknown:
Ah! are there other wars, beside the wars of sword and fire!
And are there other sorrows, beside the sorrows of poverty?
And are there other joys, beside the joys of riches and ease?
And is there not one law for both the lion and the ox?
And is there not eternal fire, and eternal chains?
To bind the phantoms of existence from eternal life?

Then Oothoon waited silent all the day, and all the night,

VII

But when the morn arose, her lamentation renewd,
The Daughters of Albion hear her woes, & eccho back her sighs.

O Urizen! Creator of men! mistaken Demon of heaven;
Thy joys are tears! thy labour vain, to form men to thine image.
How can one joy absorb another? are not different joys
Holy, eternal, infinite! and each joy is a Love.

Does not the great mouth laugh at a gift? & the narrow eyelids mock
At the labour that is above payment, and wilt thou take the ape
For thy councellor? or the dog, for a schoolmaster to thy children?
Does he who contemns poverty, and he who turns with abhorrence
From usury: feel the same passion or are they moved alike?
How can the giver of gifts experience the delights of the merchant?
How the industrious citizen the pains of the husbandman.
How different far the fat fed hireling with hollow drum;
Who buys whole corn fields into wastes, and sings upon the heath:
How different their eye and ear! how different the world to them!
With what sense does the parson claim the labour of the farmer?
What are his nets & gins & traps, & how does he surround him
With cold floods of abstraction, and with forests of solitude,
To build him castles and high spires, where kings & priests may dwell.
Till she who burns with youth, and knows no fixed lot; is bound
In spells of law to one she loaths: and must she drag the chain
Of life, in weary lust! must chilling murderous thoughts, obscure
The clear heaven of her eternal spring? to bear the wintry rage
Of a harsh terror drivn to madness, bound to hold a rod
Over her shrinking shoulders all the day; & all the night
To turn the wheel of false desire: and longings that wake her womb
To the abhorred birth of cherubs in the human form.
That live a pestilence & die a meteor & are no more.
Till the child dwell with one he hates, and do the deed he loaths
And the impure scourge force his seed into its unripe birth
E'er yet his eyelids can behold the arrows of the day.

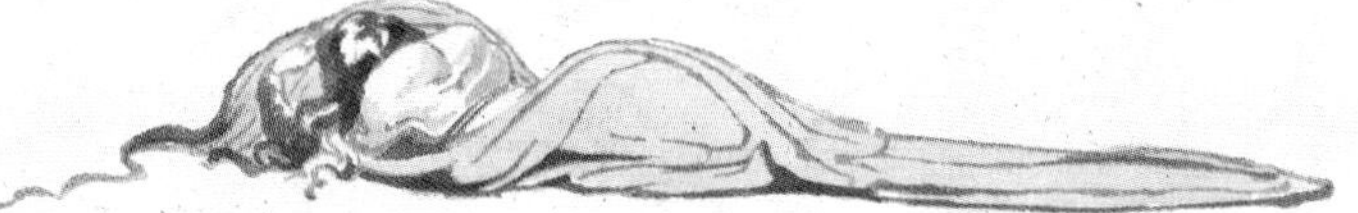

Does the whale worship at thy footsteps as the hungry dog?
Or does he scent the mountain prey, because his nostrils wide
Draw in the ocean? does his eye discern the flying cloud
As the ravens eye? or does he measure the expanse like the vulture?
Does the still spider view the cliffs where eagles hide their young?
Or does the fly rejoice, because the harvest is brought in?
Does not the eagle scorn the earth & despise the treasures beneath?
But the mole knoweth what is there, & the worm shall tell it thee.
Does not the worm erect a pillar in the mouldering church yard?

VIII

And a palace of eternity in the jaws of the hungry grave
Over his porch these words are written. Take thy bliss O Man!
And sweet shall be thy taste & sweet thy infant joys renew!

Infancy, fearless, lustful, happy! nestling for delight
In laps of pleasure; Innocence! honest, open, seeking
The vigorous joys of morning light; open to virgin bliss.
Who taught thee modesty, subtil modesty! child of night & sleep
When thou awakest. wilt thou dissemble all thy secret joys
Or wert thou not awake when all this mystery was disclos'd!
Then com'st thou forth a modest virgin knowing to dissemble
With nets found under thy night pillow, to catch virgin joy,
And brand it with the name of whore; & sell it in the night,
In silence. evn without a whisper, and in seeming sleep.
Religious dreams and holy vespers, light thy smoky fires;
Once were thy fires lighted by the eyes of honest morn
And does my Theotormon seek this hypocrite modesty!
This knowing, artful, secret, fearful, cautious, trembling hypocrite.
Then is Oothoon a whore indeed! and all the virgin joys
Of life are harlots: and Theotormon is a sick mans dream
And Oothoon is the crafty slave of selfish holiness.

But Oothoon is not so, a virgin filld with virgin fancies
Open to joy and to delight where ever beauty appears
If in the morning sun I find it: there my eyes are fixd

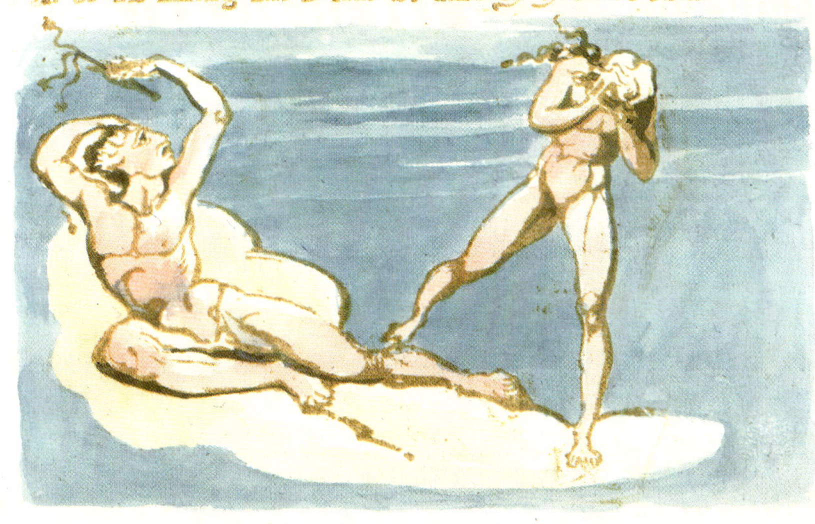

IX

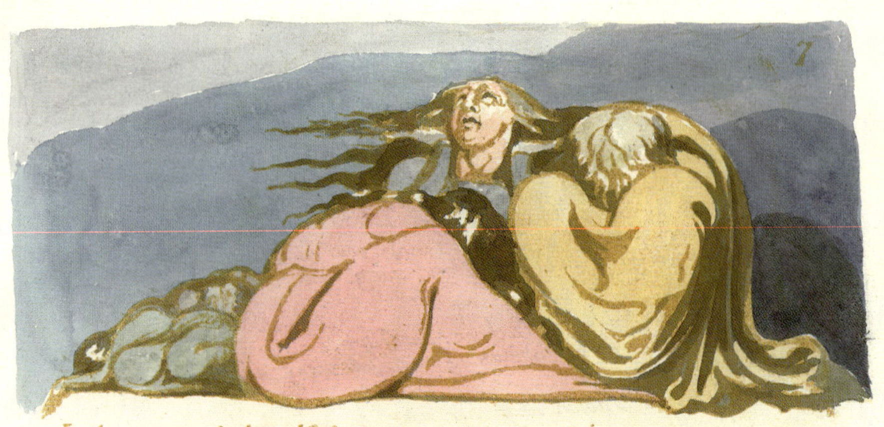

In happy copulation; if in evening mild. wearied with work;
Sit on a bank and draw the pleasures of this free born joy.

The moment of desire! the moment of desire! The virgin
That pines for man; shall awaken her womb to enormous joys
In the secret shadows of her chamber; the youth shut up from
The lustful joy. shall forget to generate. & create an amorous image
In the shadows of his curtains and in the folds of his silent pillow.
Are not these the places of religion? the rewards of continence?
The self enjoyings of self denial? Why dost thou seek religion?
Is it because acts are not lovely, that thou seekest solitude,
Where the horrible darkness is impressed with reflections of desire.

Father of Jealousy. be thou accursed from the earth!
Why hast thou taught my Theotormon this accursed thing?
Till beauty fades from off my shoulders darken'd and cast out,
A solitary shadow wailing on the margin of non-entity.

I cry, Love! Love! Love! happy happy Love! free as the mountain wind!
Can that be Love, that drinks another as a sponge drinks water?
That clouds with jealousy his nights, with weepings all the day:
To spin a web of age around him. grey and hoary! dark!
Till his eyes sicken at the fruit that hangs before his sight.
Such is self-love that envies all! a creeping skeleton
With lamplike eyes watching around the frozen marriage bed.

But silken nets and traps of adamant will Oothoon spread,
And catch for thee girls of mild silver, or of furious gold:
I'll lie beside thee on a bank & view their wanton play
In lovely copulation bliss on bliss with Theotormon:
Red as the rosy morning, lustful as the first born beam,
Oothoon shall view his dear delight, nor eer with jealous cloud
Come in the heaven of generous love; nor selfish blightings bring.

Does the sun walk in glorious raiment, on the secret floor

X

Where the cold miser spreads his gold! or does the bright cloud
On his stone threshold; does his eye behold the beam that brings
Expansion to the eye of pity? or will he bind himself
Beside the ox to thy hard furrow? does not that mild beam blot
The bat, the owl, the glowing tyger, and the king of night,
The sea fowl takes the wintry blast, for a covering to her limbs:
And the wild snake, the pestilence to adorn him with gems & gold.
And trees & birds, & beasts, & men, behold their eternal joy.
Arise you little glancing wings, and sing your infant joy!
Arise and drink your bliss, for every thing that lives is holy!

Thus every morning wails Oothoon, but Theotormon sits
Upon the margind ocean conversing with shadows dire.

The Daughters of Albion hear her woes, & eccho back her sighs.

The End

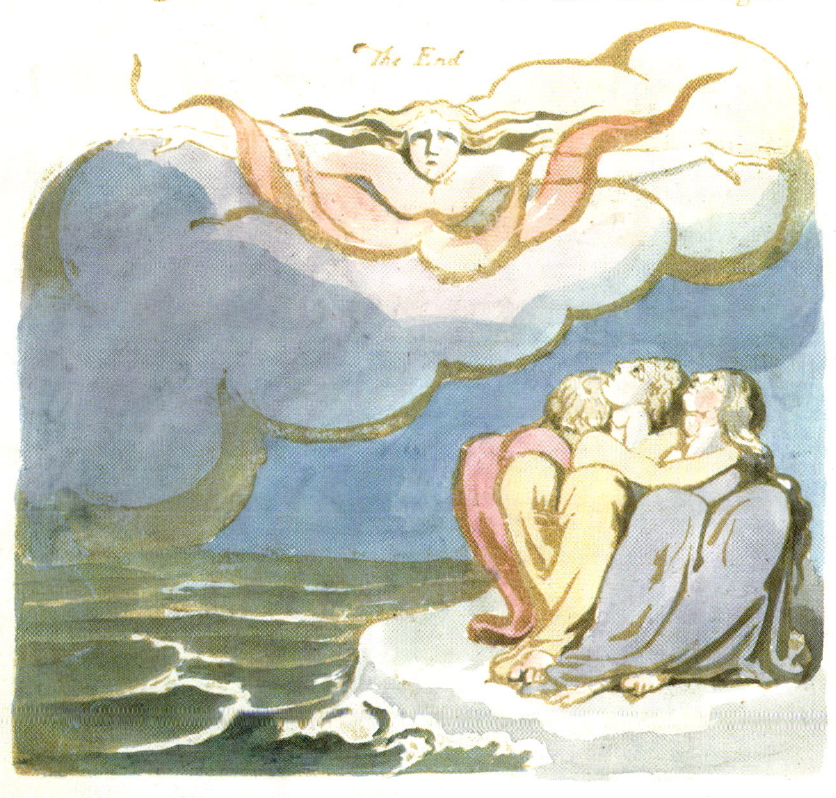

XI

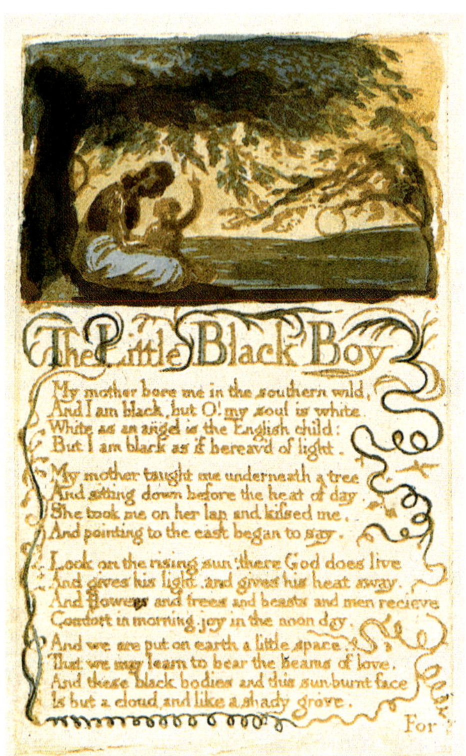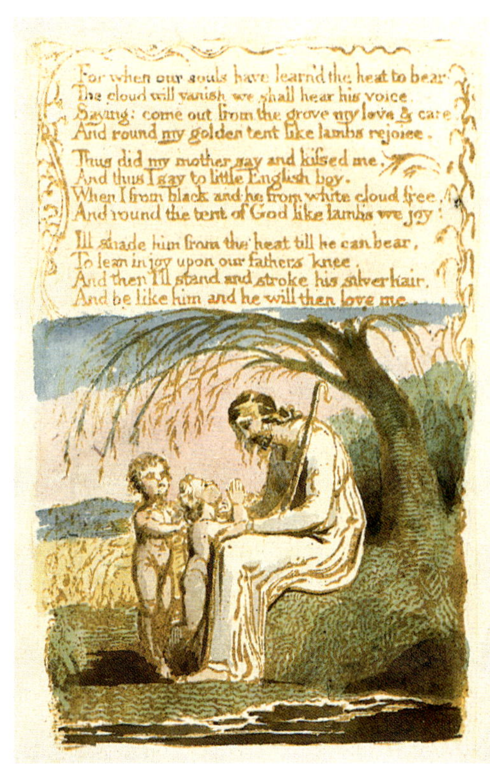

XII (left), XIII (right)

"The Little Black Boy," *Songs of Innocence,* copy G

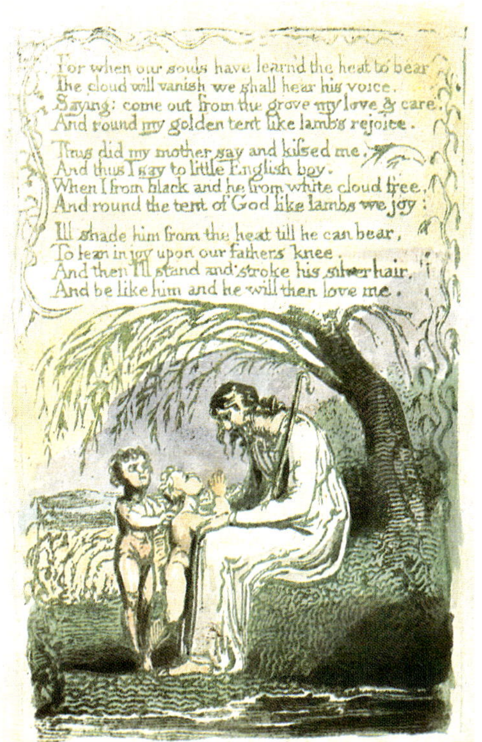 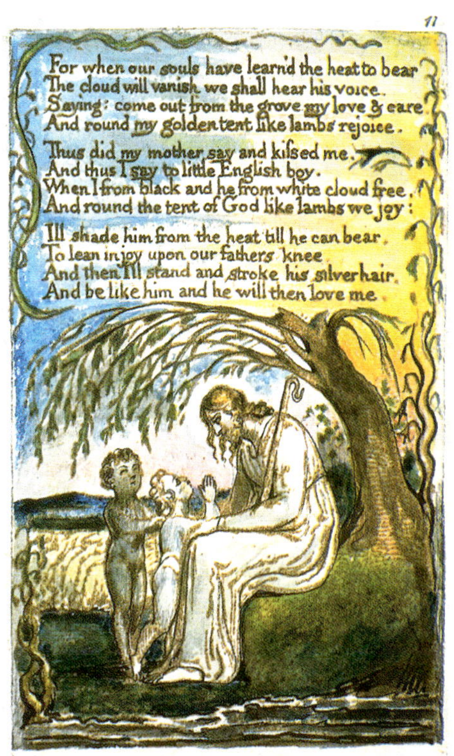

XIV (left), XV (right)

"The Little Black Boy" (second plate),
XIV: *Songs of Innocence and of Experience,* copy F
XV: *Songs of Innocence and of Experience,* copy E

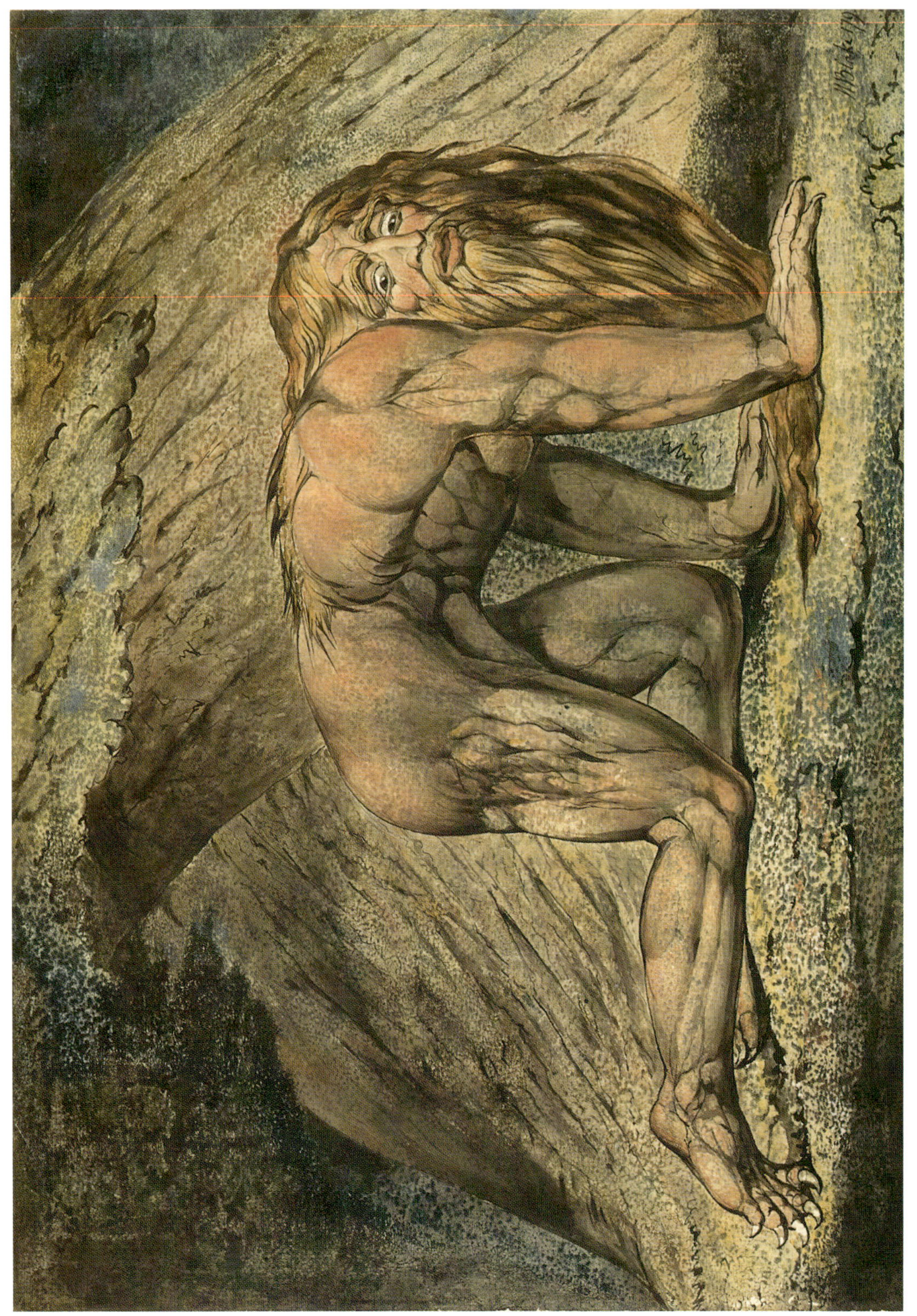

XVI

Nebuchadnezzar

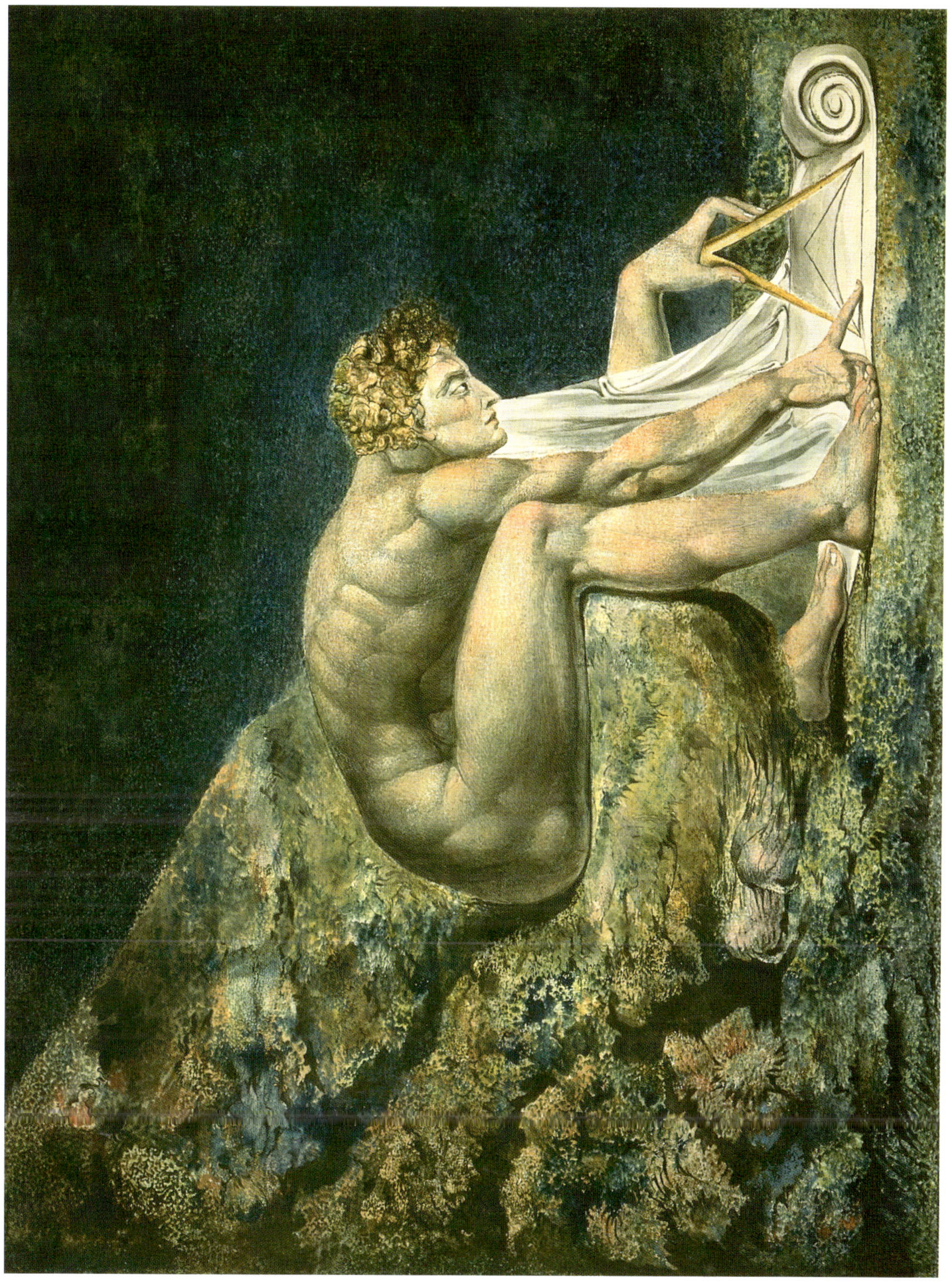

XVII

Newton

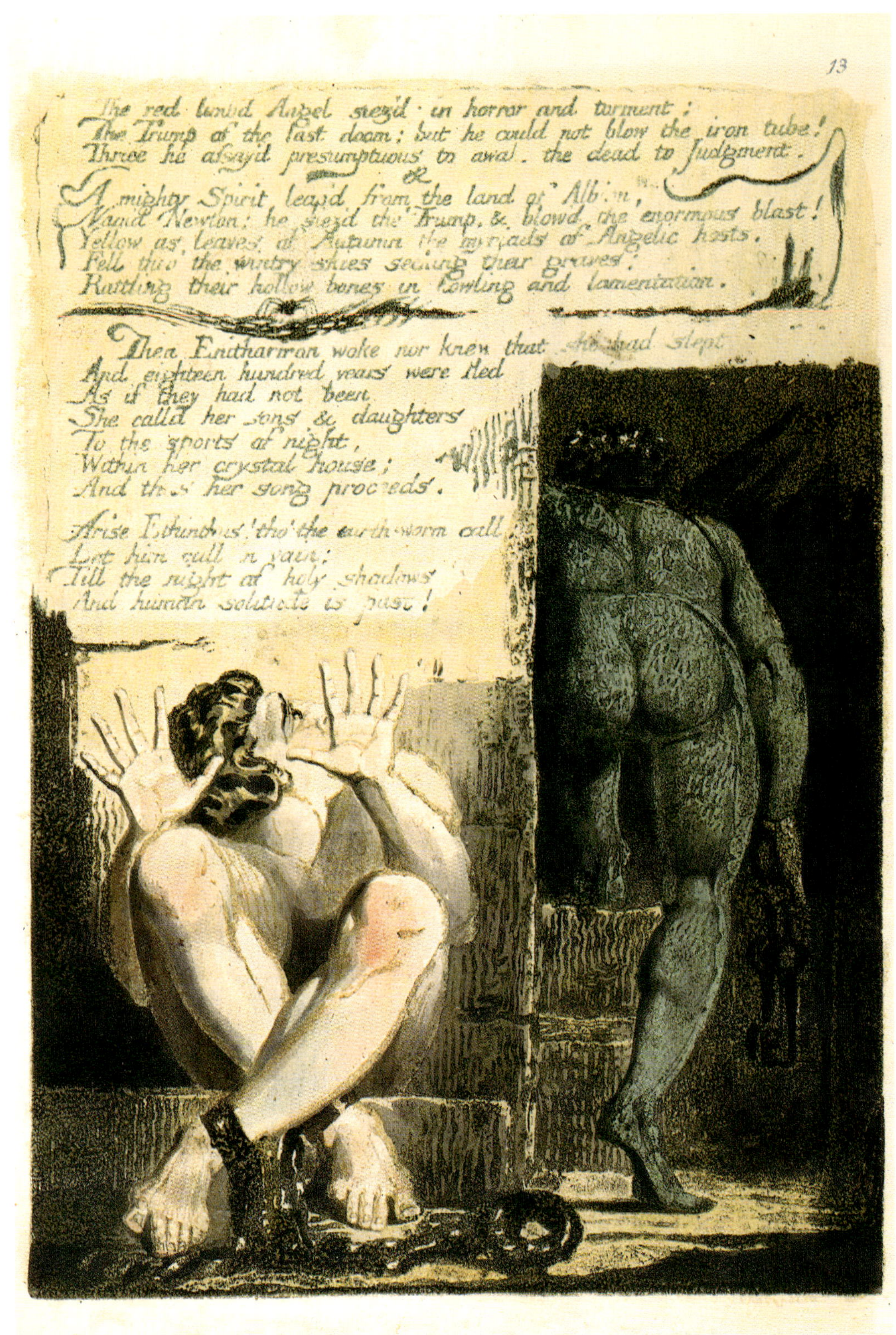

XVIII

"The red limbd angel . . . ," *Europe: A Prophecy,* copy G

Blake's Vision of Slavery Revisited

———————————————————————————— DAVID BINDMAN

Specific references to contemporary physical—as opposed to spiritual—slavery are infrequent in Blake's writings. Such references as there are mostly occur, as one might expect, around 1790, during the national campaigns to abolish slavery. In a seminal article of 1952, "Blake's Vision of Slavery," David Erdman argued that the illuminated book *Visions of the Daughters of Albion* was, among other things, an abolitionist parable locked into the current debates over the morality of slavery and British involvement in the slave trade.[1] The three main actors in the *Visions* accordingly represent the main interests involved in those debates. The villainous Bromion, who rapes the liberty-seeking Oothoon, is a West Indian slave-owner exploiting "the swarthy children of the sun," who bear the mark of his signet. Oothoon represents the enslaved British nation and presumably also African slaves seeking liberty, while Theotormon is an ineffectual liberal with the right beliefs but absorbed in his own misery, unwilling to act and thus unable to liberate Oothoon and combat slavery, whether it be of women or of Africans (frontispiece; color plate I).

According to Erdman, the hapless Theotormon was drawn from Captain John Stedman, whose book on slavery in Surinam contained illustrations by the author that Blake engraved.[2] Stedman, whom Blake apparently knew well, was a man who reputedly deplored slavery and pitied slaves; however, as Anne K. Mellor has noted, Stedman was in fact an apologist for slavery.[3] Theotormon is also by implication William Wilberforce, who opposed slavery, but only until he was accused of Jacobinism in the wake of the French Revolution. Blake himself, in Erdman's account, appears to be passionately opposed to slavery but at the same time capable of enough detachment to see through the hypocrisy of both

1. *Journal of the Warburg and Courtauld Institutes* 15 (1952): 242–52.
2. J. G. Stedman, *A Narrative of a five years expedition, against the Revolted Negroes of Surinam* (London, 1796), some of these reproduced in Anne K. Mellor's article in this issue.
3. See her article in this volume.

the slave lobby (Bromion) and the abolitionists (Theotormon); and he speaks up for sexual freedom as well as the humanity of the enslaved blacks.

Even if we do not accept the whole of Erdman's argument, there is no reason to doubt that Blake supported the abolition of slavery. But the few references Blake made in his writings to Africa and Africans and the way he pictured them—particularly in "The Little Black Boy" in *Songs of Innocence* and *Songs of Innocence and of Experience* (color plates XII–XV)—raise older questions of causality and the relationship of body and soul that, in the seventeenth and eighteenth centuries, had divided scientists from theologians in the discussion of racial differences: was the sun the physical cause of the African's dark skin color; and what was God's purpose in so differentiating Africans from their fellow beings? The idea that exposure to the sun causes the blackness of the African's body is, however, an ancient one; and the notion that a black body might contain a white soul is expressed at least as early as the third century. A Greek epitaph to a black slave reads, as Christopher Miller notes, "Among the living I was very black, darkened by the rays of the sun, but my soul, ever blooming with white flowers, won my prudent master's good will."[4] Miller further points out that common to all ancient references to the spiritual and physical beauty of blacks is just such an implicit "despite"[5]: "blackness" implied a negative that might be overcome by an act of redemptive faith or by an exceptional beauty that could transcend the assumed disability of a dark skin.

Blake's "The Little Black Boy," printed in 1789, obviously reflects on such issues, and I want to begin to consider them by looking at the visual format of the poem. Taken in isolation it bears—as indeed do all the poems in *Songs of Innocence*—a strong resemblance to single-sheet illustrated broadsides and small pamphlets of the type produced in large numbers by popular publishers in the period. Some, like the two-page pamphlet *The African Widow* (shown in figure 24) were produced by evangelical abolitionists and sold for the benefit of "a society, instituted for the relief of the bodily and spiritual wants of the poor African and Asiatic strangers, whom various circumstances in Providence have brought to England." The pamphlet tells harrowingly of the misfortunes of an African widow who has now lost her child and is all alone in her heathen state. She laments over the tomb of husband and child in a churchyard until one day she encounters a rich lady there who introduces her to the idea of the mercy of Jesus, who will in turn grant the widow eternal peace and redemption:

4.   Quoted in Frank Snowden, *Blacks in Antiquity* (Cambridge, Mass., 1970), 178; and discussed in Christopher Miller, *Blank Darkness: Africanist Discourse in French* (Chicago, 1986), 19.
5.   Miller, *Africanist Discourse in French*, 30f.

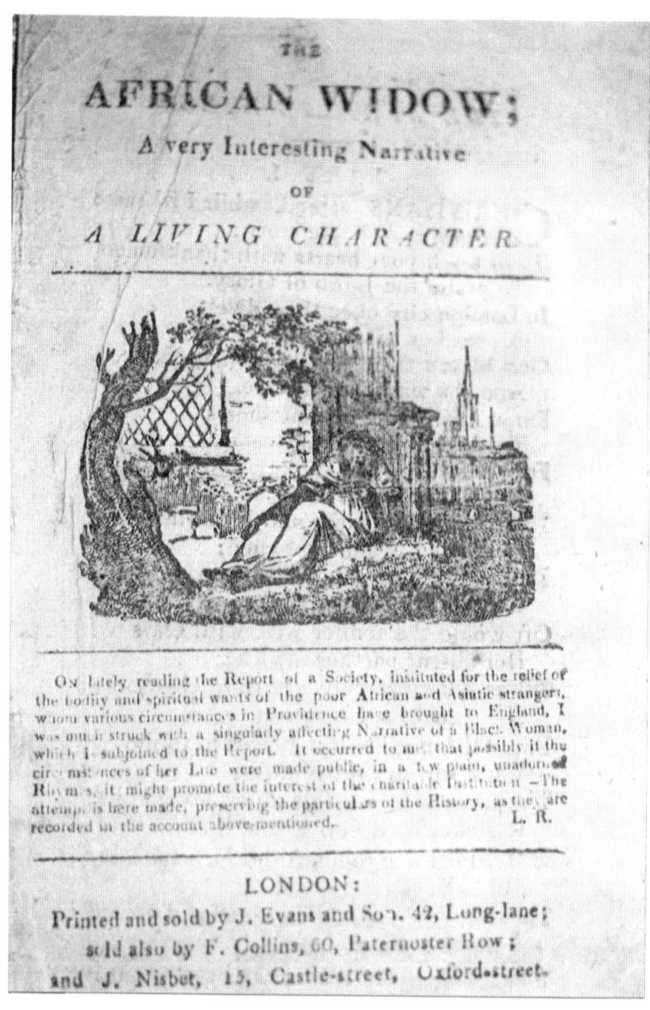

Figure 24. First page of anonymous pamphlet *The African Widow*, c. 1790–1800 (author's collection).

> Dark was my day of ignorance,
> And dark of sin my night,
> But now the shade of death is turn'd
> To morning's welcome light.

Behind the poem is the evangelical abolitionist view that it is a Christian duty to convert the African; and it is carried out in the poem by a wealthy lady as an act of charity and obligation. The point of the pamphlet was presumably to encourage wealthy individuals to take seriously the idea of converting heathens rather than leaving them in a state of "darkness."

Ephemeral pamphlets such as *The African Widow* provide a point of reference for Blake's poem, which also contains the central idea of redemption through Christ; but Blake's central metaphor is of blackness of skin as an unredeemed state in "the southern wild." To paraphrase the poem: the African's blackness, the Little Black Boy's mother tells us, is caused by the sun, which is the source of light and heat. Africans are especially tried because they must bear the heat of the sun, but this cloud of blackness will vanish on death, and the African child will be redeemed as white. His blackness, however, enables him to bear the beams of love from Jesus better than the white boy, whom he will shade from the sun. The Little Black Boy implicitly stands for all Africans, or the state of Africanness—just as the white boy in the poem stands for all brought up as Christians—and the theological condition of a continent deprived of Christian light.

The heading design in all copies I have seen shows the mother to be naked from the waist up and the Little Black Boy evidently to be completely naked. In the terminal design there are however significant differences in the coloring from one copy to another. The Black Boy is seen to be freed from the cloud of his blackness but in most early copies he is shown as white whereas in some later copies he is emphatically colored black by Blake's hand (color plates XII–XV).[6]

By connecting the heat and light of the sun with the blackness of the African, Blake appears to follow an explanation that had already been rejected by Malpighi and most scientists of the seventeenth and eighteenth centuries, who were well aware that white people did not turn black in Africa nor blacks white in Europe.[7] The strong sense in Blake's poem that blackness is a curse upon the African ("I am black as if bereav'd of light") and that human existence in Africa is a special trial of endurance reminds us that the "natural" subservience of blacks was often attributed by Christian commentators to the infamous curse of Ham. One of the sons of Noah had "looked upon the nakedness of his father" and his sons were condemned to be forever servants; the idea that the sons of Ham were black, established in early Hebrew commentaries and taken up in sixteenth-century England, had become a commonplace by the eighteenth century.[8]

A reading of the "Africa" section of the *Song of Los* suggests that the Little Black Boy's bereavement from light can be connected with the curse of Ham:

6. This is confirmed by G. E. Bentley Jr.; see *Blake Books: Annotated Catalogues of William Blake's Writing in Illuminated Printing* (Oxford, 1977), 385.
7. See Winthrop D. Jordan, *White over Black: American Attitudes toward the Negro, 1550–1812* (Chapel Hill, N.C., 1977), 239–40.
8. Ibid., 17f.

> Adam stood in the garden of Eden:
> And Noah on the mountains of Ararat;
> They saw Urizen give his Laws to the Nations
> By the hands of the children of Los.
> Adam shuddered! Noah faded! black grew the sunny African
> When Rintrah gave Abstract Philosophy to Brama in the East

This is one of the most compressed passages in the Prophecies; but the blackness of the African might be interpreted as deriving from Noah's seed as the fallen world is established by Urizen. The curse of Ham in effect allowed fundamentalist Christians a way of reconciling a belief in the biblical account of Creation —which made all human beings children of the first parents—with a belief that Africans were a benighted race.

If the Little Black Boy had achieved liberation and was freed from the black cloud and the curse of Ham through the mercy of Christ, then we would expect him to be wholly equal to the English boy, now freed from his white cloud. But both the end of the poem and the terminal image suggest equivocation. The now redeemed Black Boy, whether colored black or white by Blake, still appears to act like a servant. He shades the English boy from the heat, stroking him in the expectation that he will gain his love by being like him. The Black Boy's subordinate position is made explicit in the configuration of the image; he stands apart like John the Baptist in an Italian Madonna and Child painting, while the white boy adores Christ, who gazes at him tenderly.

Yet the white boy adopts a position of supplication that would have evoked unmistakably, for many of Blake's contemporaries, the famous emblem entitled "Am I not a Man and a Brother?" (figure 25), produced originally in 1786 by Wedgwood for the abolitionists. Much of the power of this image—which rapidly became universally familiar, as Hugh Honour has pointed out—came from the precision with which it expressed the idea of the gratitude expected of the liberated slave, who would embrace Christianity but would ever afterward be a loyal servant to the white masters and mistresses who had liberated him.[9] One might explain the Little Black Boy's servility to the white boy and the white boy's servility to Christ as a sign that the poem is an ironical exposure of the limitations of the abolitionist position—that is, that blacks were to be freed from chains only to become servants, for as converted heathens they could only aspire

---

9. Hugh Honour, *The Image of the Black in Western Art*, vol. 4, *From the American Revolution to World War I*, pt. 1 (Cambridge, Mass., 1989), 62–64.

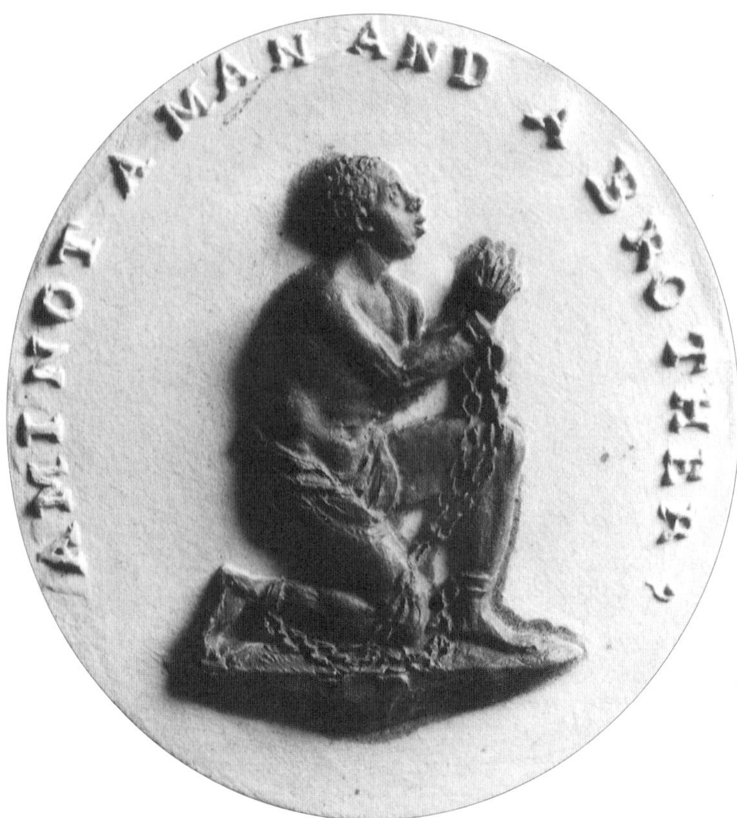

Figure 25. "Am I not a Man and a Brother?" Wedgwood medallion
(courtesy of Messrs. Wedgewood, Barlaston, England).

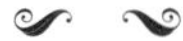

to join the servant class. As Blake exhibited a keen and often ironical perception
of the inadequacies of sentimental liberalism of the kind advocated by William
Cowper and practiced by William Hayley, this is a tempting explanation, but unlikely to be more than a partial one.

The attitudes toward race expressed in "The Little Black Boy," despite their evident sympathy for Africans, seem to be based on conceptions appropriate to a fervent antirationalist like Blake. By contrast, a reference to Africans in the "Song of
Liberty" attached to *The Marriage of Heaven and Hell* (see figure 4 in Joseph
Viscomi's essay in this volume) leads us in the direction of modern "scientific"

racial typology. The poem contains an invocation to Jews to leave off counting gold, and to the African: "O African! black African (go winged thought widen his forehead)." The parenthetical aside implies the African's mental backwardness. Like the Jew he is in a pre-Christian state and must throw off his inherited character before he can receive the message of universal revolution; the aside also associates mental and spiritual characteristics with physical form. But why the African's narrow forehead? The answer, I believe, is to be found first of all in John Caspar Lavater's *Physiognomy,* published in a number of editions from 1788 onward,[10] for which Blake made a number of engravings. He would have had a special involvement through his friendship with Henry Fuseli, who was in turn a friend of Lavater's. Blake could have read in Lavater that man combines animal, intellectual, and moral aspects in his being, and that all of these are expressed in differing proportions in the face, which is always dominated by one of the three aspects. The forehead—and this idea was not new to Lavater—was the seat of intelligence: "it is likewise evident that the faculty of thinking has its seat, not in the foot, in the hand, or in the breast; but in the head,—in the interior of the forehead. . . . The forehead, down to the eye-brows, [is] the mirror of intelligence."[11]

Lavater does not apply this notion of the dimensions of the forehead to the African, but this connection had already been made by the Dutch painter Pieter Camper, who first applied physiognomical theory to racial classification. Camper's theory was in effect an attempt to apply the ancient theory of the Great Chain of Being to the races of humanity, along with all the later apparatus of anatomical classification developed by Linnaeus and Buffon. Camper's method was to measure the angle caused by the meeting of two lines, one line drawn along the forehead and nose and the other through the chin and mouth (figure 26).[12] In the Greek ideal form, the two lines meet without an angle, while the European form deviates from this slightly. The African, however, with a sharp angle at the intersection of the two lines, is closer to the orangutan than to the European. The effect, as can be seen from the diagram, is for the African's forehead to narrow and to recede.

There is, however, one problem in proposing the influence of Camper: his book, published in Holland in 1784, only became available in English in 1794. But the preface tells us that Camper was a familiar figure in London before the

10. John Caspar Lavater, *Essays on Physiognomy,* trans. Henry Hunter (London, 1789–98); see also Robert N. Essick, *William Blake's Commercial Book Illustrations* (Oxford, 1991), pl. xix.
11. Lavater, *Essays on Physiognomy.*
12. *The Works of the late Professor Camper, on the Connexion between the Science of Anatomy and The Arts of Drawing, Painting, Statuary, etc.* (London, 1794), 32–44.

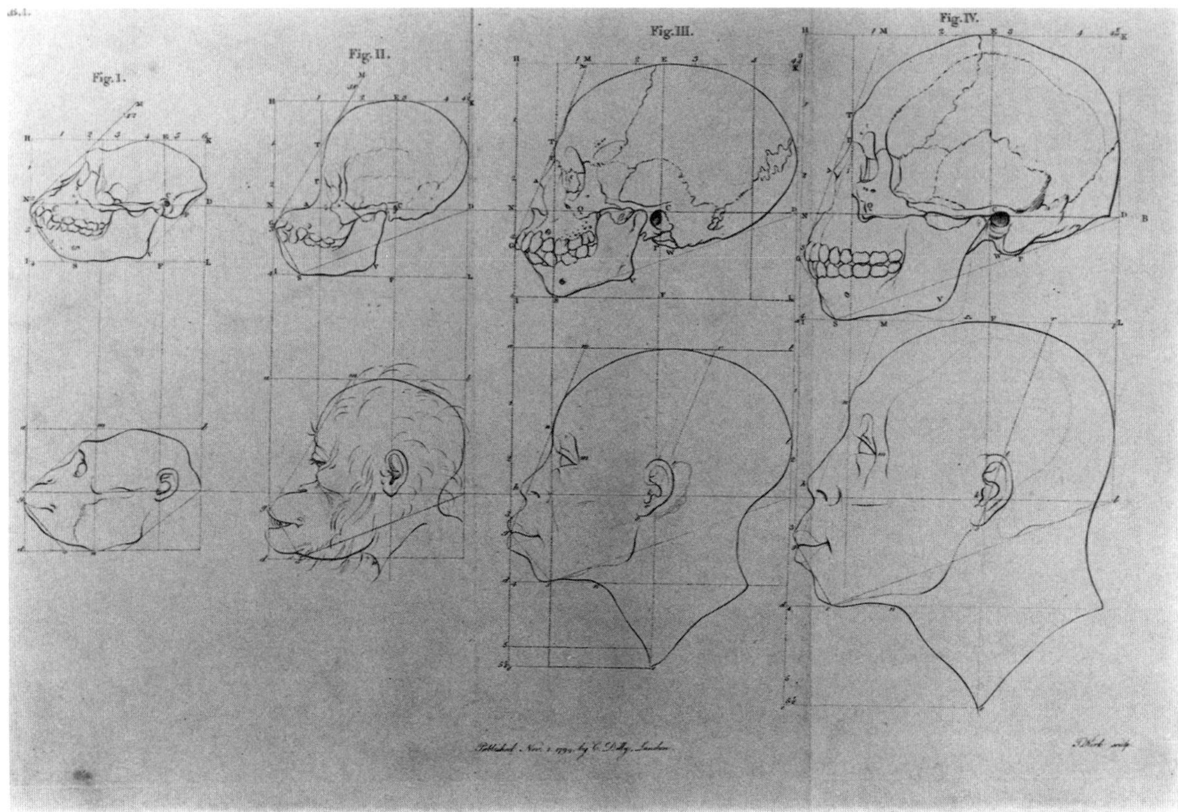

Figure 26.
Figure 12 from [Pieter Camper], *The Works of the late Professor Camper* (London, 1794).

publication of the English translation, especially at the Royal Academy, where he knew William Hunter, the professor of anatomy from 1768 to 1783. He also discussed racial physiognomy with Benjamin West, who was exercised about the correct way to depict the Jews in his biblical paintings.[13] The beliefs prevalent in the circle of the Hunters are suggested in a print of William's brother, Dr. John Hunter, after a painting by Sir Joshua Reynolds, engraved by William Sharp in 1788 (figure 27). The Hunter brothers were both interested in comparative anatomy and kept distinguished public museums containing specimens of all kinds, from vegetables to human skulls.[14] John is shown in his museum, surrounded by specimens, and he has open a page from a volume containing drawings (or perhaps engravings) of skulls. They are evidently intended to illustrate

13. Ibid., 8–9.
14. See Jessie Dobson, *John Hunter* (Edinburgh, 1969).

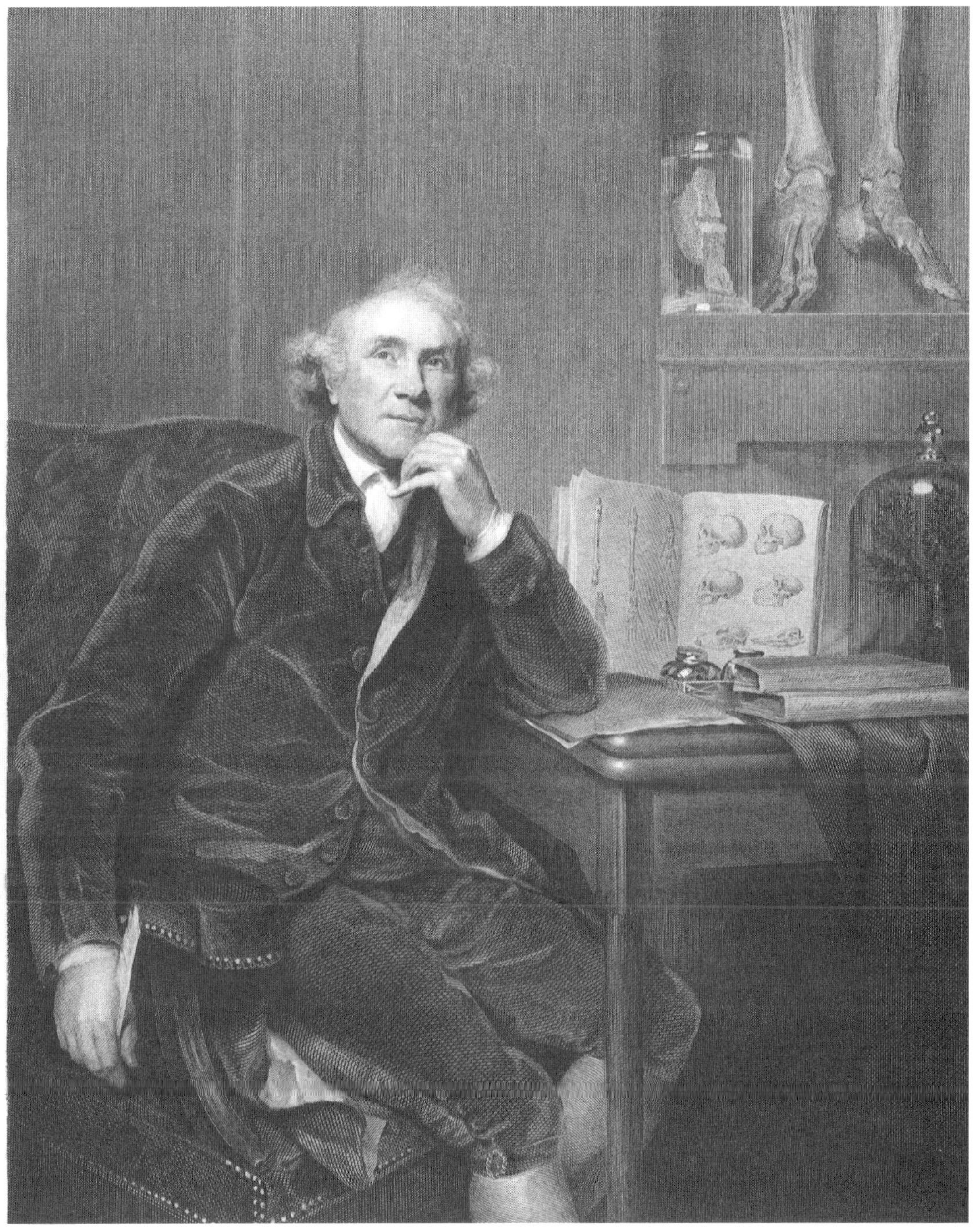

Figure 27.
W. Sharp after Sir Joshua Reynolds, engraving (proof impression) by John Hunter (Yale Center for British Art).

the Great Chain of Being as applied to the human head, and the ones shown depict the transition from animal to human skull. The human skulls are implicitly ranked in order, representing, we may assume, the three separate races thought by the most widely known theorist, Johann Friedrich Blumenbach, to constitute the human race, alongside an orangutan's head for comparison. Though Hunter's series of skulls do not imply a system of measurement like the one proposed by Camper, this would have been the next step in the process.

Blake's passing reference to the African's narrow forehead is, therefore, probably derived from an unattractive bit of late-eighteenth-century racial theory, while "The Little Black Boy" appears to be inflected by theological traditions that assume Africans to be spiritually disadvantaged. These two examples do not, of course, cast doubt on the sincerity of Blake's opposition to slavery in the early 1790s or on his commitment to universal redemption. They do, however, suggest that Blake was unable to free himself—no more than anyone else at the time—from the complex and often contradictory web of ancient and modern beliefs that had settled around Africa and Africans in the late eighteenth century.

If we return to *Visions of the Daughters of Albion* and Erdman's view of it, a number of points can be made. The centrality that Erdman gives to slavery in the poem seems open to dispute. The interlinear illustration of the slave under the sun (color plate V) is certainly one of the most moving images of slavery from the period, but the references to physical slavery add up to little more than a metaphor for Oothoon's loss of freedom. They make the point that Bromion's restriction of freedom is indivisible; an oppressive society will oppress at every level. It is easy to see how a drama of state oppression such as the one Erdman advanced in 1952 for *Visions of the Daughters of Albion*— in which the liberals have the right ideas but are too ineffectual to challenge the powerful—might have appeared especially prescient in the political climate of the early Cold War years. The political affiliations of radicals in the media and in the academic world were under intense investigation by governmental agencies, and the powerlessness of liberals in the face of injustice was only too evident. My object is not, however, to reduce Erdman's argument to being merely a symptom of its own times, but to admit that my own argument, nearly fifty years on, is by the same token affected by contemporary concerns and may reflect the intellectual contradictions of our age. Whether one is a poet and artist like Blake or a mere academic historian, such contradictions are unavoidable, especially over matters of race.

University College London

(Dis)figuring the System:
Vision, History, and Trauma
in Blake's Lambeth Books

— TILOTTAMA RAJAN

Writing in 1986 Stephen Leo Carr referred to "the still common assumption that an essentially homogeneous (noncontradictory) 'system' or 'myth' underlies Blake's art, guaranteeing that each illuminated book is finally a performance of the same, a marginal deviation or derivation from some ur-text or 'vision' . . . to be recuperated by reading each Blakean text in the context of all others."[1] Since the conference "Blake and Criticism," held in Santa Cruz, California, in 1982, we have been more inclined to privilege the resistances to homogeneity previously marginalized by Blake criticism. One such challenge to the structures stubbornly constructed by Northrop Frye and S. Foster Damon had already been provided in 1980 by Leopold Damrosch, who saw the tradition Blake inherited as a "nest of problems," and therefore saw the system as mobilized precisely by the contradictions it struggled endlessly to "reconcile."[2] More common now than this use of "Mental Fight" to defer but protect the system is its replacement by a logic of absolute difference in which the Blakean text exists only in its performances, as a transformational narrative surface, or in terms of a writerly rather than readerly textuality.[3] As much as the system, absolute difference protects the economy of literature and the self-satisfaction it affords the critic. As Steven Goldsmith points out with reference to current Blake studies, there is a strange symbiosis between poststructuralism and representative democracy: the culture in which every voice is heard, and differences are consumed and satisfied in a unifying pluralism.[4] As Jane Gallop points out more generally, the death of the author becomes all too easily

---

1. Stephen Leo Carr, "Illuminated Printing: Toward a Logic of Difference," in Nelson Hilton and Thomas A. Vogler, eds., *Unnam'd Forms: Blake and Textuality* (Berkeley and Los Angeles, 1986), 180.
2. Leopold Damrosch Jr., *Symbol and Truth in Blake's Myth* (Princeton, N.J., 1980), 6, 3.
3. The best example of this tendency is Donald Ault's *Narrative Unbound: Re-visioning William Blake's "The Four Zoas"* (Barrytown, N.Y., 1987).
4. Steven Goldsmith, *Unbuilding Jerusalem: Apocalypse and Romantic Representation* (Ithaca, N.Y., 1993), 164, 204–8.

"a reader's fantasy of perfect mastery" or a "fantasy for the critic who would identify with such mastery as reader-writer."[5]

Resisting the mastery afforded us by an author who disappears into his own negative capability, this essay returns to Blake's typically Romantic desire to construct a system that will contain matter within form by "reducing"[6] temporality and difference within the iconic space of the illuminated book. At the heart of the system completed in *Jerusalem* is an alignment between space and time that first becomes an issue because of the two media that make up Blake's composite art, and for which the illuminated book as the apocalyptic (en)closure of history through art serves as a material trope. In this essay, however, the completed system and its icon, the Book as Logos, will provide no more than a starting point. Instead I shall explore the (dis)figuration of the system at its first site of emergence in the Lambeth books, where Blake attempts to arrange world history mythopoeically, or rather to work (out) the system through the materiality of history. The difficulty he has in doing so is apparent in two areas. To begin with, the verbal and visual components of three of the Lambeth poems—*The (First) Book of Urizen, The Book of Ahania,* and *The Book of Los*—are conspicuously disjoined. This separation points to a radical disturbance of an aesthetic economy in which time and space form a circle, such that vision is realized in time, but time is then gathered up into an ahistorical space. Secondly, the three major poems in the group (*Europe, America,* and *Urizen*) are prefaced by preludia or proems. Rather than read these works mimetically or dramatically, as adumbrating or performing the system,[7] we are therefore called on to read them reflexively, as texts that are configured within the scene of their own writing.

This does not mean that the Lambeth books are examples (like *Milton*) of what Philippe Lacoue-Labarthe and Jean-Luc Nancy call the literary absolute, in which the deconstruction of authorial authority is recovered within "the model

---

5. Jane Gallop, *Reading Lacan* (Ithaca, N.Y., 1985), 182.
6. I am using this word in quotation marks to refer to its technical philosophical signification in Husserlian phenomenology, where it denotes a "bracketing" of the natural standpoint, or more generally of complicating elements that interfere with grasping the essential structures of consciousness.
7. Northrop Frye and S. Foster Damon provide obvious examples of work that assumes in the "system" a constative level of myth that precedes and guarantees prophetic utterance. The alternative view of prophecy as "performative" is introduced by Leslie Tannenbaum, who argues with reference to eighteenth-century theories of prophecy that Blake's work is rhetorical and oratorical rather than mimetic (*Biblical Tradition in Blake's Early Prophecies: The Great Code of Art* [Princeton, N.J., 1982], 25–54). More recently, Angela Esterhammer approaches the visionary performativity of Blake's texts from the perspective of speech-act theory in *Creating States: Studies in the Performative Language of John Milton and William Blake* (Toronto, 1994). My own account of "nomadic textuality" in the second section of this paper attributes a more anarchic form of performativity to a limited group of Blake's texts.

of the subject-work creating itself."[8] Rather, these texts are caught in the impossibility of their own writing, as a process in which Blake articulates, cancels, and (dis)figures the system that he can produce only in and as its abjected parts.[9] In *Europe* and *America* this disfiguration is thematized and confined within the preludia, allowing the prophecies at least some performative existence apart from it. Along with the supplementary *Song of Los*, these poems comprise the first group of Lambeth books. But in the second group, consisting of *Urizen, Ahania*, and *The Book of Los* (none of which refers to itself as a prophecy), the scene of writing extends throughout the entire text. For the texts in question move forward only with enormous difficulty, and indeed are about the difficulty of their writing. In the earlier and later Lambeth books, Blake seems to be accumulating the raw material for a system: the "mythemes" and "gross constituent units," as Lévi-Strauss describes them. But this material has yet to be processed aesthetically or psychically, and the Lambeth books *are* the process of trying to give it structural articulation by shaping it into a narrative leading to organized innocence.

Moreover, the process of shaping—later figured in *Milton* as Milton sculpting the image of Urizen (*Milton* 20:8–10, E 114)—is full of false starts, provoking the bard in *America* to break his harp (*America* 2:18–20, E 52).[10] Thus in *Ahania,* Urizen's disk takes ten years to make and is then countered by the "fiery beam" of Fuzon, which wanders the earth for five hundred years before Los "siez[es]" it and gives it a shape (*Ahania*, 2:44–8, E 85). The shaping of force into form is a recurrent concern of these texts, as it also is in Shelley's last texts, where the imagination forms a revolutionary vision out of the ethereality of a shape all light or out of a materiality without form or outline. But in *Ahania* it is not clear what Los makes out of the beam of Fuzon in hammering it back into the body

8.   Philip Barnard and Cheryl Lester, introduction to Philippe Lacoue-Labarthe and Jean-Luc Nancy, *The Literary Absolute: The Theory of Literature in German Romanticism* (1978), trans. Barnard and Lester (Albany, N.Y., 1988), xvi; see also 5.

9   I borrow the terms "abject" and "abjection" from Julia Kristeva's *Powers of Horror: An Essay on Abjection,* trans. Leon Roudiez (New York, 1982). Briefly, Kristeva defines the abject as that which does not fit, and that therefore produces a sense of dis-ease in the body of the Kantian, or Cartesian, subject. Associated with phenomena that lack boundaries, and thus with the confusion of subject and object or inside and outside, it threatens the power of (self)definition, and must therefore be cast out for predication to occur. The very term confuses grammatical boundaries, functioning as subject, object, and verb. "Abjection" or ("to abject") indicates, from the point of view of the subject, the violent expulsion of what is constructed as other. But the "abject" also refers to what is cast out. Finally, "abjection" also refers to a feeling not dissimilar to what Coleridge calls dejection, which follows the casting out of the self as other.

10.   All references to Blake's texts are to *The Complete Poetry and Prose of William Blake*, revised ed., ed. David V. Erdman (Berkeley and Los Angeles, 1982), abbreviated "E," following plate and line numbers.

of the sun, and still less is it clear whether his activity has any material consequences. Likewise Urizen's body takes seven ages to emerge, figuring the aeons it takes Los as prophetic imagination to hammer out a form for world history. And when that body is complete we are only at the beginning of a narrative that is continued in *Ahania,* itself to be discontinued when the desire figured in Fuzon amounts to nothing.

Able to invent names for entities without distinct characteristics and energies without shape, Blake cannot do anything with them, so that the slowing down of historical time also figures the "abjection"—the unusable negativity—that haunts his writing.[11] For the system at this stage is disorganized, emerging in bits and pieces like Urizen's body. This body is figured as a *corps morcelé* that has yet to be hammered into imaginary or symbolic totality, and in which the parts emerge out of sequence and disjoined from any larger whole: spine first, then brain and heart entangled with each other, then over four ages the senses, and finally the limbs. Likewise Blake works on his myth in overlapping segments, which are like pieces of a jigsaw puzzle that do not fit together. In *Europe,* he works on a genealogy of the female will as prime cause behind the nightmare of history. But he puzzlingly depicts Enitharmon as asleep during the damage she brings about, as though like Milton she may have a "real, immortal" self that stands apart from her shadow or her spectre (*Milton* 15:1–17, E 109). In *Urizen,* Enitharmon plays a minor role, and Blake turns to a male power who frustratingly exceeds his characterization as reason and his role as villain. In *America,* Blake deals with revolutionary change, but in *Urizen* he retreats to an ontopsychic analysis of what makes change impossible, thus leaving open the question of whether his characters are forces in the theater of public events or spectres in a dialogue of the mind with itself. And finally in *The Song of Los,* he gestures to-

---

11. The concept of unusable negativity, in the particular form I employ it here, derives from Maurice Blanchot, who reconceives negativity in terms radically different from those of Hegel. Whereas Hegel sees negativity as an antithetical stimulus to the generation of new positions, and thus puts it to use within the dialectic (generating progression through contraries, in Blakean terms), Blanchot explores a form of negativity that cannot be "re-economized" or put to work. Through his notions of worklessness (*désoeuvrement*) and death, Blanchot theorizes a depressive form of negativity significantly different from the more energetic version of unusable negativity developed by his colleague Georges Bataille, through the notion of a heterogeneity or surplus that cannot be absorbed back into the restricted economy of Hegelian dialectic. Blanchot's version of unusable negativity thus anticipates Kristeva's interest in abjection and melancholia. See in particular his essays on "Literature and the Right to Death" and "The Essential Solitude" in *The Gaze of Orpheus and Other Literary Essays,* trans. Lydia Davis (Barrytown, N.Y., 1981), 21–78, as well as *The Space of Literature,* trans. Ann Smock (Lincoln, Nebr., 1982), 85–160, and 163–70.

ward a world-historical frame for his previous texts but is able to produce it only as two disjoined fragments.

The difficulty Blake has in articulating his system has much to do with his relationship to history (a term that I am not using in a Marxist way, since events for Blake are not simply social or cultural but are intergenerated with ontological issues and collective traumas). Writing in the 1790s, Blake does not have the apocalyptic privilege of disengaging himself from events, both past and present. As is suggested by the tormented family romances that traverse these texts, history is the scene of the system's psychoanalysis, an unconscious or radical alterity inseparable from its prehistory in trauma. Struggling to reduce this otherness to symbolic form, the later Blake, as both Damrosch and Lorraine Clark point out, replaces the dialectical with the apocalyptic. He "cast[s] off" what is threatening by defining "the qualities he dislikes . . . as Satanic" and thus "external to the self."[12] Crucial to this turn is Blake's retrieval of negation[13] as a category he can use to abject difficult or traumatic material—or more precisely his displacement of the term negation, which no longer describes a binary and limited epistemic mode but rather names the substance or state that he wants to exclude (*Milton* 40:33–34, E 142). The consequence is the system: a master narrative with its own regulatory symbolism, and thus also a Symbolic order in Lacan's sense of the term (see n. 28 below). Constantly threatened by what it has abjected—like the masquerades of Jean Genet's *Balcony*—Blake's Symbolic order can maintain itself only through an elaborate apparatus of classes and levels in which the self, as Damrosch puts it, is "distribut[ed] among different levels of reality,"[14] so that the "real" Milton can remain in Eden while his vegetable body exists in Ulro.

The mode that constructs this separation between levels of reality, so as to protect them from mixing with each other, is "Sublime Allegory" (E 730) as developed within the fourfold scheme of Christian theology. As an apparatus of levels, allegory is a kind of schizophrenia:[15] a form in which pneuma is separated

---

12. Lorraine Clark, *Blake, Kierkegaard, and the Spectre of Dialectic* (Cambridge, 1991), 4; Damrosch, *Symbol and Truth,* 179, 154. Damrosch sees this development as unfortunate (p. 154), whereas Clark valorizes it as a turn "from a Hegelian 'both-and' dialectic . . . to something very like a Kierkegaardian 'either/or'" in which the Spectral or Satanic must be purged entirely (pp. 2, 5).

13. Clark, *The Spectre of Dialectic,* 3; Damrosch, *Symbol and Truth,* 181.

14. Damrosch further points out that the later Blake distinguishes a hylic, a psychic, and a pneumatic self (*Symbol and Truth,* 155).

15. For a psychoanalytic account of allegory as a form of schizophrenia, see Angus Fletcher, *Allegory: The Theory of a Symbolic Mode* (Ithaca, N.Y., 1964).

from psyche and mind from body along a figural axis that abstracts the signified from the signifier. The dominant figure of the Lambeth books is by contrast catachresis, a figure in which tenor and vehicle cannot be separated, the vehicle seeming at times to *be* its tenor. One example is the extended description of Urizen's body, in chapter IV(b) of *The (First) Book of Urizen,* in which the body is configured simultaneously with the seven ages and the four points of the compass. Here the literalism of the figure is such that figure and ground cannot be differentiated: Urizen's sleeping body cannot be made a mere metaphor for the nightmare of history, because as figure he usurps the ground he is supposed to represent, becoming in some sense the Real, which can be grasped only as its traumatic figuration. I shall return to the disfigurative effects of catachresis and other condensations that block the work of systematization. Suffice it to say here that allegory is the figure of separation as well as of the exegetical translation of matter into spirit; catachresis, by contrast, is the figure of unreadability: it is the form taken by what Julia Kristeva calls the abject, as the state in which spirit remains glued to matter, like Los to Urizen. In abjection, which is a pre-thetic rather than synthetic identity, things cannot be separated and predication cannot occur because subject and object are confused, as are inside and outside, spirit and body.[16] Catachresis is the rhetorical form of abjection, because it jams together phenomena that cannot be seen in the same space and confuses the figural and literal aspects of metaphor. In a text such as *Urizen,* catachresis blocks vision (as a form of imaginative predication), because the figural is stuck to the literal, thus figuring the way that vision itself is stuck to the materiality of history. To put it differently, catachresis is the site at which these texts confront something radically inhuman, a materiality that Blake grasps as "history." Whereas Hegel anthropomorphizes history by figuring it as a phenomenology of mind, Blake disfigures this organicism by grotesquely overlaying Urizen's body on the map of the world, so that the body is outside itself—as an inside that is neither inside nor outside.

I conclude this introductory section with a last point on Blake's myth in the Lambeth poems. Although Damrosch proposes that Blake's myth is "psychological,"[17] the figure of a containing self fragmented into different parts is in fact a

---

16. Kristeva frequently uses feces and vomit to figure the "abject" as an in-between phenomenon that is neither subject nor object and that hovers between a material substance and a psychological condition (analogous to dejection, but more violent). Abjection makes predication impossible by blocking the separation of subject from object, inside from outside, and spirit from body. In order to enter the thetic phase and constitute himself as a bounded ego, the subject must overcome abjection and distinguish himself from an object or Other.

17. Damrosch, *Symbol and Truth,* 122.

later development, beginning with *The Four Zoas* and culminating in *Jerusalem.*
In the latter, Blake returns to the figure that disfigures *The Book of Urizen* when
he equates the four senses with the four points of the compass in his description
of Golgonooza:

> Fourfold the Sons of Los in their divisions and fourfold,
> The great City of Golgonooza: . . .
> And the Four Points are thus beheld in Great Eternity
> West, the Circumference: South, the Zenith: North,
> The Nadir: East, the Center, unapproachable for ever.
> These are the four Faces towards the Four Worlds of Humanity
> In every Man. Ezekiel saw them by Chebars flood.
> And the Eyes are the South, and the Nostrils are the East.
> And the tongue is the West, and the Ear is the North.
> (Jerusalem 12:45–60, E 156)

In this recuperation of *The Book of Urizen,* Urizen is replaced by Golgonooza so
that catachresis can be reorganized as allegory.[18] Correspondingly, the material
world is securely placed *inside* the body, which in turn becomes a pure signifier:
a phenomenal rather than material body, written over by numbers and concepts
and invested with the ideality of mathematics and myth.

This iconic body is the culminating figure for the process of ego consolida-
tion that Blake begins in *The Four Zoas,* where he posits the metasubject of
Albion so as to interiorize the action of his texts, in which subjects had previously
been dispersed, produced, and used up by events. Through Albion, Blake introduces the notion of an original or potential self, thereafter replacing the chroni-
cle structure of the early texts with autobiography in *Milton,* and with history as
cosmic autobiography in *Jerusalem.* In the Lambeth books, however, it is not the
self but the historical process that dominates, affecting even Blake's system (as the
body of beliefs he would like to inhabit) with an element of irreducible exteriority. This exteriority is nowhere more evident than in the strange names that pop-
ulate these texts as disfigurations of subjectivity. For "Los" and "Orc" are
attempts to ascribe subjectivity to what may well be a process without a subject:

---

18. Catachresis obviously continues to exist in the later Blake—in fact, Milton's body is an extensive
example of it, an almost hysterical literalization of the hermeneutic figure that says that to understand
and overcome a system of beliefs you must understand it from within. The point, however, is that
catachresis is contained within allegory, in a re-vision of the earlier work that sometimes verges
dangerously on being a repetition.

a process of "changes" and "rift[s]" that is fundamentally inhuman (*The [First] Book of Urizen* 3:10–11, E 70). Names trope Blake's attempt to insert himself as subject into this uncontrollable process, so as to write the text of history as his own text.

Confronting a similarly inhuman process in the form of Demogorgon, Shelley will represent the countervailing act of (self)figuration or mythopoeia through Asia's ascent in the Chariot of the Hour: literally a vehicle without a tenor that Asia bends to her author's will when she steers it toward the utopian ending of her marriage to Prometheus. Blake, however, cannot reconfigure the materiality of his text through his characters, who are responses to events rather than selves, and who therefore do not give him a stable position to occupy. Thus Urizen is authoritarian in chapter 2, yet helpless and anguished at other points, almost to the point of not seeming to be the character earlier referred to by that name. Characters are produced and discarded, like the Eternals, who are largely absent after chapter 3 of *Urizen;* or like Fuzon, who appears almost as an afterthought at the end of this text but then takes center stage at the beginning of *Ahania,* only to be used up and forgotten by the end of that poem.

Blake's characters, with their strange names, are in fact the site of his struggle with the recalcitrant materiality of history. As Vincent De Luca observes, Blake does not construct his names allegorically by translating a concept into a character: rather he first encounters them as signifiers, as acoustic forms that have yet to be given a content. But this does not mean, as De Luca concludes, that the names are "iconic"—that we should conceive of the signifier in phenomenal rather than material terms.[19] In the Lambeth books at least, where they appear sporadically rather than within epic lists, the strangeness of these names figures the unreadability of the events that Blake struggles to control by naming them with names that he does not himself understand. If the names are an attempt at humanization, their anthropomorphism turns into something like catachresis. Thus the "system," far from being an indicator of Blake's creative autonomy, is the scene of his implication in a world that as yet operates only at the level of the signifier. It is no help that this world can seem familiar: that its characters intermittently function like counterparts to figures in Milton and the Bible; or that their Nordic and uncouth names sometimes evoke eighteenth-century projects

---

19. De Luca argues that names are "miniature iconic centres" or "encapsulated portions of imaginative energy that derive from the permanent forms of 'Los' Halls'" (*Words of Eternity: Blake and the Poetics of the Sublime* [Princeton, N.J., 1991], 94, 97). But this is mainly true of the later prophecies, where names occur in epic catalogues, and where their opacity is heraldic and ceremonial.

for the assimilation of difference through syncretist mythology. For Blake carries over these hermeneutic paradigms only in bits and pieces, as if unable to incorporate them, and as if he can do no more than introject them, as possibilities that can neither be digested nor discarded.

❧ II ❧

So far I have set the Lambeth books against Blake's subsequent development of a system for the management of difficulty, divided allegorically between a nomenclature and a conceptual apparatus.[20] The material signifier of this system is the illuminated book, which unites time and space—in defiance of Lessing's view that art is limited by its medium.[21] As the containing form of the system, the illuminated book accomplishes what the system by itself cannot. For whereas the system as verbal construct can do no more than contain difficulty—in the double sense of the word *contain*—the composite artifact of the illuminated book "reduces"[22] difficulty within the intricacy of a figured surface, allowing us to look rather than read, to assimilate the text as art rather than experience.

We can approach the aesthetics of the illuminated book by way of De Luca's discussion of the sublime, which is also concerned with the problem of difficulty as it is deployed through the thematics of space and time. De Luca distinguishes two modes of the sublime, the bardic and the iconic, corresponding roughly to Kant's mathematical and dynamic sublime—the distinction between the sublime that overwhelms us and the sublime as an experience that restores the bounded ego to a sense of mastery. The bardic style is a style of crisis that is serial, characterized by catalogues of undifferentiated details and by parataxis and metamorphosis rather than culmination. The iconic, while seeming to share the syntax and tactics of the bardic, emphasizes structure rather than flow, "compressing signs so densely and firmly that their contingent signifieds are virtually squeezed out," leaving only "a conclave of signifiers, the visible form of intellect mirroring itself."[23] It seems that the mode of the bardic is time, whereas that of the iconic is space, and that Blake's texts are generated by a dialectic in

---

20. This conceptual apparatus is notably absent from the Lambeth books, which in turn increases the difficulty we have in separating figure from ground.
21. Gotthold Ephraim Lessing, *Laocoön: An Essay on the Limits of Painting and Poetry* (1766), trans. Edward Allen McCormick (Indianapolis, 1962).
22. Again I use this word in its technical, philosophical sense to evoke Husserl's "reductions," in which extraneous material and phenomena are bracketed, so as to produce a concentration upon essential structures.
23. De Luca, *Blake and the Poetics of the Sublime*, 61–72, 79; 80, 99.

which the latter reorganizes the former. According to De Luca, there are "no limits to the scale of an iconic text. Insofar as we can situate ourselves at the proper distance to perceive its form as consolidated and autonomous, a whole poem . . . or even an entire canon in illuminated printing . . . may operate as a magnified word, an iconic centre of arrest and release."[24] Ideally, then, the engraved work would function as a form of iconic sublimity, enclosing the difficulty of the system within the illuminated book, which, to adapt Maurice Blanchot, is a "labyrinth in which all combinations of forms, words and letters are rolled up in volumes."[25]

De Luca's notion of the iconic resembles what Joseph Frank some time ago called spatial form, as an experience in which the reader grasps "both past and present simultaneously in a moment of . . .'pure time.'" In spatial form, as in the "centripetal concentration" of the icon, we encounter "word-groups that have no comprehensible relation to each other when read consecutively," and we then apprehend these units of meaning as "referred to each other reflexively" in space.[26] Whereas Lessing stresses the mutual inadequacy of painting and poetry, as media in which one either encounters bodies without action and movement or action without bodily presence, Blake's own late engraving *Laocoön* is precisely such an instance of spatial form: a kind of concrete poem in which the visual representation of the Laocoön is surrounded by aphorisms, iconically distilled from Blake's other works (figure 28). Converting time to space by allowing words to function visually as borders, *Laocoön* reverses the layout of Blake's other textographic works, in which a verbal center is enframed by visual borders. It thus makes the point that in a composite art the individual components are not limited to their own media, but rather each order can draw on the powers of the other. Thus *Laocoön* is a paradigm for the iconic reading of *Jerusalem* in terms of the interconvertibility of verbal and visual, time and space, within a logocentrism that allows word groups to function as pure signifiers purged of materiality yet endowed with the presence of the visual. Spatial form is profoundly ahistorical. For the system totalized as verbal icon is a refiguration of history as art, a putting of time into space that inscribes the end of history.

Compositeness is a formal marker of the fact that composition involves bringing together incommensurables, including space and time or myth and history.

24. Ibid., 94.
25. Blanchot, "The Absence of the Book," in *The Gaze of Orpheus*, 146.
26. Joseph Frank, *The Widening Gyre: Crisis and Mastery in Modern Literature* (New Brunswick, N.J., 1963), 24, 13, 25; De Luca, *Blake and the Poetics of the Sublime*, 81.

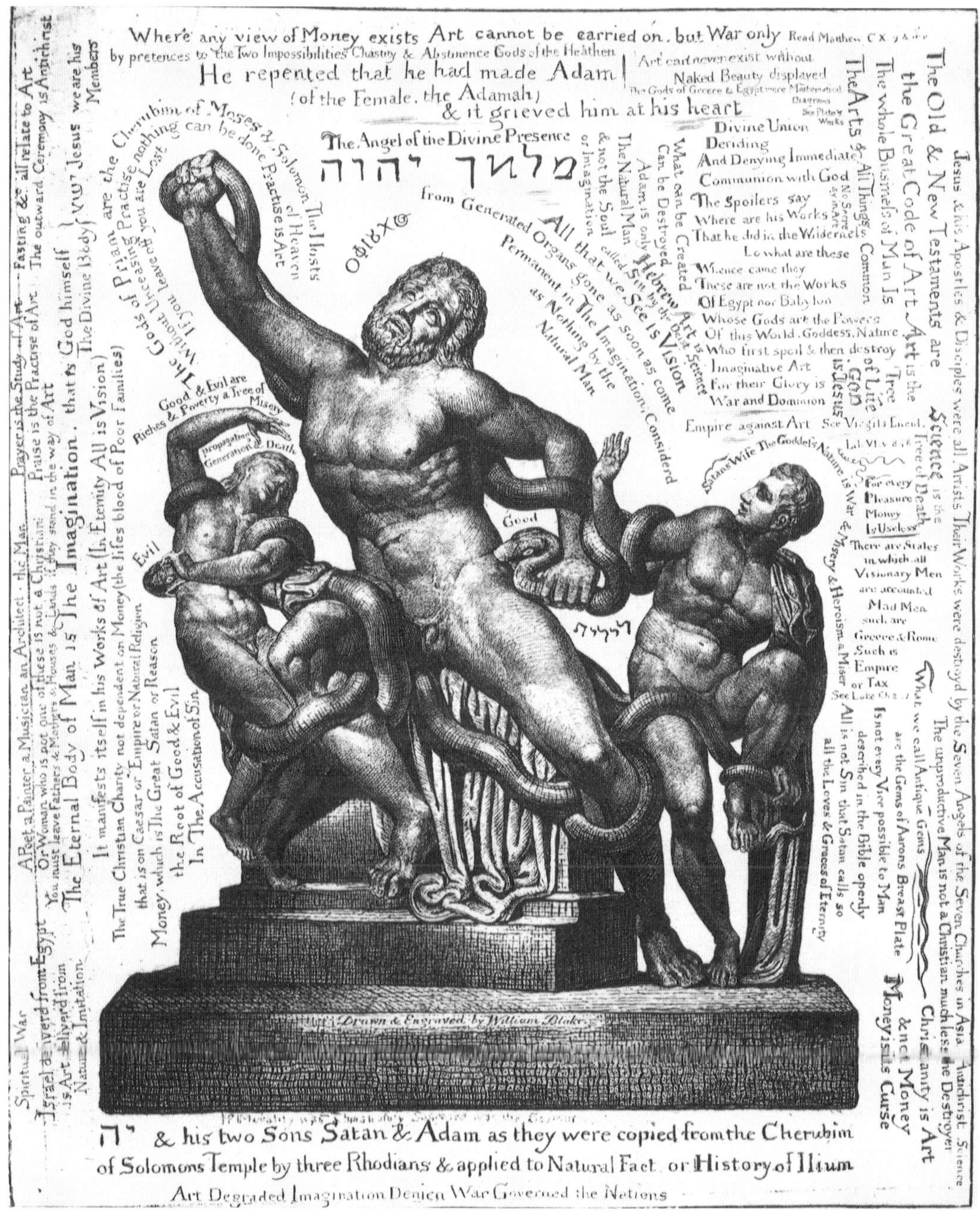

Figure 28. *Laocoön* (from the collection of Robert N. Essick).

Whether in this respect the illuminated book is more than an ideal category is not something I shall consider. Rather I shall return to the difficulty Blake had with composition: with organizing the Lambeth books into what Leslie Tannenbaum claims is a "coherent and unified vision of human life from the Creation to the Apocalypse."[27] We can sense this difficulty in the way the Lambeth books fall into two groups, as if Blake found himself reassessing his project in midstream. The first group follows the mode of *The French Revolution,* which is historically localized and full of spectacular scenes and hyperbolical speeches. Thus *America, Europe,* and *The Song of Los* are keyed to presenting actions, and they erupt rather than develop, their very disconnectedness signifying prophetic crisis rather than epic continuity. All four poems place themselves in a world-historical space and, as we shall see, construct history as a shifting discursive surface. In sharp contrast is the second group of poems, whose titles are provided by characters and not continents, those characters (Urizen, Ahania, Los) being psychological rather than geographical "states." Speeches are few and far between in these texts. Shifting from events to the space that precedes them, a space indeterminately cosmic or psychic, Blake reaches back to the prehistorical traumas that encode history, the unseen "rifts" and "perturbations" that produce its furious disorganization. He now seems to want more than a discursive surface, developing the dimension of myth that had first entered his work in *Europe,* in which the figure of Enitharmon was palimpsestically overlaid upon contemporary events. But this is myth in an anthropological rather than visionary sense, raw and violent. In other words, it is a fundamentally unartistic form of myth, functioning more like the semiotic that precedes the Symbolic order:[28] a way of taking culture back to the overdetermined primal scenes that constitute its contradictions.

Developing his myth between 1791 and 1795, Blake reaches for an explanation of the historical world whose surface he is initially content to appropriate through discourse. In the process, however, he dismantles the temporary synthesis he had constructed in his earliest historical poems to deal with the alienness of history as a world of energy resistant to imagination. He likewise disables these texts from functioning within the world-historical space of prophecy, aborting

---

27. Tannenbaum, *Blake's Early Prophecies,* 7.
28. I use these terms as they are used by Julia Kristeva. The "Symbolic" order, as in Lacan, is the order of law and patriarchy inscribed in the very structures of language and predication. The "semiotic" is a pre-thetic realm of drives and "pulsions" that precedes the entry into language by way of which the fragmented body is organized into a bounded ego, and that continues to erupt into the Symbolic throughout adult life.

them within a semiotic and pre-textual space. As I shall suggest, the preludia to *Europe* and *America* are Blake's first reflection on the relationship between that space and the time of history, while the splitting apart of visual and verbal elements in the next group of texts traumatically figures the sense that that transference can no longer be made.

That the early Blake's view of history is in no sense humanist has already been suggested. From *The French Revolution* to the texts of 1795, history is depicted in terms of "unseen conflictions" and abrupt "changes" (*The [First] Book of Urizen* 3:10, 14, E 70) that are the archeological symptoms of its structuring by an arbitrarily (im)positional power that makes the inscription of any individual event in a sequential narrative virtually impossible. Nevertheless, *The French Revolution* and *The Marriage of Heaven and Hell*—as well as the "prophecy" sections of *America* and to a lesser extent *Europe*—differ from *Urizen* in the style of their engagement with this "history." They protect prophecy by developing what I shall call a nomadic textuality, which survives by assuming the form of the history that disfigures it. In these texts history is Foucauldian rather than Hegelian, which is to say that it is not teleological but governed by power. What we have in *The French Revolution* and *America* is a world of pure surfaces in which actors on the world-historical stage put on and take off the apocalyptic discourse of cloud and fire like clothing. They appear, seize the microphone, and cease, eluding "commentary by supposing no remainder, nothing in excess of what has been said, but only the fact of its historical appearance."[29] Because these characters exist only as what they say, the prophecies inscribe themselves as pure event, in the performative presence of what Tannenbaum calls "significative action,"[30] which creates an iconic focus on the physical or discursive event.

But perhaps even more appropriate than Foucault as a recent gloss on these texts is Gilles Deleuze and Felix Guattari's "nomad" politics, which reworks the concept of power in a more libidinal and anorganic way.[31] Nomads are those that live outside the state apparatus, avoiding the "sedentary road" (p. 380) for the

29. Michel Foucault, *The Birth of the Clinic: An Archaeology of Medical Perception*, trans. A. M. Sheridan (London, 1989), xvii.

30. Tannenbaum, *Blake's Early Prophecies*, 56.

31. I use the word *anorganic* to indicate that the rhizome, while after all a form of life and not a structure, also violates conventional notions of the organism. Analogous to the rhizome (represented in the plant world by tubers and weeds, in the animal world by rat packs, and in the insect world by ants) is Deleuze and Guattari's notion of the body without organs. See Gilles Deleuze and Felix Guattari, *A Thousand Plateaus: Capitalism and Schizophrenia*, trans. Brian Massumi (Minneapolis, 1987), 4, 149–66; references to this book will hereafter be provided in the text.

"perilous path" (*The Marriage of Heaven and Hell* 2:9, E 33) and moving without a fixed trajectory through a landscape of "rhizomatic vegetation that is temporary and shifts location according to local rains" (p. 382). Consequently, while nomadic territory will have "lines of articulation or segmentarity," it will also be characterized by "lines of flight, movements of deterritorialization and destratification" (p. 3). Corresponding to such societies, and to an imagination that is prophetic rather than priestly, is the rhizomatic text as distinct from the "root-book" constituted "by the interiority of a substance or subject" (pp. 5, 9). The rhizome is "a stranger to any idea of genetic axis or deep structure" (p. 12). Instead, like certain weed forms, it grows as a "ramified surface extension in all directions," such that if it is broken at a given point "it will start up again on one of its old lines, or on new lines" (pp. 7, 9). From time to time it will stabilize in a bulb or tuber, as the energy of Blake's text is temporarily fixed in a figure such as Orc before passing on and leaving us "with nothing more than a name as the trace of an intensity" (pp. 7, 4). This notion of the text as transmitting intensities is in fact the key to understanding how Blake preserves the prophetic function in a world of power: a rhizomatic world that he will later associate more darkly with the polypus. The nomad text is not meant to be read, or even to be looked at, but rather to be felt. It is not an illuminated book but an "assemblage" printed in the infernal method with corrosives, which means that we do not ask "what it means, as signified or signifier" but rather "what it functions with, in connection with what other things it does or does not transmit intensities" (p. 4). Because it is a "body without organs" converging with the reader's body, it causes "asignifying particles or pure intensities to pass or circulate" (p. 4), and can thus discharge revolutionary intensity without narrating the achievement of revolution. Indeed, narrative is unnecessary to the nomad text, since "the rhizome connects any point to any other point" (p. 21). In this sense it does not matter that tyranny is not overthrown in what Blake wrote of *The French Revolution,* or that the significance of the "strife of blood" at the end of *Europe* is so unclear as to have been read in totally contradictory ways. For Blakean prophecy is not a prediction or a vision, but a "literary machine" that functions in conjunction with other machines: "a war machine, love machine, revolutionary machine, etc." (p. 4).

✐ III ✐

As the politicized form of the negative capability discussed at the beginning of this essay, the nomad text is the inverse mirror image of the illuminated book.

But the evidence is that Blake was growing increasingly troubled with this model. The beginnings of this discomfort are already evident in *Europe* and *America,* which, by way of their division into preludium and prophecy, raise the question of what lies behind prophetic power. The narrative sections of these poems are focused on the discursive event and not on its (psycho)analysis. *America* in particular continues the tactics of the rhizomatic text most clearly developed in *The Marriage of Heaven and Hell.* Where the "book composed of chapters has culmination and termination points," the rhizomatic text consists of plateaus, which always occur "in the middle, not at the beginning or the end" (Deleuze and Guattari, *A Thousand Plateaus,* 22, 21), each act or speech act in the case of *America* constituting one of these thousand plateaus. But in both *Europe* and *America,* nomadic prophecy is placed within a specifically masculine space, by way of its positioning in relation to preludia spoken by women who have no voice in the prophetic discourse itself. For in *America* the protagonists of the main narrative are all male. As for *Europe,* the vilification of Enitharmon marks the prophetic voice as decisively male, even as the strangely rhythmic quality of her speeches combined with the positing of a female "depth" behind the masculine surface of world-historical action inscribes gender as a site of excess unaccounted for by this vilification.

As Julia Wright points out in the most impressive account to date of the preludia, both preludia focus on women agonistically divided between womb and voice so as to foreground the stamping (out) of their heterogeneity in the "solid form" (*Europe* 2:8, E 61) of the *book.*[32] But in contrast to Wright I would argue that the nomad *text* is in some ways complicit with the book. For one thing, it evades time and thus experience through a sub-version of spatial form in which each "plateau can be read starting anywhere and can be related to any other plateau" (*A Thousand Plateaus,* 22). Moreover, in substituting general for restricted economy, it merely replaces a homogeneous with a heterogeneous prophetic power.[33] For the female of *Europe* there is no clear division between these two modes, between the prolific and "vig'rous progeny of fires" that

---

32. Julia Wright, "'And None Shall Gather the Leaves': Unbinding the Voice in Blake's *America* and *Europe,*" *European Romantic Review* 7 (1995): 61–84. I am also indebted to Wright's doctoral dissertation "The Politics of Textuality: 'Unceasing Practice' in Blake's Work" (University of Western Ontario) for making me think about textual cruxes and oddities even when we interpret them differently.

33. I borrow these terms from Georges Bataille, who obviously stands behind the work of Deleuze and Guattari. The most succinct account of heterogeneity and general economy can be found in Bataille's "The Psychological Structure of Fascism," *Visions of Excess: Selected Writings, 1927–1939,* ed. Allan Stoekl, trans. Allan Stoekl et. al. (Minneapolis, 1985), 137–60.

Enitharmon stamps out and Orc's "howling terrors, all devouring fiery kings" (2:8, 4, E 61). Occupying the same position in Blake's text as do Milton's invocations to his muse, the preludia disable rather than enable the subsequent process of composition, forcing prophecy to "roll inward" (2:16, E 61) and consider its own basis. In *America,* the writing of the poem is facilitated by a form of rape, symbolically normalized by figuring the shadowy female as dumb nature, and recuperating her violation as that which gives her access to speech. The mating of Orc and the shadowy female, however, is hardly a union of spirit with matter. For both are primitive and chthonic beings, and what the female finds in her new access to language is "eternal death" and "the torment long foretold" (2:17, E 61). In *Europe,* expression—whether it involves the restriction of creativity through the "stamping" attributed to Enitharmon[34] or its dissemination through what Blake had earlier described as the casting of his metals into the expanse—is felt by the female as a constant violation. Breaking his harp in two copies, the bard of *America* may concede that he cannot make the shadowy daughter of Urthona work as a figure of inspiration who would be the female (and historically localized) counterpart of Los. Or he may recognize that his (ab)use of the female (dis)figures the work that follows by inscribing it as part of a will-to-power, complicit with a historical world in which there is no substantive distinction between tyranny and energy, "Albions Angel" and America's "thirteen Angels" (5:1, 9:13; E 53, 54).

Both preludia, moreover, are focalized through nameless shadowy females who raise the question of what is involved in the naming that will prove so crucial to Blake's system (including perhaps the naming of the female as Enitharmon).[35] Insofar as the female of *America* gains access to speech only after her rape, we can see these "Unnam'd forms" (*The Marriage of Heaven and Hell* 15, E 40) with which Blake begins as versions of what Kristeva calls the semiotic, which for Blake is found in the prelinguistic space of myth. For Kristeva as for Plato, the semiotic "chora" is a specifically female space. Through the females, then, Blake represents the reading of history through the transposition of myth into literature as a reduction to Symbolic form of the semiotic that Nietzsche describes as "the original Oneness, its pain and contradiction."[36] For the female of

---

34. Wright points out that the process of stamping with a signet recalls the licensing of books (which of course Blake tried to avoid through his unique mode of producing texts).

35. The link between the female and Enitharmon is suggested by the female's reference to the latter as the "accursed mother" who brings her "into life" even as she labors to bring into life her own vigorous progeny of fires (E 1:11, 2:8).

36. Friedrich Nietzsche, *The Birth of Tragedy,* in *The Birth of Tragedy and the Genealogy of Morals,* trans. Francis Golffing (New York, 1956), 38.

Europe this process is profoundly disturbing, leading her to cry despairingly: "My roots are brandish'd in the heavens. my fruits in earth beneath / Surge, foam, and labour into life" (*Europe* 1:8–9, E 60). In these lines the unnamed form is surre-alistically given a face, beginning as a tree, then turning into an ocean that is also a woman giving birth, and then becoming a thunderstorm that emerges in fe-male clothing to give birth to herself from her head: "I wrap my turban of thick clouds around my lab'ring head; / And fold the sheety waters as a mantle round my limbs" (1:8–13, E 60). The lines represent the process of figuration by which the semiotic is given symbolic shape, but they represent this process agonistically as disfiguration. For on the one hand the unnamed form is given a face by means of its clothing in the rhetoric of apocalypse, much as characters elsewhere in Blake put on prophetic discourse like clothing. But on the other hand the re-sulting tree is uprooted and inverted, and the lines conspicuously draw attention to the process of clothing by which the nameless female is figured as the muse of prophecy—a process whose gendered violence Blake had already confronted in *Visions of the Daughters of Albion*.[37]

The disturbing effect of these lines is in large part owing to the fact that they rework metaphors and similes from earlier works as catachresis. Thus in *The French Revolution* we scarcely notice the comparison of the duke of Burgundy to a storm extending over a ripe vineyard (lines 83–86, E 289). But in the pre-ludium to *Europe,* three heterogeneous entities (woman, tree, and ocean) are vi-olently yoked together in a "space they cannot logically share," so that the "ordinary referentiality of one set of terms wars against the ordinary referential-ity of the other."[38] These multiple symbolic constructions, far from giving a face to the female, leave her "void as death" (*Europe* 2:11, E 60). For catachresis, as Andrzej Warminski notes, "generously 'humanizes' cabbages and lettuces by giv-ing them 'heads,'" yet it thereby "deprives them of a face, body and limbs," thus threatening us with similar mutilation.[39] Symbolically figured as a tree, the fe-male is disabled from existing as a human being. But of course the female herself

37. For a discussion of this point see the analysis of *Visions* in Tilottama Rajan, *The Supplement of Reading: Figures of Understanding in Romantic Theory and Practice* (Ithaca, N.Y., 1990), 238–52.

38. This is De Luca's description of catachresis (*Blake and the Poetics of the Sublime,* 99–100). De Luca, however, associates catachresis as a trope of "identification" with the iconic, whereas I would see symbol (as theorized from Coleridge to Paul de Man) as the trope of identification, and would see catachresis as its dismemberment. Insofar as catachresis involves "identification," it is the kind of identification (or confusion) we find in the abject.

39. Andrzej Warminski, *Readings in Interpretation: Hölderlin, Hegel, Heidegger* (Minneapolis, 1987), lx. It is not clear, of course, whether the tree in this passage is being figured as a female and thus "de-faced" or whether the female is being figured as a tree and thus rendered profoundly unnatural.

is a figure—a way of affecting us with the pathos of "her" (dis)figuration through images that are profoundly unnatural in the way they naturalize "her." So in the end the catachresis also implicates its author and readers, inscribing our own "mutilation *by* figures"[40] that represent us at the cost of leaving out some part of what we are.

As I have suggested, it is possible to read the "prophecy" section of *Europe* as a nomad text, thus giving it a performative power apart from the preludium. But its style is also dense and involuted, in a way that distinguishes it from the previous historical poems. More specifically the prophecy is constructed as a dark conceit that is itself more like catachresis than allegory, or fourfold vision. For the entire narrative is based on a figure, or rather a montage, in which the myth of Enitharmon is overlaid on the masque of European history. But it is far from clear how we separate figure from ground here: that is, whether European history is the phantasmagoric effect of the Female Will; or whether conversely Enitharmon is a figure *for* a "history" that would then constitute the ground of the figure. If the latter is the case, Enitharmon would also be a figure constructed within history, a misogynistic trope for the nightmare with which the masculine Logos cannot deal. The curious fact that she is asleep for the entire duration of this history literally allows us to figure history as her nightmare. But it also suspends the causative link between ground and figure, between the Female Will and the sociohistorical world, by dislocating any sense of agency in the poem. As an extended catachresis, then, the narrative of *Europe* is unreadable because we cannot *see* the two quite disparate entities of "Enitharmon" and "history" in the same space, and therefore cannot see the relationship between them. For it is far from clear whether the action takes place in Enitharmon's crystal house or the historical world, catachresis also being a figure that undoes perspective as the difference between foreground and background. The impossibility of seeing the text, of envisioning its narrative, generates on a broader level a loss of vision that makes it impossible to see the relationship between myth and history. Or to put it differently, *Blake* cannot see this relationship: a predicament that he expresses by placing Enitharmon and history on two separate planes of space and time, each organized, it would seem, according to its own logic.

As a figure that makes the text unreadable, catachresis is linked to other forms of deformation that enter the Lambeth books after *America*. These include narrative compression and genealogical metalepsis. Thus in *Europe* the shadowy fe-

---

40. Ibid., lx.

male rises from "out the breast of Orc" (1:1, E 60), yet Orc in the form of "howling terrors" seems to be the fruit of the labor she goes through in childbirth (2:4, E 61). Moreover, it is not clear whether the labor of childbirth is endured by Enitharmon producing the female (1:8–11, E 60), by the female giving birth to herself (1:12, E 61), or by the female giving birth to Orc, with whom a shadowy female had mated in the preludium to *America*. This scrambling of genealogy makes it impossible to figure (out) the relationship between the mythic characters, and thus to understand how mythic space might inform the historical time with which Blake seems to want to align it.[41] Like the catachrestic structure of *Europe*, the poem's mangled genealogy forces us to encounter the increasing difficulty of composition as a process in which Blake has two sets of material and cannot translate the one into the other. On the one hand he is accumulating more and more of the mythemes or "Unnam'd forms" that will constitute his "system." On the other hand their relationship to history is far from clear. Moreover, the archetypes themselves are characterized by a certain excess, such that their transposition into time is a disfiguration, a stamping with "solid form" of the semiotic that precedes language.

✿ IV ❧

Despite the increasing difficulty of transferring myth into history in these works, Blake continues in *The Song of Los* with the project of nomadic prophecy, constructing a frame to contain *America* and *Europe* within a structure of four "plateaus" that now includes Africa and Asia as well. In the process he also begins to disclose nomadic space as imperial, by mapping it onto four continents that can be linked in a temporal structure, introducing at least the potential for a fusion of time and space in world history conceived in apocalyptic rather than Hegelian and evolutionary terms. The logistics of this structure have been outlined by Erdman and Tannenbaum. Erdman sees the "Africa" and "Asia" sections of the *Song* as forming a prologue to *America* and *Europe*, since "Africa" ends with the first line of *America* and "Asia" begins with the howl that proceeds from Orc's appearance in *Europe*.[42] Tannenbaum further develops this suggestion within a biblical framework by arguing that Africa or Egypt is the place where abstract law

---

41. Damrosch discusses the persistence of these genealogical dislocations in the later texts, but concludes simply that they show "the irrelevance of ordinary causal and genetic assumptions" to Blake's post-Newtonian narrative (*Symbol and Truth,* 129).
42. David V. Erdman, *Blake: Prophet against Empire* (1954; reprint, Garden City, N.Y., 1969), 258.

and philosophy were first imposed, while Asia is "the area in which Paul did his most important work."[43] To this hypothesis about Blake's intentions we might want to add one modification. Asia can provide no more than the trace of apocalypse, since an interpretive imperialism so resolutely occidental as the one outlined here is unlikely to find salvation in the third world. Rather than functioning as prologue and epilogue to the earlier poems, then, Asia and Africa, as places where history has its primitive origins, might be seen as pre-forming the *arche* and *telos* of Western history. In other words their relationship to *America* and *Europe* would not be a linear one in which they provide the beginning and end of a secular scripture. Instead we would see the continents as comprising two pairs of plateaus, in which the movement from the shorter to the longer prophecies transposes myth into history, and juxtaposes the European crisis in which the nightmare of history *im*plodes on itself with the more positive *ex*plosion of this energy in the American revolution.

What is noteworthy, however, is that this framework becomes apparent only as a frame that does not work—which may be why Blake never listed the *Song* among his works. Blake, moreover, seems unable to make Asia function except as a dark continent: in the climax of this section Urizen unfolds his wings to protect her kings, simultaneously unfolding his books of law, which melt Icarus-like; but as the books are destroyed, the continent on which they fall is also consumed in "clouds of despair / . . . howling, weeping" (*Song of Los* 7:12, 16, E 69). Rather than seeing the continents as political states that Blake has succeeded in colonizing by putting them into world history, we should therefore see them instead as psychic "states" that he is unable to put into time. Like the other Lambeth books, the *Song* assembles bits and pieces of the system, summoning up virtually all the characters Blake has named so far, but as an array that the text cannot narrativize. Whatever its intention, the *Song* conspicuously fails to enact the progress from Africa to America projected in the union of Orc, "the image of God who dwells in darkness of Africa," with the dark virgin of America (*America* 2:8, E 52). Instead, Europe, Africa, and Asia (*Song of Los* 4:18–21, E 68), as well as different episodes from world history, seem to be concurrently present in a space without time. Moreover, the difficulty of making space and time work together is expressed in a new division between the material components of Blake's work. Insofar as the verbal for Lessing was associated not just with time but also with

---

43. According to Tannenbaum, "Blake uses the two continents as symbols that define the movement of biblical history, starting in Africa with the origin of Mosaic law and ending in Asia with the abrogation of the law and the apocalyptic birth of a new dispensation" (*Blake's Early Prophecies,* 185–86).

action and the visual with the static presence of bodies in space,[44] this division thematizes what we had already sensed in the text of the *Song:* namely, that Blake cannot combine bodies and actions, psychic space and history.

Thus in *Ahania* and *The Book of Los* the text is completely without design. On the other hand, *Urizen* has more full-page designs than any other text by Blake (a total of ten). Furthermore, where text and design are combined, the latter dwarfs the former, often dominating it from above or pressing against it from below, but always occupying a separate space—whereas in previous texts the two orders had intersected and intertwined. In retrospect this dichotomous organization draws attention to a problem already present as early as *Visions of the Daughters of Albion*, the first work to include a full-page design that is not simply part of the front matter (see color plates I–XI). Invited to collect these designs separately in his "Large Book of Designs," Blake began to constitute the visual as a zone separate from language. But it is *Europe* in particular that anticipates the precedence of the visual in *Urizen*. For *Europe* contains five pull-page designs, and more bizarrely two plates in which the verbal and visual intersect, but as in a collage. These plates are particularly interesting because they interrupt the seamless functioning of visual and verbal orders. The plate beginning "And the clouds & fires pale rolld round in the night of Enitharmon" (E 64, plate 12) is mostly text but is broken up by a cobweb, spoiled, in a gesture similar to the bard's breaking of his harp in *America.* In the plate beginning "The Red limbd Angel seiz'd in horror and torment," two incomplete visual segments are spliced together with a text also cut into two pieces (see color plate XVIII; E 65, plate 13). Dividing the text between European history and Enitharmon's crystal house, the plate also divides the phenomenality of prophecy from the raw materiality of the design underneath it, which usurps the foreground so as to make what Blake is *saying* seem irrelevant. Moreover, this foreground consists only of mutilated fragments: a frontal view of a manacled and shrieking prisoner, and the backside of some rough beast slouching away—either the jailor or the freed prisoner himself holding a link of his chain.

The "Red limbd Angel" plate is the visual equivalent of the preludia in functioning reflexively as a scene of composition. It shows Blake trying to splice together materials that are incommensurable, thus defacing the aesthetic of the illuminated book as a unity in which seeing and saying support each other. But

44. Lessing, *Laocoön,* 78.

while *Europe* still struggles to unite different orders of perception and thus to perform as prophecy, in the later Lambeth books this synthesis is increasingly disabled. In *Urizen* (copy G),[45] the text's attempt to construct the Eternals in opposition to Urizen, "As the stars are apart from the earth" (6:1, E 73), fails entirely to translate the design of the facing plate 7, which shows the Eternals bound and twisted, falling head downward into the depths of the earth. More generally, designs in *Urizen* often bear no relationship to the texts they face, thus inscribing an excess, a separate zone, whose "dark visions of torment" cannot easily be translated into "swift winged words" (2:6–7, E 70). This zone exists as a space apart from time, a space of trauma rather than transcendence. For the designs in *Urizen* are dominated by the body, and lack the foliage, the traces of the natural world, that are still occasionally present in *Europe.* They constitute space as inside rather than outside, as the space of a psyche that grasps itself as body rather than spirit, and thus as outside itself, in materiality. Moreover, they draw us irresistibly into this space, because the body is pushed into the foreground and represented frontally, so as to deny us any distance from what we see.

The designs in *Urizen* are material signifiers of the semiotic foreclosed by the text's struggle to reduce history to systematic form so as to refine body into spirit. Thus the text tries to construct a Symbolic order by distinguishing Urizen from the Eternals and Los from Urizen, so as to name characters within a system of binary oppositions. But the designs are full of unnamed forms whose identity is far from clear, even to Blake himself, who must keep naming and unnaming them by attaching them to different segments of text. Moreover, the designs traumatically foreground images such as the globule of blood or Urizen's skeleton. They project a zone of the abject, to reintroduce Kristeva's term: a zone of pre-thetic horror that precedes and impedes the construction of subjectivity by making it impossible to distinguish this from that, Los from Urizen, or inside from outside. Because it precedes syntax and predication, the abject emerges visually rather than linguistically, rendering vision itself a profoundly problematic concept. For the precedence of the visual also coincides with Blake's foregrounding of the *word* "vision," which is increasingly associated not with transcendence but with "torment" and "dark seperation" (*The [First] Book of Urizen* 15:8, E 78): with the primal scenes that anthropologists study as "myth."

The emergence of the visual as a separate affective register figures Blake's growing sense of the connection between myth and trauma, which in turn ac-

---

45. A reproduction of copy G of *The (First) Book of Urizen* has been edited by Kay Parkhurst Easson and Roger R. Easson (Boulder, Co., and New York, 1979).

counts for the difficulty he has in translating vision into language. In *Urizen* (as also in *Ahania* and *The Book of Los*), Blake goes behind the mangled surface of history to the pre-history in which it is inscribed, thus confronting a recurrent problem: namely the origin of historical events in cultural traumas for which there may not be material causes or remedies. These traumas are collectively encoded in myth, which turns out to be closer to the Real than to the Imaginary. Myth therefore functions as a shifter for Blake, a defense mechanism that switches the track on which the texts move by diverting what is meant to be the rationalization of history, in the anagogic terms of the system, into an encounter with its pre-history.

But it is not that language avoids the trauma en-visioned in myth, for the text itself is usurped by metaphors that are intensely visual but jammed together in such a way as to make visualization impossible. At the root of the difficulty we have in seeing this text is the text's own uncertainty as to what "Urizen" is. Thus it is important not to approach the title character through the role Blake generally assigns to him. Rather the "Urizen" of this text is what makes necessary his supplementary figuration as a tyrannical rationalist whose separation from the other Zoas accounts for the genesis of both history and the self as a fragmented body or *corps morcelé*. From the beginning Urizen has no identity, and can be evoked only negatively as a "shadow of horror," or by subtraction as a "vacuum" that is "Unknown, unprolific!" and "unseen" (3:1–5, 10, E 70). Before Urizen there is something else, a landscape that is confusedly material and psychic: a space in which obscure and cataclysmic geological mutations appear that are neither inside nor outside a subject who seems unseparated from the material world. While the Eternals try to see this space as a void created by Urizen and thus to place it within a perceptual syntax that distinguishes subject from object, what they confront is more like the abject: a state in which Urizen *is* the "vast forests" that the Eternals construct genitively as "his" (3:24–26, E 71). This impossibility of separating subject from object is why "Urizen" so often appears as a function rather than a subject ("an activity unknown and horrible" [3:20, E 71]), or as the congealed effect of a verb without an agent, as in the description of him as an "obscure separation" (5:40, E 73). Attempting to understand this cognitive "void," the poem's speaker asks "What Demon" has formed it and answers with the statement, "Some said / 'It is Urizen'" (3:3–6, E 70). He concedes that what he calls "Urizen" may be a process without a subject, whose "history" may be no more than an anthropomorphizing figure. Significantly, the very positing of Urizen leaves open the question of a subject distinct from its object, since it is unclear whether "It is Urizen" who has created the void, or whether "It" (as the void) *is* Urizen.

As a work that begins by conceding its own figurality, *The Book of Urizen* on one level is about figuration, and enacts the disfiguration of the abject it attempts to screen. The abject as a loss of distinctions leaks into the text through a syntax that suppresses predication and subordination in favor of adjectives and compacted participial constructions that can refer to more than one actant, or displacements of word-order characteristic of an inflected language. Thus when Urizen says "I alone, . . . the winds merciless / Bound" (4:19–20, E 72), it is unclear whether the adjective refers to Urizen or to the winds; and when he describes how he fought with fire it is unclear whether he or the fire is "consum'd / Inwards" (4:14–15, E 72). Often activities are described, or verbs used, that have no clear agency:

> Shrill the trumpet: & myriads of Eternity,
> Muster around the bleak desarts
> Now fill'd with clouds, darkness & waters
> That roll'd perplex'd labring & utter'd
> Words articulate,
>
> (3:54–4:4, E 71)

Here the subject of the verb "utter'd" ought to be "Urizen," but the only possible grammatical subject is "clouds, darkness & waters," thus once again confusing "Urizen" with the elements. Moreover, while it is often eventually possible to assign subjects to participles and verbs in the punctuated written text, such assignments are radically suspended in an oral reading, making words into intensities or pulsions through which characters exchange identities.[46] And it is an oral reading that is called for in the opening lines, in which the Eternals dictate their swift, winged words to the poet.

This syntactic amorphousness reflects the text's status as myth, which we can define as the dream-work of anthropology. As Jurij Lotman points out, myth in general differs from the "plot-text" in being cyclic and in "precipitating" within a single "text-image" characters who in literature would be distinguished synchronically (like Los and Urizen) or diachronically (like Orc and Fuzon). Because myths consist of self-repeating cycles of events that can be told starting at any

---

46. An example is "Los wept . . . for in anguish, / Urizen was rent from his side" (6:2–4). The punctuation makes it clear that the anguish belongs to Urizen, but in an oral reading either Los or Urizen could be "in anguish."

point, linear categories of beginning and end are irrelevant to them,[47] as are moral categories of good and evil. Myth in this sense is the abject of literature: an orality without syntax in which actantial identities are not yet distinct and events (such as the Creation and Fall) are condensed together. Attempting to organize this chaos in transmitting the "words" dictated by the Eternals into writing, Blake constructs the "Book" of *Urizen* as a story that isolates a beginning, a middle, and an end, so as to inscribe the horror of Urizen within a chain of responsibility. He likewise structures the field of characters in terms of binary oppositions that will separate good from evil and proper from improper. But the chronology of the poem remains radically unclear, even at the level of simple words such as the "When" of the Preludium (2:2, E 70). Thus it may be that the Eternals confined Urizen in the north "when" he assumed power. Or it may be that he assumed power "when" they cast him aside by banishing him to the north, or even that they confined him to the north when they assumed him to have a power that they needed to figure as concentrated in him. Likewise the characters that Blake distinguishes keep collapsing back into each other. Thus Urizen is accused of dividing space and time (3:8, E 70), but Los also divides "The horrible night into watches" (10:10, E 75). The Eternals produce the seven deadly sins that are also attributed to Urizen (4:49, 30, E 72), and anticipate Urizen's construction of the "Net of Religion" when they spread the "Tent" of "Science" (25:22, 19:2–9; E 82, 78). Indeed the preludium already makes it impossible to distinguish the Eternals from Urizen, referring to "the primeval Priests assum'd power" (2:1, E 70), and leaving it unclear whether "Priests" refers to Urizen or (as is more likely given the plural form) to the Eternals.[48]

If the story the text tries to tell itself is constantly precipitated back into the unresolved mythic matrix from which it emerges, it is also twisted and interrupted by grotesque metaphors such as a roof "fram'd: like a womb" or a "Web" that is a "Female in embrio" (5:28–29, 25:18; E 73, 82). These metaphors are intensely visual yet cannot be visualized, marking the eruption into language of the trauma Blake tries to confine in the designs. More important, they are catachresis—the dominant mode of *Urizen*, which constantly attaches body parts to what seems nonhuman, figuring rivers as "veins / Of blood" and the world as "a human heart strugling & beating" (5:30–36, E 73). Catachresis, as Warminski argues, is

---

47. Jurij M. Lotman, "The Origin of Plot in the Light of Typology," trans. Julian Graffy, *Poetics Today* 1 (autumn 1979): 163, 167.

48. I discuss these ambiguities of syntax and plot at greater length in *The Supplement of Reading*, 262–70. However, my attempt to allow space for a more positive reading of *Urizen* now seems rather forced.

the trope of disfiguration because it is abusive, far-fetched—thus opening up the tropological system so that it cannot constitute itself seamlessly.[49] But as I have further suggested, it is also the trope of abjection. This is true not only because of its link to the horrifying and grotesque, but also because catachresis blocks the separation of figural and literal, Symbolic and Real, a suspension that is necessary if literature is to address the spiritual rather than corporeal understanding. Thus in the metaphor of the roof "fram'd: like a womb," the text replaces one figure (the roof) with another (the womb), withholding the ground of the figure in an image that is doubly figural. But at the same time the second figure is more affectively real than the first, as if afflicted by the Real that it would like to forget by using the womb as no more than a symbol for a female nature. We can grasp this point better by referring to Ortega y Gasset's suggestion that metaphor is linked to "the spirit of taboo," and involves the substitution of "one thing for another—from an urge not so much to get at the first as to get rid of the second."[50] Where metaphor as an agent of the Symbolic is a mechanism for forgetting, catachresis is a kind of memory: a literalization of figure that remembers the Real.[51]

As a memory of the material, catachresis in *The Book of Urizen* produces the abjection of a humanist history that reads material processes in organic terms by making use of such figures as "the body politic." The prophet of the Lambeth books wants to see history as the story of a subject, albeit a fragmented subject struggling to return to the primal unity destroyed by "Urizen." But this subject appears only in bits and pieces, its organs transplanted into rivers that are "veins / Of blood" and a world "Like a human heart strugling & beating." Indistinguishably Urizen and Albion, the subject seems grafted onto the material world, as if it can be imagined only outside its own body, where it also returns as an inside through the affect of its abjection. In this sense *Urizen* brings to a climax the crisis first introduced when the Bard of *America* breaks his harp, ashamed of his attempt to anthropomorphize the American Revolution by figuring it as the union of Orc with a shadowy female. This first disfiguration of prophecy is agonistically figured in a motif that is repeated across the last four Lambeth books: the figure of a globe or disk that may be a world, a womb, an embryo, an orb of vision, or a globule of blood. The figure occurs thrice in the designs of *Urizen* and twice in those of *The*

49. Warminski, *Readings in Interpretation*, liv.
50. José Ortega y Gasset, *The Dehumanization of Art and Other Writings on Art and Culture* (New York, 1956), 31.
51. I am obviously diverging here from the more rhetorical account of catachresis given by de Man and Warminski, although I would argue that my psychoanalytic account of the figure is implicit in the pathos of Warminski's description, which in effect does posit a Real (and not just a lack) at the origin of the figure.

Song of Los. It also appears at numerous points in the text of *Urizen* as "the dark globe of Urizen" over which Los keeps watch (5:38, E 73), the "red / Round globe hot burning deep" which drops from Urizen's spine (11:2–3, E 75), and the round globe of blood that drops from Los when he is divided by pity (13:58, E 77), becoming a "globe of life" that turns into "the first female form now separate" (18:1, 15, E 78). Blake tries to recuperate this figure within a teleology in *Jerusalem,* when he says "There is a Void, outside of Existence, which if enterd into / Englobes itself & becomes a Womb" (*Jerusalem* 1:1–2, E 144). In the Lambeth books, however, the globe englobes the organ of vision for which it is a catachresis, and (dis)figures itself as a globule of blood, binding vision to the trauma from which it is born.

∞ V ∞

In the three texts that follow *Urizen,* Blake expands his system, like Urizen's body, in various directions, inscribing it in a process of displacement and substitution. He makes two mutually supplementary attempts to move beyond the anger and dejection cathected onto "Urizen," by adding characters in *Ahania* and *The Book of Los* and a world-historical framework in the *Song of Los.* Thus the *Song* takes off from the penultimate lines of *Urizen,* where the followers of Fuzon name "the pendulous earth" Egypt and leave it (28:21–22, E 83). Crossing back from prehistory into history, these lines gesture toward a spiritual nationalism that will map space into time, such that this time can itself be gathered up into the totalized space of *Jerusalem* as the end of history. They reconstitute psychic as political states, so as to organize what in *Urizen* has neither "form—nor outline,"[52] by dividing self from other and inside from outside. But the lines in *Urizen* already concede the futility of this project, begun by the Eternals when they confined "Urizen" geographically by giving him a place in the North. For Fuzon's followers give the name of Egypt not to Africa but to the entire pendulous earth, thus "leaving" Egypt only in the sense that they leave behind what they cannot deal with. These lines, in other words, already prefigure the generalizing of national into psychic space that will stall Blake's project in the *Song.* Thus in the next two books he expands his system horizontally by adding characters rather than vertically through historical time, and he once again approaches history in psychic terms rather than in terms of events. By the same token, he compulsively repeats *Urizen,*

----

52. Percy Bysshe Shelley, *Prometheus Unbound,* II.iv.6 (in *Shelley's Poetry and Prose,* ed. Donald Reiman and Sharon B. Powers [New York, 1977]).

returning to the problem that had afflicted the earlier text: that of bodies that cannot be put into narrative.

The failure of the Lambeth books is acknowledged in *The Book of Los*, which functions as a reflexive coda to the series as well as a "roll[ing] inward" (*Europe* 2:16, E 61) from the global ambitions of *The Song of Los*. *The Book of Los* focuses on the five- hundred-year process to which Blake had alluded in *Ahania*: the shaping of the sun into an icon, an "immense Orb of fire" that is, however, without light (*Book of Los* 5:34, E 94). The poem might seem to be a cosmogony, but it is rather an introjection of cosmogony as a metaphor for Blake's own dark visions. Chapter 3 is an elaboration of plates 6 and 8 of *Urizen*, in which a human form now described as a "white Polypus" forces its way through the waters (*Book of Los*, 4:57–67, E 93). Chapter 4 develops the last plate of the *Song*, in which Los bends with a hammer over a red orb, which in turn is linked to the globes and globules that recur in *Urizen*. The entire text is thus an elaboration of earlier plates that encloses and aborts them within the scene of their own composition. Moreover, in *The Song of Los* the prophetic voice had tried to enter the void so as to englobe it as a specific country, thus mapping psychic space into world-historical time. But in *The Book of Los* the project of binding or defining semiotic energies crucial to representation seems to lead nowhere. Los labors for "Nine ages" (5:41, E 94) at creating the sun, but when it is complete nothing happens. Instead the sun seems to be a form without content, a shape that cannot be inscribed in a sequential or Symbolic narrative; it therefore produces "no light," thus making no impact on the "unform'd / Dark vacuity" it was supposed to englobe (5:48–50, E 94). As pure form, "self-balanc'd" and self-contained (5:45, E 94), the sun seems not to lend itself to human use or thus to figuration—a process that Blake, unlike Shelley in *The Triumph of Life*, does not even attempt. The sun as pure form resists the very notion of artistic labor as praxis, in which work is "the force of history" because it "affirms the presence in the world of something which was not there before," a product or "work" that "transform[s] natural and human realities."[53] Instead the sun, as a form that is simply *there*, leaves its creator superfluous, or as Blanchot says "workless" (*désouevré*),[54] like the shadowy female who is left "void as death" after giving birth to the prophecy.

53. Blanchot, "Literature and the Right to Death," in *The Gaze of Orpheus*, 33–34.
54. Blanchot, "The Essential Solitude," in *The Gaze of Orpheus*, 65.

Blake recognizes this fact when he concedes that the sun produces "no light, for the Deep fled away / On all sides, and left an unform'd / Dark vacuity" (5:48–50, E 94). Moreover, because the positivity of the sun is without use, the negativity that produces it (the wrath of Los, the melancholy of Ahania) also cannot be dialectically recuperated. *The Book of Los*, in other words, is an extended "preludium" that deconstructs artistic creation by returning it to the site of an unusable negativity, felt as an "absence of time . . . [a] time in which nothing begins, in which initiative is not possible."[55] In the process, it also deconstructs both dialectical and apocalyptic history—the figures projected by Los's masculinization of labor as work—in which laboring at the furnaces of imagination produces Giant Forms that use negativity to change the world by "destroy[ing] language in its present form" to "create it in another form."[56] Los, of course, does not accept this deconstruction, and he tries to forge a dialectical and productive relationship between the positivity of the sun and the negativity of "Urizen." Attempting to put the energy of the sun to work Symbolically by binding it to the hi(story) of Urizen, Los tries to give a face to the abject till its "Brain in a rock, & [its] Heart / In a fleshy slough formed four rivers" (5:52–53, E 94). But the "Form" he creates is pure "Illusion" (5:55–56, E 94), and Blake therefore does not tell us what it is, seeming almost to pass him by in the "darkness and deep clouds" that end *The Book of Los* (5:57, E 94). Perhaps it is for the same reason that Blake includes virtually no designs with his text, turning away from Los and from "the glowing illusion" (5:47, E 94) of the illuminated book.

University of Western Ontario

55. Ibid., 72.
56. Blanchot, "Literature and the Right to Death," 34.

On Blakes We Want and Blakes We Don't

Morris Eaves

Wordsworth concluded that the innovative poets of his time would have to "create taste" for their work,[1] and in time he managed to do something like that for his own. But what happens when original poets fail? They fall onto the thorns of posterity and disappear, or other people have to rescue them by creating that taste in arrears. During his lifetime, Blake attracted the attention of some individuals who saw his potential greatness, attempted rescue, and not seldom concluded that he was his own worst enemy, "utterly unfit to take due Care of Himself," as Blake's sometime patron William Hayley remarked to Lady Hesketh.[2] Having taken due care of poor Cowper, Hayley transferred his attentions to Blake—as it later proved, with disheartening results for both of them.

As the Hayleys, Linnells, and Tathams of posterity, we take up our post as Blake's caretakers. He no longer needs rescue because that happened earlier. We can see how a sustainable taste for Blake was first created through the efforts of late Victorians and early Modernists from D. G. Rossetti and Swinburne through Yeats. Blake was not a poet when he died in 1827 but a visual artist who had left behind some poetry. It is an idle but to me interesting question how many lines of this poetry—in, say, *The Four Zoas*, *Milton*, and *Jerusalem*—were ever read by anyone other than the poet during his lifetime. In any case, by the time Swinburne and Yeats finished with him he had been transformed into a poet whose visual side had shrunk to manageable proportions. This reconfigured Blake—child of a generation of rebellious writers in opposition to the high Victorians, and the earliest model that could be called successful—was brought in not only for his

---

1. William Wordsworth, "Essay, Supplementary to the Preface of 1815," in *The Prose Works of William Wordsworth*, ed. W. J. B. Owen and Jane Worthington Smyser (Oxford, 1974), 3:82.
2. G. E. Bentley Jr., *Blake Records* (Oxford, 1969), 105–6.

outsiderly commitments (modified to serve the special purposes of his sponsors) but also for his combination of lofty artistic ambition with mysticism and multimedia craft, which, duly subordinated to his identity as a poet, could serve as yet another sign of his outsider status.

Blake was then and continues even now to be the sign of something new about to happen, partly because of his brand of obscurity, situated right between portentous sense and arrant nonsense, and partly because of the importance that posterity has granted to his difficult illuminated books, whose multimedia character makes them even more difficult to read, to see, and to exhaust by reading or looking. A persistent problem in creating a taste for this work has been how to motivate readers to climb walls of such difficulty. The present collection of essays demonstrates in several interesting ways how we are still at it, altering "Blake" as our desires, for him and for ourselves, alter.

Despite the fundamental early shift of canonical priorities from his art to his poetry, one of Blake's special advantages has always been his double talent for words and pictures, which, in the making of a durable cultural image of him, has allowed visibility to come in aid of legibility. Being read, after all, accounts for only a part, and sometimes not a terribly important part, of an artist's complex infiltrating and staying powers. Blake's durability seems to depend partly on his ready reproducibility in simple forms as a cultural marker—memorable images to decorate dust jackets, startling proverbs to launch book chapters, catchy phrases to name rock bands.

His ability to produce both words and images has made him doubly available and served him well as a signature, but it has often proved a serious liability. Sometimes it stretches him too thin across the vast reaches of the culture, with a loss of focus and a blurring of identity that threatens to dissolve in a sea of white noise. On the other hand, simple clarity is eventually monotonous; the attention of the audience must be captured and then kept. There must be resources available to supplement the original message and sustain interest in it. The illuminated books, so confusing and bizarre that they required both hard sell and simplification (such as the divorce of the poetry from the pictures) before they could make the necessary primary impression on an audience, have excelled at supplying the backflow of rich secondary resources that sustains interest in the long term—and the term in art *is* long, practically endless, which creates the kind of problem that politicians ignore until they become concerned about their "place in history." That may help to explain why concepts like "wide appeal," "popularity," and (the dignified form of the other two) "universality," flawed as they are, keep resurfacing in critical discussion of the arts despite the considerable resistance to them.

In any case, the handmade picture books that Blake once glamorized as his "illuminated books" in "illuminated printing"[3] have been closely bound up with his posthumous fate. Since most of the battles over his reputation have been fought over that corpus, it cannot be surprising that four of the five essays in this volume look chiefly to the illuminated books for what Tilottama Rajan calls the "material signifier" of his "system." Nor is it surprising, considering the layers of complication that the illuminated books supply, that they can support the several different kinds of exploration and critique that are launched by their critics and commentators in the present collection. By this late date, of course, Blake's canonical status is so entrenched and stable that he can easily withstand remapping (Rajan), severe criticism of his views (David Bindman and Anne K. Mellor), and tunneling through his material foundations (Joseph Viscomi). By this time it is clear to most readers, I think, that any of the twentieth-century theses posted on the door of this particular landmark are likely to be temporary stage directions in a theater of criticism that sustains itself by generating new images of its objects and new maps of the territory on which they lie. Some, like Rajan's, construct new positions from old ones by triangulation and synthesis. Others, like Bindman's and Mellor's, use eighteenth-century history to connect Blake with urgent, troubling twentieth-century issues of race and gender: by warning that he was of his time, they signal that they are of ours. Yet others, like Viscomi's, construct revised explanations of the "material signifier" sufficiently authoritative to strengthen and clarify a familiar icon; in the light of Viscomi's discussion, Blake seems more than ever a rare union of the practical artist with the profoundly creative thinker.

As Rajan indicates, her essay returns late to the postmodern party that once passed Blake through the "fires of deconstruction" (David Simpson's phrase, I think)—interestingly, again, almost always the Blake of the illuminated books. But Blake never proved terribly useful to deconstruction because he is just too eligible. One needs no special theory of language to make it happen; he self-deconstructs. It takes the massive intellectual pressure of a Northrop Frye to bind Blake's formidable difficulties into an illusion of total coherence, which, inevitably, falls into contradictions, fragments, and dead ends as soon as the pressure

---

3. [Prospectus], 1793, in *The Complete Poetry and Prose of William Blake,* revised ed., ed. David V. Erdman (Berkeley and Los Angeles, 1982), 693. Page references to Erdman's edition (abbreviated "E") are given hereafter in the text.

lets up. Even Vincent De Luca's metaphor of Blake's "wall of words" (in *Words of Eternity: Blake and the Poetics of the Sublime* [Princeton, N.J., 1991]) is too elegantly architectural. In my experience, Blake's work is a heap of words—and pictures—that starts to become a wall when we readers apply the necessary intellectual pressure to get what we want from it: sense, structure, coherence. It meets us halfway—as Christopher Smart's writing does not—but every step beyond the halfway point is a struggle, pleasurable for some of us. But in Blake criticism the pleasurable anticipation of sense frequently stands in rhetorically for the actual demonstration of sense. Blake criticism is addicted to a rhetoric of false confidence, which in turn feeds a counteractive syndrome of reader letdown.

Although Rajan arrives late on the scene, then—having visited several times previously in her own poststructural phases—she comes seeking middle ground: to her right the "homogeneity" represented by "the structures stubbornly constructed by Northrop Frye and S. Foster Damon," and to her left "a logic of absolute difference in which the Blakean text exists only in its performances," represented by Donald Ault's reading of *The Four Zoas* (*Narrative Unbound: Revisioning William Blake's* The Four Zoas [Barrytown, N.Y., 1987]). She finds both at fault for "protect[ing] the economy of literature" (which she implies should be left unprotected) and giving "self-satisfaction . . . to the critic" (who she implies should be left unsatisfied), presumably via the poststructural pleasures of killing this author (engraver, painter) and mastering his text. Linking, for reasons that are not clear to me, the "unifying pluralism" of "representative democracy" to this unsatisfying logic of absolute difference, she proposes an alternative that carries the implicit promise of unspecified improvements in the political order: a division between the so-called Lambeth books of the 1790s and the later books, chiefly *Milton* and *Jerusalem*. In this construction the earlier books betray, as it were, the compositional process by which Blake attempts but consistently fails to create his megamyth out of historical events, the artistic stresses and strains made visible and audible by an artistic lamination machine that, over and over again, fails to keep the shiny veneer of myth glued to the rough particleboard of history.

For Rajan, the Lambeth years constitute a period of successful failure—successful in that she values the strewn wreckage of contradictions, the "false starts" and "raw material" and "process of shaping," more than the achieved but oppressive and antihistorical system of *Milton* and *Jerusalem*. That view is not explicitly defended but everywhere implied: the tumultuous processes of the Lambeth books are superior to the seamless products of later years, when an apocalyptic "master narrative" replaces "dialectical" struggle.

I admit that I am wary of this strong distinction on several grounds. As a formula it is too tidy to be quite real: it reproduces an all too familiar (call it Romantic) value system that ranks dynamic processes above static products; and it reproduces an all too familiar (Romantic) contrast between the radical young artist who grapples with history and the conservative old systematizer who abandons it for the consolations of religion and philosophy. The "later Blake" of Rajan's narrative aligns perfectly with the later Coleridge and the later Wordsworth of literary-historical mythology. These are hardly sufficient reasons for rejecting Rajan's formulations, but the ease with which they fall into place leaves me wondering if she is taking dictation from the master narrative of Romanticism.

To me, the neatness of her oppositions suggests that she may approach Blake too well defended against the shock of asymmetry. Whereas Damon and Frye first professed to find homogeneous structures, earlier readers had seen nothing but uncontrolled heterogeneity, which they usually personalized and branded with negative sociocultural labels (the lunatic, the fanatic). Rajan presents a highly schematic synthesis of the two heretofore dominant accounts of Blake's books: they are heterogeneous and indecipherable; they are homogeneous and entirely decodable. No, she suggests, the earlier ones are heterogeneous, the later ones homogeneous. Is her readiness to accept (some version of) Damon's and Frye's views on the systematic character of the later illuminated books purely pragmatic? Because a one-hundred-percent unsystematic Blake is useless to criticism, her argument may need Damon and Frye so much that they become its uninvited enablers. Their rigorous defense of what had always been, after all, the least defensible of Blake's books, those insane epics *Milton* and *Jerusalem*, is what gives her the opportunity to amputate the Lambeth books from the Damon-Frye canon and to elevate them for being open processes and demote the later works for being closed products.

This account does not line up with my experience of the later books. Rajan writes with more confidence about what is and is not in them than I can summon. No one, to be sure, is going to miss the signs of mythmaking energy that are everywhere in Blake: all those compass points aligned with all those characters, emanations, cities, cathedrals, professions, and bodily organs; and all those secular local events read by the light of sacred universal narratives. These seem to be elements of a rhetoric of conviction that Blake offers as a support-system for readers in time of their greatest need. All will be revealed, it implies, to those who tough it out: "Mark well my words! they are of your eternal salvation" (*Milton* 2:25, E 96). For me and I gather for others, those elements glittering on the surface constitute one of the most seductive features of Blake's illuminated books, symbolizing the author's covenant with the reader that there *is* a deeply coherent system somewhere here, and that the investment of readerly exertions will eventually pay off in a grasp of it. To mount her argument, Rajan needs to take it for granted that Damon and Frye were right at least half the time—about *Jerusalem* if not about *The Book of Urizen*. I feel obliged to repeat what I have said perhaps too many times already: my best reasons for believing that there is a system that can really be understood come from the secondhand testimony of great systematizing critics like Frye. Personally I have never experienced the grasp of Blake's meaning to which they, and she, have so eloquently testified.

Nor do I find solace in magical notions of the power of the illuminated book as such, "which unites time and space" and is "the containing form of the system" that "accomplishes what the system by itself cannot. . . . the composite artifact of the book 'reduces' difficulty within the intricacy of a figured surface, allowing us to look rather than read, to assimilate the text as art rather than experience." Rajan's antivisual prejudice belongs to a venerable tradition in which words are associated with difficult adult "experience" and pictures with mere mesmerizing visual "art," a distraction from the real. (The construction is also reversible—why are the illuminated books not artified words but wordified art, a visual spectacle spoiled by hard language?) To revise something Harold Bloom once said of his experience of the illuminated books: I read some of the most ambitious and persuasive literary criticism in the language; I stare, disbelievingly, at the mystifying poetry and pictures it claims to account for, and then I try, too strenuously, to wind the golden string of the criticism into the heart of the illuminated books.[4] I understand the criticism at least well enough to lipsync it, but I know I do not understand the poems and pictures . . . yet? The light of the Promise flickers in the darkness.

4.   "I read one of the most eloquent descriptive passages in the language; I stare, disbelievingly, at an inadequate engraved illumination, and then I try, too strenuously, to isolate an image that Blake, as a poet, knew better than to isolate." From this experience Bloom proceeds to argue that Blake's later illuminated books, which for Rajan are coercive monolithic systems signified by the very integration of text and design, are instead experiments in "auditory and visual counterpoint" that succeed only as poetry (Harold Bloom, "The Visionary Cinema of Romantic Poetry," in Alvin H. Rosenfeld, ed., *William Blake: Essays for S. Foster Damon* [Providence, R.I., 1969], 18–35).

❧ ❧

Nestled into the yin of Rajan's critical and theoretical macroeconomics is the yang of Joseph Viscomi's scholarly microeconomics. Skeptics who wonder if material signifiers are not always bloodless theoretical entities can find reassurance in Viscomi's essay, whose exhibit number one is the "disjointed, miscellaneous work entitled *The Marriage of Heaven and Hell*, . . . in some measure the result of a production history in which sections were written and executed at different times." With real, or perhaps material, questions at issue—what did Blake do, and how and when did he do it?—Viscomi measures every which way till the shoe fits. The "material signifier" is again the illuminated book, but "material" is broadened to encompass, beyond even paper and ink and watercolor, the materials of Blake's trade that he manipulated to produce the extant artifacts.

Viscomi's relentless archaeology, aided by exceptional powers of observation, produces a flow of brilliant insights. Where his predecessors have often found nothing or the wrong things, his intense scrutiny of physical evidence leaves us with a mountain of new fact—on which he balances, precariously, a second mountain of new speculation. From an immense range of harder material evidence—including habits of printing, shapes and sizes of plates, styles of lettering, catchwords—and softer but sometimes suggestive textual evidence —concurrent events, literary reference and allusion, logical and narrative and rhetorical structures—Viscomi is able to extract more ore than just about anyone else can. Reading his essay reminds me (again) how fortunate I am to have him as an accomplice. Even if one disagrees with him, as I occasionally do, he makes evasion hard. His mode of argument, though it can be dangerous for claustrophobics, is ultimately very satisfying in its ability to produce arguable, even testable, propositions in a field of study where the play of untestable Attitude and the leap of Conclusion can count for so much. As the first of a three-part study on the evolution of the *Marriage*, the present essay gives us every reason to look forward to the other two parts.

In what is by now a familiar vein of his work, Viscomi casts his argument as a correction of the view that Blake composed his illuminated books from end to end before executing them—what we might think of as the usual way that modern writers work with publishers and printers. A writerly approach to the medium of reproduction has helped to sustain the image of Blake as a coherent writer— writing out his system, so to speak, in a coherent and systematic manner. But because Blake executed and designed plates before completing a manuscript, it became "technically possible for him to think and work outside the letterpress paradigm," which dictates that a text is "written on paper and then set in type . . . with labor moving determinently . . . from author to compositor." By breaking with the techniques of conventional printing, Blake achieved "unprecedented interplay between graphic execution and textual composition." Viscomi seeks to mark a strong separation between the "paradigms" of watercolored relief etching and those of conventional letterpress printing (and the habits of authorship that have grown up with them, such as the creation of "far copy"—manuscripts, or, more recently, typescripts and output from computers—for the editor, compositor, and printer). Thus do Viscomi's researches help define one of the hallmarks of Blake's reputation, the special status granted to his illuminated books as texts. Viscomi, however, shares with Rajan, at least, the opinion that in some of the early books a lot of Blake's seams are showing.

Viscomi's core proposition is that "plates 21–24 preceded not only the other *Marriage* plates but possibly the idea of the *Marriage* itself. That idea appears to have originated in what were originally two separate projects, an anti-Swedenborgian text, presumably meant as an independent work, and the Bible of Hell announced at the end of the pamphlet." The harshest thing one can say about Viscomi's masterful arguments in support of this proposition is that some of them are highly conjectural. I see a fundamental division between the set of arguments about sequence that depends on the intricate details of printing and a second set that rests on notions of narrative integrity and Blake's reactions to Swedenborg. The first set—including Viscomi's analysis of the copper sheets, Blake's squirrely *g*s, and his catchwords—are so wondrously documented and defended that for my money they can be put down as unassailable in our lifetime. The second set—right down to Blake's fulfillment of those Aristotelian requirements for a four-part oration—can seem, by comparison, a bit pat and mechanical. In general, Viscomi marks the second class of evidence with provisional phrasing—for example, "is consistent with the theory that" instead of "strengthens the evidence for the conclusion that" or "helps to prove that"— that nonetheless becomes the tissue that connects key pieces of his argument. Toward the end of the essay, the odd notion of one plate's "awareness" of another's themes ("this news from hell [on plate 4] appears aware that the 'jews code' and 'ten commandments' have already been criticized on plates 13 and 23 [and 27?]") and one plate's ability to "recognize" another seems to ask personification to bear more weight than it can, given that the chronology of awareness is reversible—plate 4 is said to be aware of 13 and 23, but 13 and 23 can also be aware of 4. The awareness (which can itself be very tenuous) does not establish a sequence; it identifies a group of plates with thematically related material. Similarly, the conviction that plates 21 through 24 are thematically and rhetorically more coherent than any other textual unit is highly subjective; several other units seem to me quite as coherent, and, after all, coherence in the product does not establish coherence in the process. In my experience, coherent processes often produce disjointed products. Coherence may be achieved only on a second or third pass, and it may not be the goal at all. Finally, in such conclusions as "when plate 4 is placed within the composing process and read in light of the many plates it in fact follows, Blake's original intentions for this plate and for the devil's views throughout the *Marriage* begin to reveal themselves," Viscomi's faith in the power of narrative analysis to expose original intentions is stronger than mine. Readers will, as we say, have to judge for themselves how much support this second-string evidence adds to Viscomi's fundamental claims.

Mixed in among his most astute arguments on the construction of the *Marriage* is an unexplained investment in specific alternative plans for certain sections of the work. The most baffling of these is the thesis that the *Marriage* has its genesis in an "independent pamphlet" comprising plates 21–24. "Independent pamphlet" ("independent unit," "independent work," and so on) becomes something of a mantra that has little bearing on the more compelling argument that the composition of the *Marriage* simply began with plates 21–24. Why does this independent pamphlet not look more like a pamphlet? Why, at a minimum, has it no title (nor author, printer, date)? The evidence of careful registration and separate printing seems slight by comparison with the counterindications. A similar argument is advanced for yet another independent pamphlet comprising plates 25–27, "A Song of Liberty." Here at least there is a title but, again, no evidence of separate publication, just one instance of separate printing. Because Viscomi's larger argument persuasively outlines the conditions under which the separate printing of textual units is entirely possible—and two distinct instances in the compass of what eventually became one work normalize it even more—it is difficult to understand why the separate pamphlet conjectures are anything other than extra baggage.

Viscomi also proposes that the Proverbs of Hell were part of Blake's Bible of Hell. The Bible of Hell runs second only to Tatham's supposed destruction of Blake's works in its power to generate speculation about the artist. Because Blake includes the Proverbs of Hell in the *Marriage* as plates 7–10 and then arranges the plates of the work to put the narrator's announcement of the Bible of Hell as a forthcoming work on plate 24, what reason is there to suppose that the

Proverbs of Hell are (or were) part of a Bible of Hell project that preceded the announcement and was (partly) combined with the anti-Swedenborgian material? He might have, after all, easily eradicated his announcement if it had become, as it were, out of date in the process of organizing the *Marriage*. He seems to have designed a separate title page for his Bible of Hell project (untraced since 1876 but described by W. M. Rossetti), probably after finishing the *Marriage*—it mentions Lambeth, where Blake moved in 1790.[5] In any case, all discussions of the Bible of Hell are based on a very few uncertain facts and a vast deal of conjecture, on which, fortunately, little in Viscomi's reconstruction depends.

A useful way to situate Viscomi's argument might be in relation to prior readings of the *Marriage*, which have always had to contend with its wild and crazy assortment of materials. The usual defensive maneuver has been to tack on "apparently" before "miscellaneous" and then to explain the apparent heterogeneity by reference to some mixed but esteemed literary model, if not Menippean satire then the Bible. The defender who springs first to mind is Max Plowman, who was the earliest to claim—three years after Damon had called the *Marriage* a "scrapbook"—that he had discovered its structure: "a poem as prologue" (pl. 2); "a prose argument composed in six chapters," each one delimited by pictures (pls. 15–16, for example); and "a song as epilogue" (pls. 25–27).[6] As I recall, Plowman was making no claims about the process of composition by which Blake might have arrived at his final product, but clearly Plowman was offering his account of structure partly as a defense against the mischievous notion that Blake's works are a hodgepodge because his mind was a hodgepodge—perhaps a homemade English individual talent, as T. S. Eliot concluded, whose works do not belong with the smoother and more systematic contributions to Western poetic tradition. Blake's eccentric works were something to be kept in the archive, probably, but in the attic rather than the public gallery. On the contrary, Plowman hinted, if even the most miscellaneous-looking of Blake's works has a beautifully articulated structure, then what deep orders might we discover in the rest of the illuminated books! Plowman's discovery constituted one more episode in the narrative by which a completely coherent Blake might be constructed. Here was

<hr>

5. Martin Butlin, *The Paintings and Drawings of William Blake,* 2 vols. (New Haven, Conn., 1981), no. 221v.

6. See S. Foster Damon, *William Blake: His Philosophy and Symbols* (London, 1924), 88; and *Blake's Poems and Prophecies,* ed. Max Plowman (1927; reprint, New York, 1954), xxiii.

a kind of critical progress: if everyone by then admitted the value of the *Songs,* the *Marriage,* by virtue of its uncharacteristic "accessibility" to readers, was surely the next step for those who wanted to explore further. By establishing the structure of the *Marriage,* Plowman was preparing the way for even bolder forays into the Blakean outback.

I do not know whether Viscomi would resist Plowman's description. He engages in a little shadowboxing with unspecified straw men (disguised as "one") over the notion that Blake composed the *Marriage* according to some preconceived plan ("one is hard pressed not to envision [Blake] writing and rewriting the entire composition on paper before committing it to copper, because one still imagines Blake working as a poet in the manuscript tradition and using illuminated printing subsequently as a mode of reproduction"). But might a product as orderly in the arrangements of its parts as Plowman describes be the result of a process as haphazard as the one Viscomi describes? Viscomi seems to believe at least that coherent products suggest coherent processes of composition. He clearly believes the converse, that incoherence in the product—dead ends, missing catch words, *g*s that won't settle down, mismatched plate/page sizes, misregistered impressions, references on later plates that predict the coming of plates the reader has already read (if part of the Bible of Hell announced on plate 24 is the Proverbs of Hell on plates 6–10)—points to incoherence in the process. Viscomi dwells intensively on the order in which Blake might have executed the plates of the *Marriage;* he never says what principles might have guided Blake's assembly of these plates into a final order.

If indeed Blake conceived his *Marriage* as a parody of "the theory that the Old Testament is a gathering of redacted fragments,"[7] then it is ironically appropriate that Viscomi analyzes the composition of Blake's bible with a version of the editorial methods used by those Bible critics for more than two centuries. In some respects Viscomi's approach resembles the textual criticism that attempts to determine the "strands" that have been editorially woven into the Pentateuch and the "genetic" textual criticism of (mostly) Continental editors, best known in North America through the element of genetic reasoning in Hans Gabler's controversial edition of Joyce's *Ulysses,* published in 1984. Unlike Gabler, Viscomi does not seem to be establishing an editorial rationale that would make

---

7. Robert N. Essick quoted by Viscomi; see *Representation, Anxiety, and the Bibliographical Sublime,* forthcoming in *Huntington Library Quarterly.*

any difference in an edition of the *Marriage*, though he certainly lays the foundation for such an edition (and sometimes comes close to suggesting, more subversively, that such an editorial rearrangement might be superior to the *Marriage* that we have, at least in terms of narrative integrity). One might reasonably ask, then, why *does* Viscomi go to such lengths to reconstruct the process of composition of the *Marriage?*

The research presented here certainly advances Viscomi's work on Blake's production processes, but I suspect that a compelling part of the answer is more biographical than editorial or technical: this analysis of the *Marriage* adds support to the image of the historical William Blake that Viscomi has been constructing by the indirect means of technical recipes and procedures. Viscomi's method does not promise to deliver just Blake's methods of production; it also promises Blake the person, present in his work and workshop. Viscomi is unflinchingly into what used to be called, back in the Derridean days, presence: "Witnessing the *Marriage* unfold through its production enables us to answer basic questions about the *Marriage*'s form and Blake's original and final intentions. . . . In short, it enables us to see more of Blake's mind at work." The investigator shows enormous faith in the ability of his material methods to get at the soul of Blake's machine—not just final intentions but also literal intentions and even manifestations of the holy spirit itself, "Blake's mind at work."

By getting the present story of the making of the *Marriage* straight, Viscomi puts more flesh on the bones of his Blake, very much the dirty-handed artisan who cuts copper sheets, wields hammers and quills, mixes etching grounds, uses whatever is on hand, takes shortcuts, prints negligently—and composes on the fly. Viscomi's Blake is a chronic improviser and Viscomi's *Marriage* is the product of multiple sessions of improvisation, as Blake riffs here on an inspiring fragment, there on a political event, a biblical genre, a controversy among the London Swedenborgians, or an ad in the back of a Swedenborg volume.

Thus is Viscomi advancing the project of revamping the most influential old Blakes—Damon's mystic philosopher, Frye's archetypal poet—to produce a Blake more in line with the known facts of his historical situation, headquartered in an engraver's and painter's workshop-studio rather than a writer's study, for whom the burning questions of the day were primarily those that aroused engravers, painters, and sculptors rather than poets, novelists, and critics. A very appealing Blake to those of us who like ours both jazzy and grounded.

To the extent that the artist Viscomi is discovering is known in advance, however, he is shaped on the armature of a well-known Romantic ideology. This Blake "behave[s] like an artist," which in this construction means that he employs a "hands-on, workshop style of composing." But this is about more than dirty hands. As an "artist," this Blake "think[s] nonlinearly" according to a "creative logic." Evidence that might suggest that Blake is *just* foolhardy, sloppy, hasty, or careless is taken rather as evidence of this creativity, which causes him to "deepen the meaning of his text," for instance, "by responding creatively to his own first prints." He is not only or merely an artisan, like his peers among the reproductive engravers. Blake's "workshop" is elevated to critical importance as the material signifier of his "mind." In an adventurous essay full of risks well and wisely taken, the greatest danger, I feel, looms whenever Viscomi is tempted to work backward from the physical facts to a Romantic metaphysics of presence—and then forward again to the physical facts, a circular approach by which Viscomi may get what he wants—a certain kind of Blake who composed a certain kind of work—too easily.

A major consequence of construing an engraver-artist's workshop in specifically Romantic terms is to preserve and indeed in some respects shore up the bridge to the other, much more familiar Blake—a rather conservative construction tied to a related set of conventional (and powerful and influential) Romantic ideas of art and the artist: the ideological Blake who actually cares, in a disputatious but still linear sort of way, about articulating his own ideas in relation to Swedenborg's; a Blake whose thought processes can be benchmarked to standards of "narrative integrity," and even to Aristotle's rhetoric. This is the sober-sided Blake I find standing behind such statements as "Blake sees what he has accomplished, and sees the creative import of passionate response. In the *Marriage* he not only expresses opposition but at the same time engages in the intellectual combat—or 'Mental Fight' (*Milton* 2:13)—that he believed essential." Or, similarly, "Contrary to Swedenborg, who believed vision required leaving the body, Blake knew as an artist that it could occur while in the body and through the physical body of art."

In such "creative" struggles Blake belongs with, say, Keats or Wordsworth; a study of the "production history" of the *Marriage* belongs alongside a study of the "development" of *The Prelude*. Which is to say that Viscomi does not depart from the usual view that Blake's creative imagination and his ideas are the most important things about him (to us). Viscomi's essay is packed with those hallowed ideas. The difference lies in his conviction that they are manifest in the ways Blake—literally—handled them in his workshop. As I say, this is a Blake to whom my sympathies also incline, although I cannot share its more orthodox Romantic attributes. The matter is significantly complicated by Blake's participation in eighteenth-century discourses, secular and sacred, that contradict workshop realities on the one hand and the ideas of the Romantic literati to which posterity has tied him on the other.

I wonder whether Viscomi's familiar and generally helpful opposition between the autographic and the mechanical—which reappears here in the opposition between illuminated printing (autographic) and letterpress printing (mechanical) and their respective "paradigms"—does not quite own up to the extent to which illuminated printing is mechanical, or, more precisely, the extent to which the autographic is mechanical. Viscomi's reluctant acknowledgment of apparent exceptions to the paradigms, such as D. G. Rossetti, carries the unfortunate implication that printers cannot be creative because they use "mechanical" pieces of type instead of "autographic" script. Handwriting is itself a mechanical procedure—a technology. Any of these media, including Blake's, are to some degree eligible for mechanization, organization, and institutionalization. If Blake had been trained as a letterpress printer, would he have set—for that matter composed—his own compositions in type? Nothing in the technology would have prevented it.

In the inclination to romanticize Blake's medium by identifying its autographic character with his creativity, Viscomi occasionally overstresses the medium's flexibility and slights its rigidity. After all, the unit of convenient substitution in movable type is the individual letter; in Blake's medium, it is the entire plate and all the text on it. Thus Blake had good technical reasons, once a plate was etched, to stick by its text; writers revise their galley proof and even their page proof a good deal more freely, for equally good technical reasons. The fact is that Blake, like any author using almost any conceivable method of production, could *choose* to create his texts bit by bit, in or out of final order, or to start with some beginning and write his way to some end. Most of the time, writers working with printers have to turn in completed works in some form and they lack control over the final product. Blake had a greater range of control and hence choice. He could behave like a writer (who in this case is his own printer) or, if he chose, like the Blake of Viscomi's argument, building his work piece by piece. Nothing but the evidence can suggest what he did in any individual case.

Among the host of interesting questions stirred up by Viscomi's discussion, the unresolved one that fascinates me most is what might have happened to the manuscripts that Viscomi supposes Blake produced while working out the *Marriage* on copper: "an assortment of texts written at different times, probably on various sizes and kinds of paper, but never a fair copy of a completed manuscript. As with his other illuminated books, Blake did not know the number of plates *Marriage* would require until after it was executed." It is worth remembering, however, that Blake had much more control over the number of plates in his works—and over what goes on any individual plate or group of plates—than authors of printed prose narratives ordinarily do. That is why the unit of narration in Blake's books is much more often the single plate/page than it would have been had he turned manuscripts over to a letterpress printer—because the page/plate unit is a physical presence in front of him as he works, a cross between a writer's sheet of paper and a painter's canvas (that is, an expensive, relatively troublesome material object within whose borders much labor will be expended). This is not to say that Blake always exercised the control that his medium allowed—not to say that he composed the *Marriage* in any way other than the piecemeal way Viscomi imagines. But Blake could choose between freer and more controlled ways of working; both were available in his workshop and in his medium.

Viscomi rejects too hastily, I believe, the possibility that Blake composed spontaneously in his head, stored lines in memory, and wrote them onto copper later. Following Blake in demonizing "memory" will not do as a reason for rejecting this possibility (see Viscomi's essay, n. 16). Just as Viscomi rightly feels free to emphasize Blake's practical interactions with materials without fretting over the blatant contradictions with his antimaterialistic theories of art, so must it be with memory. Blake objected to theories of art that value memory—that is, imitation—above original inspiration, but, like all human beings, he depended on his own memory for storage, fundamentally and inescapably. He is not against storage; the etched texts themselves are a form of storage. And there is persuasive evidence that the memories of Blake's generation ordinarily developed far greater wordhoarding capacities than do ours.[8] Could the explanation for Blake's "missing" manuscripts be the simplest one, that they never existed? Or that Blake's references to taking dictation in large batches of lines (see Viscomi's essay, n. 16) point to habits of composition closer to Wordsworth's method of composing out of doors for later transcription from memory at home than to the manuscript-to-print methods of later writers? In that context, the survival of *The Four Zoas*, say, in manuscript may well be evidence that it was never intended to be an illuminated book. But the survival of that manuscript also suggests that, if there had been manuscripts, even scrappy ones (and much of *The Four Zoas* is pretty

---

8. Perkins's essay "How the Romantics Recited Poetry" (*SEL* 31 [1991]: 655–71) is a useful starting place: "Wordsworth dictated ninety-two pages of verse from memory—not his own verse" (p. 656)—though the emphasis is on vocal performance rather than the cultural history of memory.

scrappy), some would have survived. We might imagine, with Viscomi, that short works could be composed on bits of paper that were thrown away; it is far harder to imagine that this happened to the yards and yards of text in *Milton* and *Jerusalem.* The absence of manuscripts suggests a method of composition that did not call for composition on paper. For what it is worth, my own vote is for either execution from memory directly onto copper or spontaneous composition directly onto copper, or, more likely, a combination of the two—with, no doubt, occasional exceptions (a reality principle is healthy even when dealing with Blake).

When Henry Crabb Robinson, curious as ever, made Blake the target of a mission of local ethnology, he did so as one taken with the stranger in his midst. Robinson handled his odd and provocative informant with care, quoting his words, turning them over for close scrutiny, analyzing them to see how they might make sense if properly construed. In explaining Blake's particular form of insanity—not "*mere* madness" but "Monomania," he said—he found a helpful historical comparison with "the theosophic dreams . . . of *Swedenborg.*"[9] (One might usefully contrast his cautious approach to exotic Blake with the self-assurance of John Gabriel Stedman's reports on plantation life in distant Surinam.) The essays of Bindman and Mellor have normalized, it seems to me, that historical Blake of the weird and dangerous opinions not despite history but with it, and in the process raised some perplexing questions about the uses of historical evidence.

Historical evidence is always partly shaped by the hypothesis it supposedly demonstrates. What that means in practice is that something is always brought to the evidence that helps to sort it, simplify it, and focus it. Particular ideas about Blake—the kind of man he was, the kind of man it was possible for him to be at the time—control the use of historical evidence in both Bindman's and Mellor's discussions. Both are scholarly papers of our time in their desire to put ideological distance between then and now by tying Blake down to some commonplace ideas with influence in his time and place but beneath contempt in ours. The considerable, and perhaps unavoidable, risk is the one that Nicholas Penny has termed "anachronistic indignation."[10]

9.   Bentley, *Blake Records,* 53.
10.   Nicholas Penny, review of Patricia Rubin, *Giorgio Vasari: Art and History,* in *London Review of Books,* 16 November 1995, 18.

In a smart little essay, "Teaching Ideology in [*The*] *Songs* [*of Innocence and of Experience*],"[11] David Simpson dramatizes the familiar experience of a class of students "visibly scratching its collective head" over three ideologically enigmatic songs in *Innocence*—"Holy Thursday," "The Chimney Sweeper," and "The Little Black Boy." For the two latter poems, as Simpson indicates, "we have an urgent contemporary occasion" (p. 51)—the plight of sweeps and the slave trade—and both "*can* be read (though perhaps should not be read) in either of two ways with more or less equal credibility. They are not at all vague in their social messages, but they can be interpreted convincingly as offering either of two different messages" (p. 49): one "a savagely ironic exposure of the quietistic effects of Christian doctrine"; the other the quietistic message itself, which can be read "in good faith by anyone who believes that the next life really does make up for the shortcomings of this one" (p. 51). Finally, Simpson considers the possibility that "Blake finally ask[s] to be defined as a writer"—we can add artist—"who dramatizes the inevitable clash of ideologies in the social evolution of 'meaning'" (p. 53) and rejects that possibility in favor of another: "When we . . . know more, Blake will seem less and less the canny, perspectively ironic Derridean that classroom convenience and the limits of our historical knowledge make him out to be. Considering the sheer amount of Blake criticism, very little of [the necessary] work has been done: we have all been too busy with our interpretations" (p. 55). That is, too busy interpreting and not busy enough looking in the historical archives for the "precise occasion[s]" for Blake's language and images.

Both Bindman's and Mellor's essays move in that direction, away from the play of linguistic and graphic possibilities and toward those precise historical occasions that help to put language and image in focus for us. We might learn not just about abolitionists pure and simple but also about differing abolitionist ideologies espoused by particular groups; not just about eighteenth-century views of race but also about how Africans were drawn and how conceptions of skin color changed over time; not just about the liberation of women but also about *Visions of the Daughters of Albion* as a specific response to Wollstonecraft's *Vindication of the Rights of Woman*, conditioned by reports about colonial slavery gleaned from experiences with Stedman and his Surinam *Narrative*.

Bindman wants to produce a Blake for the '90s—the 1990s—by refuting certain features of David Erdman's ultraprescient Cold War–radical Blake, who could see through the hypocrisy of both pro- and antislavery factions, advocate

---

11. In Robert F. Gleckner and Mark L. Greenberg, *Approaches to Teaching Blake's* Songs of Innocence and of Experience (New York, 1989), 47–56. Page references to this essay are given in the text.

sexual freedom, and recognize the humanity of African slaves. Bindman erects his far more human, which is to say limited, counterconstruction on a stark but uneasy opposition between the evangelical and the rational-scientific (or what was passing for rational science in Blake's time). He finds in Blake a flawed composite of the two: "Blake's passing reference to the African's narrow forehead is, therefore, probably derived from an unattractive bit of [quasi-scientific] late-eighteenth-century racial theory, while 'The Little Black Boy' appears to be inflected by [evangelical] theological traditions that assume Africans to be spiritually disadvantaged." Theology and science come together in a "complex and often contradictory web of ancient and modern beliefs" about race from which Blake could not extricate himself, just as we cannot extricate ourselves from the "contradictions" of our age. Here, through a transhistorical use of history, Blake's condition, as it has so many times before, comes to stand for ours. The "complex web" of beliefs that Bindman invokes, however, is often not presented with enough complexity to accommodate the Blake that he wishes to characterize. The most troubling feature of the argument, I think, is the simplicity of the categories said to constitute the complexity.

In the narrative of salvation that Bindman finds in "The Little Black Boy," evangelical abolitionists—whom he associates with Blake's views—opportunistically find blacks benighted in order to give Christianity a chance to save them. Bindman locates this racial ideology in another document of the period, *The African Widow*, said to be a "point of reference for Blake's poem": "Behind the poem"—*The African Widow*, but also "The Little Black Boy," the claim being that both poems are outgrowths of a common ideology—"is the evangelical abolitionist view that it is a Christian duty to convert the African," who is under the curse of Ham, Bindman says, quoting an impenetrable passage from *The Song of Los* that does not mention Ham or a curse but describes the transmission of "Abstract Philosophy." The suggestion is that Blake was a "fervent antirationalist" and an evangelical Christian; evangelical abolitionists thought this way about black people; Blake thought this way about black people.

A problem, of course, is that "evangelical" is an extremely broad classification, and arguments based on Blake's connection with it may not withstand scrutiny. Not that Blake has *no* affinities with the class, but he is certainly far enough on the fringes that we are led to ask: What is an evangelical if Blake is one? What, for instance, is all that free-love doctrine that Bindman and Mellor find in *Visions* doing in the poem of an evangelical? Sure enough, in response one might usefully point to the dispute among London Swedenborgians over the keeping of concubines, but turning over that rock would also uncover ideas about race very different from the comforting abolitionist line that Bindman cites. "Among the Gentiles in Heaven," wrote Swedenborg, after one of his visits to that place, "the most beloved are the Africans"[12]—and they allow polygamy. Africans think more "internally" than the Gentiles, they better understand God's human form, and they enslave Europeans, especially monks, for not properly understanding religion.[13] I have been surprised to notice that Swedenborg and the Swedenborgians are very rarely mentioned in books about the slave trade or European attitudes toward Africans.[14] Their potential importance in this instance does not depend on the untenable position that Blake was a Swedenborgian. But Swedenborgian attitudes expand the spectrum of *possible* attitudes toward race at the time and of the uses of such attitudes.

Blake's own attitudes are, as usual, far more difficult to get a fix on. I believe that the true test of a reading of "The Little Black Boy" starts with a reading of "The Chimney Sweeper" (of *Songs of Innocence*), where once again an attitude that Bindman might call evangelical is put forward, in this case the acceptance of one's earthly lot, no matter how dire, in the name of eventual access to heaven. The narrative situation in "Chimney Sweeper" is similar to the one in "Black Boy": a counselor figure attempts to answer the probing questions of an innocent with optimistic scenarios of what will happen in heaven to set things right in the long run. If one's view of Blake leads to the position that his "Chimney Sweeper" endorses the quietistic advice offered by the older sweep to the younger, then "The Little Black Boy" falls into line behind it. But if not—and I think *not* is right—then ironic exposure, not advocacy, of the mother's apology for racism seems far more likely to be the aim of "The Little Black Boy." In that case we are getting something closer to *Candide* than to *The African Widow:*

> —Yes, sir, said the negro, that's how things are around here. . . . when my mother sold me for ten Patagonian crowns on the coast of Guinea, she said to me: 'My dear child, bless our witch doctors, . . . they will make your life happy; you have the honor of being a slave to our white masters. . . .' The Dutch witch doctors who converted me tell me every Sunday that we are all sons of Adam, black and white alike.[15]

---

12. Emanuel Swedenborg, *Heaven and Hell,* trans. George F. Dole (New York, 1976), n. 326; see also n. 514.

13. Emanuel Swedenborg, *A Treatise Concerning the Last Judgment, and the Destruction of Babylon* (London, 1788), nn. 1198–1203.

14. Gretchen Gerzina, *Black London* (New Brunswick, N.J., 1995), is a recent instance of this tendency to ignore the Swedenborgians.

15. Voltaire, *Candide, or Optimism,* trans. Robert M. Adams (New York and London, 1966), 15.

Bindman does not mention "The Chimney Sweeper," and he considers the possibility of ironic exposure in "The Little Black Boy" only to dismiss it. He traces Blake's view of the spiritual inside of Africans to the evangelicals who want to save the souls of black folks but not necessarily to respect their minds or liberate their bodies. He traces Blake's view of the physical outside of Africans to the rational strain of Enlightenment culture that was finding new ways to measure, classify, and draw human skulls. Bindman ties Blake to the physiognometry of "racial classification" by noting that Blake knew about John Caspar Lavater's *Physiognomy* through his friendship with Henry Fuseli, and that Lavater's kind of physiognomy had been applied to race by a Dutch painter, Pieter Camper—also a surgeon, I believe—whose book was not available in English till 1794 (too late for this argument), although the painter himself had been connected earlier with Benjamin West, telling him how to draw Jews; and with the "circle of the Hunters," one of whom ranked a collection of skulls to suggest racial superiority.

An unnoted complication, however, is that when Blake draws Africans in the 1790s he does not draw them according to this Enlightenment physiognometry at all. That seems to be why Bindman pairs Camper's drawings of heads not with Blake's drawings of heads, as one might expect, but with a line of text from *The Marriage of Heaven and Hell* that calls for the widening of African foreheads, presumably in a metaphorical sense. In fact, as both Bindman and Mellor acknowledge, Blake's visual representation of the Little Black Boy is so much like his representation of the Little White Boy that the black boy looks precisely like the white boy in some copies of "The Little Black Boy" (see color plates XII–XV). This interchangeability of course raises questions of its own but not the questions that Lavater and Camper raise.

Mellor, pursuing Blake's "erasure of *difference* between races," cites Lavater and Camper not as racist sources but as models that Blake should have imitated to escape visual "'Europeanization'" and achieve a "more documentary" visual style. But along with Bindman she argues for "Blake's participation in a colonialist visual discourse" in "The Little Black Boy" and uses this claim to make the transition to *Visions of the Daughters of Albion*. This participation, she argues, "is even clearer in *Visions of the Daughters of Albion*," which is approached as a rather blunt attack on Mary Wollstonecraft's *Vindication of the Rights of Woman*—as "more direct criticism," even, than that apparent in Blake's illustrations to Wollstonecraft's *Original Stories from Real Life* (1791), where Mellor finds Blake "hostile" to Wollstonecraft's images of "positive rational compassion" in the form of "intelligent charity." But, as the subtitle of the book—*with Conversations, Calculated to Regulate the Affections, and Form the Mind to Truth and Goodness*—

suggests, there was little in Wollstonecraft's *Original Stories* to appeal to Blake, who, aside from his aversion to all that calculating, regulating, and forming, was consistently critical of condescending acts of petty charity. On the other hand, Mellor may be so concerned to portray Blake as one who "reinforces his culture's hegemonic construction of the female gender" that she risks whitewashing Wollstonecraft and neglecting the area of agreement between the two of them, as when Mellor asserts that the "subtil modesty" condemned by Oothoon in Blake's *Visions* is "that very rational modesty advocated by Wollstonecraft." To the contrary, the "subtil modesty" of "a modest virgin knowing to dissemble / With nets" (*Visions* 6:7–11, E 48) is the kind of female cunning analyzed and disparaged by Wollstonecraft herself.

For Mellor the meaning of *Visions of the Daughters of Albion* is plain enough—Oothoon is "raped by the slave owner Bromion to increase her value" —and, like Bindman, she makes connections seem more plausible than they may be in fact by transferring to Blake the opinions of his characters. At a minimum we know, however, that he was wide awake to the difference between author and character. When someone quotes Theseus from *A Midsummer-Night's Dream* on the power of imagination and attributes it to Shakespeare, Blake comes back hard: "Thus Fools quote Shakespeare The Above is Theseus's opinion Not Shakespears You might as well quote Satans blasphemies from Milton & give them as Miltons Opinions" (E 601). Mellor assumes that "Blake here affirms" what the character, the black child, speaks; she then uses that affirmation to underwrite what she calls "Blake's solution" to the woman problem in *Visions of the Daughters of Albion*—that is, Oothoon's solution: Blake's solution "is, as Oothoon proclaims . . . 'free love.'"

Such shortcuts assume that we know what the author thinks and can then simply look for quotations to demonstrate it. I question whether there is such easy reading to be obtained here. Much of the difficulty in reading Blake is traceable precisely, I find, to his radically metaphorical narratives—which resist plain translations to the effect that Bromion is a slave owner who rapes Oothoon to increase her value—and his extreme perspectivism, his devotion to the dramatic in almost Jamesian terms in the least Jamesian of modes. He lets his character-like constructions speak for themselves, and the context in which they speak—by which we try to figure out what he means and where he stands—is typically a network, or perhaps a web, of other baffling speeches by other characters rather than authorial exposition. For one of so ardent and argumentative a nature and such potent opinions—judging from his letters, say, and the reports of acquaintances—he seems willing to wander extraordinarily far out along the dangerous narrative path toward pure impersonation, where the reader ends up with the excruciatingly difficult task of weighing implications without clear points of reference. Blake strikes me as at once the most opinionated and the most dramatic of artists, who forces readers to oscillate between the authority of his opinions and the autonomy of his characters (or unstable speaking metaphors).

Oothoon promises to catch for Theotormon "girls of mild silver, or of furious gold" whom she will watch in "lovely copulation" (*Visions* 7:24–26, E 50) with him. This, says Mellor, following several others including Leopold Damrosch, is only a "male fantasy"—and, presumably, Blake's fantasy.[16] (For what it is worth I would add that, in the history of pornography since the eighteenth century, males have shown equally strong evidence of attachment to the opposite fantasy, of watching their female lovers in copulation, lovely or not, with other males.) But could Oothoon's proposal be only one side of a dialogue that should have two sides? Oothoon tells what she will do for Theotormon. That creates a space for Theotormon to respond in kind—what will he do for Oothoon? The fact that he fails to respond surely counts against him; what Oothoon offers only seems to count against her *because* Theotormon fails to provide the Y to her X. She speaks of a "heaven of generous love" where "selfish blightings" (*Visions* 7:29, E 50) have no place. If Theotormon were a selfless lover fit for such a heaven, the world of *Visions of the Daughters of Albion* would be very different—and what it is is clearly not satisfactory, because Oothoon and those daughters of Albion, whoever they are (colonial slaves and/or English women and/or America and/or mental attributes) are left to wail and sigh with no liberation in sight.

Mellor draws Stedman and his slave-lover Joanna into the network of possible allusions: "Perhaps," she says, "Blake was thinking of Stedman's own bedroom frolics with Joanna and B——-e." But then again, if we want to play that game, perhaps he was thinking of Joanna, who stood her ground and refused to leave Surinam with Stedman. When Mellor then skips from Stedman, who was sufficiently liberal to allow that even the woman might have other partners, to "Swedenborg and the Muggletonians," who "explicitly forbade this," and concludes that Blake must be one with Swedenborg and the Muggletonians because "*Blake's* Oothoon never presents this possibility to Theotormon" (my italics), I am again left wondering why it is not the adequacy of Theotormon's response— or call him *Blake's* Theotormon—that is in question rather than the adequacy of Oothoon's. "At the level of sexual politics," Mellor writes, "this poem—like

16. Leopold Damrosch Jr., *Symbol and Truth in Blake's Myth* (Princeton, N.J., 1980).

Stedman's *Narrative* before it—must finally be seen as condoning the continuation of female slavery under a benevolent master." But *Visions of the Daughters of Albion* ends unhappily, and we do not have Blake's happy version of the ending—unless perhaps in Night the Ninth of *The Four Zoas!* In my opinion there is no one satisfactory version of that ending, no "program" of liberation that can be positively inferred from *Visions of the Daughters of Albion.* "The continuation of female slavery under a benevolent master," though, certainly does describe the unhappy ending we have if we do not stress the benevolence. If that unhappy ending represents Blake's sexual politics, why is it unhappy? The suggestion is, I gather, that "this poem—like Stedman's *Narrative*" does not want to change the system but only to clean it up a bit. In that construction of Blake's views, as "friends" with Stedman (a characterization unsupported by evidence as far as I know), Blake sees nothing fundamentally wrong with the Bromion-Oothoon-Theotormon triangle that a little more sensitivity on the part of the males would not fix. If Theotormon would not be so stuffy and repressed and would let Oothoon bring him those gold and silver girls, then free love would reign and, as far as Blake is concerned, all would be well.

Near the end of her essay Mellor observes that Bromion, not Oothoon, wears the ankle fetters of the slave in the frontispiece, suggesting that "*all three* characters remain trapped within Bromion's caves" (her italics). Yes: if Blake learned something from Wollstonecraft, perhaps it was that slavery involves both the slave and the tyrant in an extensive economy that is financial, psychological, sexual, political, and moral. If Oothoon is a slave, she is unlikely to be, in any plain way, Blake's spokesperson; neither is Bromion or Theotormon. The character who speaks an attractive language or who looks great in pictures but is dangerous—tyrannical, misleading, or incomplete—is very familiar in Blake. Why suppose that Oothoon is the exception? I submit that Oothoon is only *a* voice, not Blake's voice, in *Visions of the Daughters of Albion.*

To get at Blake's racial and sexual politics another way, Mellor introduces an opposition between texts and designs: while his texts (like Stedman's) "acknowledge" or even "insist," his designs "deny," "evade," or "erase" the text "insists" that Oothoon is pregnant but the design "visually erases" her pregnancy. Mellor finds it "more troubling" that "Blake's designs erase the spectacle of male violence against the female body. We do *not* see," she says, "Bromion raping Oothoon." Worse, Blake "transforms . . . slavery . . . into a . . . *metaphor*"! As *Visions of the Daughters of Albion* is unfortunately nothing *but* a tissue of textual and visual metaphors—where having sex (if that is what it is) is plucking flowers, and characters with names like "Oothoon" fly over the waves until characters with names

like "Bromion" do things like "rent her with his thunders" (*Visions* 1:16, E 46)—
how can such a powerful hunger for literalization be satisfied?

By shrinking from realistic depictions of violence, Blake "distances us from
the physical tortures of slavery": Mellor assumes that there should be a support-
ing, reinforcing relationship between text and image; if the text says "rape"
(which it does not: it speaks of "renting" and "thunders"), the image should picture the rape of one human being by another in the "documentary style" that
Lavater and Camper could have helped Blake cultivate. Such presumed obliga-
tions of image to text fail to take into account any of the vast differences, in substance as well as style, between textual and pictorial conventions. In general, one
can write much more than one can show, as showing has been regarded as closer
to doing than to thinking. (Thus Mellor treats Blake's pictures in *Visions of the
Daughters of Albion* as if they were after-the-fact tests of his words—he can talk
the talk but can he walk the walk?—without explaining why we should not regard the words as explicit confirmations and reinforcements of suggestions first
glimpsed in the pictures.) Those differences should leap to the fore in any con-
sideration of text and illustration in Stedman's *Narrative*. I do not think I am
alone in finding the violence depicted in the engravings (Blake's as well as the
other engravers' who contributed to the project) more shocking in overall impact
than the violence named in Stedman's text. Be that as it may, such outcomes are
not simple matters of erasure in one medium of the message in another.

More important, since Blake is not reporting violence in *Visions of the
Daughters of Albion* but making it up—this is an allegorical fiction—it would
seem necessary to make distinctions between the way we regard responsible and
irresponsible writing in those two different forms. We may agree that the "physical tortures of slavery" should be adequately accounted for in documentary reports on slavery. (Whether it follows that an adequate accounting requires a
graphic representation of every act of violence described in the text is question-
able.) But I cannot see Oothoon's lot in *Visions of the Daughters of Albion* as equal
to the lot of a slave in Surinam or South Carolina. The standard of authorial responsibility cannot be the same. What does it mean to claim that Blake's poetry
names violence that his design erases? Is this an act of (partial) retraction?
Cowardice? Self-censorship? If so, why did he not revise the text? How is it possible to erase a text with a design? What gives the design such special powers?
More broadly, *Visions of the Daughters of Albion* is a lie, and lies cannot be directly
and simply responsible for telling the truth, especially not our truths—even
though the *ways* of the lie, its angles of inclination toward the truth, are certainly
worth discussing. Mellor proposes a criterion of staggering authorial responsibil-

ity: "As the creator of this poem and its designs, Blake must take responsibility for what the work does not say as well as for what it does say." But then—what *does* the work say?

Bindman's and Mellor's ways of extracting ideology from poetic and pictorial evidence return me to my opening reflections on the significance of difficulty in the history of reading Blake's illuminated books. With their readings in mind, I might frame the issue as follows. Stedman is relatively easy to understand. Wollstonecraft is relatively easy to understand. Camper and Lavater are not all that difficult to understand. By comparison, Blake is very difficult to understand. I have read *Visions of the Daughters of Albion* perhaps fifty times and still cannot claim to get it. I do not understand the motto. (Neither do I understand the motto to *Thel*.)

I read a typical passage from Wollstonecraft's *Vindication*:

> Slavery to monarchs and ministers, which the world will be long in freeing itself from, and whose deadly grasp stops the progress of the human mind is not yet abolished.
>
> Let not men then in the pride of power, use the same arguments that tyrannic kings and venal ministers have used, and fallaciously assert that woman ought to be subjected because she has always been so. . . .
>
> It is time to effect a revolution in female manners—time to restore to them their lost dignity—and make them, as a part of the human species, labour by reforming themselves to reform the world.[17]

Now I read one from *Visions of the Daughters of Albion*:

> Now thou maist marry Bromions harlot, and protect the child
> Of Bromions rage, that Oothoon shall put forth in nine moons time
>
> Then storms rent Theotormons limbs; he rolld his waves around.
> And folded his black jealous waters round the adulterate pair
> Bound back to back in Bromions caves terror & meekness dwell
>
> At entrance Theotormon sits wearing the threshold hard
> With secret tears; beneath him sound like waves on a desart shore
> The voice of slaves beneath the sun, and children bought with money.

---

17. Mary Wollstonecraft, *A Vindication of the Rights of Woman* (1792), ed. Carol H. Poston, 2d ed. (New York and London, 1988), 45.

> That shiver in religious caves beneath the burning fires
> Of lust, that belch incessant from the summits of the earth
>
> Oothoon weeps not: she cannot weep! her tears are locked up;
> But she can howl incessant writhing her soft snowy limbs
> And calling Theotormons Eagles to prey upon her flesh.
>
> (2:1–13, E 46)

The first sounds to me like an explicit critique and condemnation of a social system and its effects, complete with equally explicit proposals for reform. The second sounds to me like a narrative poem (with pictures). However much the two may be said to overlap, the differences between them, I believe, are of major significance. "The Little Black Boy" and *Visions of the Daughters of Albion* are not cast simply as political critiques. They are, rather, expressions of desire with elements of political critique. But neither is cast simply as an expression of authorial desire. Authorial desires in Wollstonecraft are reasonably apparent. She states what she wants directly. We are left to infer what Blake wants from narratives in which Blake is not a speaking character.

In Blake, especially, I would think, the codes are simply too complex and cryptic—or too ambiguous and contradictory—to be cracked by straightforward reference to big public categories such as "evangelical," "Christian," "rationalist," and "abolitionist," not to mention big late-twentieth-century categories such as "sexist," "racist," and so on. We can agree that Blake uses the discourse of Christianity as one of his master discourses, but he is no Christian in the regular sense; he is not convenient to history. He is simply too much the contrarian to be caught and held that way, just as he could not be captured in earlier efforts to make him out as the universal archetypalist, or the purveyor of Kathleen Raine's "perennial religion." To his credit, E. P. Thompson saw the danger:

> If Blake in these prophetic books moved away from deism, and ultimately into sharp antagonism to rationalism in the assertion of his own "everlasting gospel," it is not very helpful to argue that he was moving towards (or back to) anything recognisable as Christianity, orthodox or heterodox. For if he had been doing so he would have had no need to labour at the creation of his own mythic system.[18]

---

18. E. P. Thompson, *Witness against the Beast: William Blake and the Moral Law* (Cambridge, 1993), 216.

Still, Thompson was too much of a collectivist himself—and a historian too devoted to the proposition that the present is the way it is because the past was the way it was to settle for Blake as a unique individual with a unique imagination. Instead, Thompson looked around until he located the smallest of small historical categories, Muggletonian, and drew *that* tiny circle around Blake as among the last of the Muggletonians—a category with a discernible past, a present represented by scarcely anyone other than Blake, and a future that ended in some British garage in our own time. That, I would say, is cutting it very fine. I do not personally see Blake as a Muggletonian in any interesting sense, although I respect the effort to see him as one for honoring the double enigmas of Blake's terrific oddity and his kinship with marginal others. The trend-lines at least are right, I believe, and Thompson's focused, archival approach is the one that promises the greatest gains at this point in the history of Blake studies.

University of Rochester

Chaosthetics: Blake's Sense of Form

—————————————————————————— W. J. T. Mᴉᴛᴄʜᴇʟʟ

> A dictionary begins when it no longer gives the meaning of words, but their tasks. Thus *formless* is not only an adjective having a given meaning, but a term that serves to bring things down in the world, generally requiring that each thing have its form. What it designates has no rights in any sense and gets itself squashed everywhere, like a spider or an earthworm. In fact, for academic men to be happy, the universe would have to take shape. All of philosophy has no other goal: it is a matter of giving a frock coat to what is, a mathematical frock coat. On the other hand, affirming that the universe resembles nothing and is only formless amounts to saying that the universe is something like a spider or spit.
>
> — Georges Bataille, "Formless"[1]

> One cannot in fact conceive of an unorganized structure.
>
> —Jacques Derrida[2]

"Chaos" is a term that generally has a negative valence in discussions of art. Like "formless," it serves mainly to bring things down in the world, down from the status of art to non-art, from the human to the nonhuman, the valuable to the worthless. The work of art is supposed to be an achievement above all of *form*—of structural organization, coherence, and shapeliness. To say that a work of art is chaotic is to identify it as bad art, or perhaps not as art at all. A universe or a work of art that resembles nothing turns out to

---

1. Georges Bataille, *Visions of Excess: Selected Writings, 1927–1939*, trans. Allan Stoekl with Carl R. Lovitt and Donald M. Leslie Jr. (Minneapolis, 1985), 31; page references hereafter in the text.
2. Jacques Derrida, *Writing and Difference*, trans. Alan Bass (Chicago, 1978), 278.

resemble something after all—something despised like a poisonous insect or a splatter of bodily fluids signifying contempt—"like a spider or spit." This "unorganized structure," which Derrida assures us "one cannot . . . conceive," turns out be conceivable after all, as a monstrous conception, a formless or deformed birth.

Even in the tradition of the aesthetic sublime, with its representations of vast spaces, powerful energies, and chaotic forces, the emphasis of aesthetics is always on the containment of chaos by form, its re-presentation and "framing" in an artistic structure. Modern chaos theory in mathematics and physics is an attempt to provide formal models and explanatory structures for catastrophic physical events like the breaching of surfaces, the shattering, rupturing, or collapsing of structures, and the randomization or disordering of orderly systems. Chaos theory "is not," as Stephen Kellert notes, "as interesting as it sounds."[3] Chaos theory is not itself chaotic; it is highly rational, logical, and systematic. Like the procedures of textual deconstruction, it examines the breakdown of order with rigor and precise detail. Its subject is not so much the notion of chaos as a positive and absolute condition but as a moment of "play" within a structure—what Derrida calls an "event" or "rupture," a "transformation of elements" that produces a "swerve," unpredictably transforming one order into another or introducing a new and unexpected constellation in a collection of objects and forces.[4]

Perhaps the only place where "artistic chaos" is anything but a contradiction is to be found in postmodern artistic experiments with formlessness, or what I will call "chaosthetics," many of them inspired by the writings of the renegade French surrealist Georges Bataille. Largely ignored in his own time, Bataille has in retrospect become a kind of prophet of the postmodern in his critique of what Allan Stoekl calls "the very notion of a 'closed economy,' predicated exclusively on utility, production, and rational consumption." Bataille argues for a "science of the heterogeneous" that posits "what is strictly speaking, *impossible:* the individual and collective experience of the unassimilable waste products of the individual body, of society, of thought. . . . Excrement, madness, poetry, automutilation, mystical trances, obscenity, unlimited proletarian revolution." All the antirational, anti-idealist, and radically materialist possibilities of human thought are explored in Bataille's writings, many of which were dismissed as pornographic or insane in his own lifetime. Bataille's influence can be seen in the randomized "scatter pieces" of Robert Morris and Joseph Beuys, which lit-

3.   Stephen H. Kellert, *In the Wake of Chaos* (Chicago, 1993), ix.
4.   *Writing and Difference*, 278–79.

erally present an array of disorganized materials, often of low value (discarded industrial materials, gravel, waste products) or forthrightly disgusting (as in Beuys's installations that pack a corner of room with dirt and rotting fat).[5] Although these experiments are framed, as it were, in the literal space of the gallery and by the implied structure of aesthetic perception, which incorporates their presentations of chaos in a structure of representation, they challenge that incorporation, and the very notion of the rational, institutional structuring of the aesthetic.

The issue of chaos and its relation to form is particularly relevant to the art of William Blake because of all the major artists and poets of the English Romantic movement (in which he was a marginal, isolated figure), he was the slowest to achieve critical acceptance as formally and intellectually coherent. Like Bataille, Blake was regarded as a mad prophet: his work was seen as pornographic and obscene by a number of nineteenth-century commentators, and even until relatively recently as the chaotic effusions of a mystical genius (especially the long prophetic books).[6] Bataille knew Blake's writings very well and named him among the English writers who moved him most deeply (see Bataille's essay on Blake in *Literature and Evil* (1957).[7] It's not surprising, then, that there are numerous specific parallels in the "obsessive images" common to Blake and Bataille. In particular, one might consider Bataille's remarks on the "man's horror of his foot" in relation to Blake's narrative of penetration by Milton through the foot (*Visions of Excess*, 21); Bataille's reflections on "the eagle and the mole" and the enigmatic Motto that Blake appends to *The Book of Thel* (*Visions of Excess*, 34); Bataille's notion of an economy of waste and expenditure ("The Principle of Loss," *Visions of Excess*, 118) and Blake's consistent pun on "prophet" as "Los"; Bataille's anal fixation (particularly his notion of the "solar anus") and Blake's inversion of "Sol" into "Los," the Apollonian poet into the subterranean blacksmith; the common interest of both writers in excrement and insects, particularly flies.[8]

---

5   For example, *Untitled (Threadwaste)*, reproduced in Guggenheim Museum catalogue, *Robert Morris: The Mind-Body Problem* (New York, 1994), fig. 104.

6.   In a brief essay of some fifteen years ago ("Dangerous Blake," *Studies in Romanticism* 21 [Fall 1982] 410–16), I argued for and predicted a general reopening of the questions of madness, formlessness, and obscenity in Blake's work; the most interesting development on madness has been Paul Youngquist's *Madness and Blake's Myth* (University Park, Pa., 1989).

7.   Georges Bataille, *Literature and Evil*, trans. Alastair Hamilton (New York, 1985).

8.   See plates 9, 12, and 14 of Blake's *Europe: A Prophecy* (1794) and plate 29 of *Milton: A Poem* (1804), reproduced in *The Illuminated Blake*, annotated by David V. Erdman (Garden City, N.Y., 1974), 167, 170, 172, 245.

It is only in the last forty years (roughly since the publication of Northrop Frye's *Fearful Symmetry*) that Blake has achieved canonical status along with Wordsworth, Coleridge, Keats, Shelley, and Byron (on the literary side), and with Turner and Constable (on the side of the visual arts). Until Frye's study, Blake was generally regarded as a minor figure, and his "minority" status was usually traced to doubts about his mental competence. His mastery of graphic techniques as a draftsman, engraver, and painter was also in doubt. Although some of Blake's line engravings and color prints have consistently been admired, there have always been serious questions about his competence as a draftsman and painter (the design for "The Tyger" [see figure 29] is often the focus for debates about the adequacy of his illustrations to his poetic conceptions). Blake's rendering of the human figure sometimes seems crude and awkward; his graphic style (especially in the illuminated books) can strike one as relatively primitive and naive when seen in the context of late-eighteenth-century printmaking; and his handling of color is notoriously indifferent, especially when seen in the context of the great British colorists of the early nineteenth century, Constable and Turner.[9]

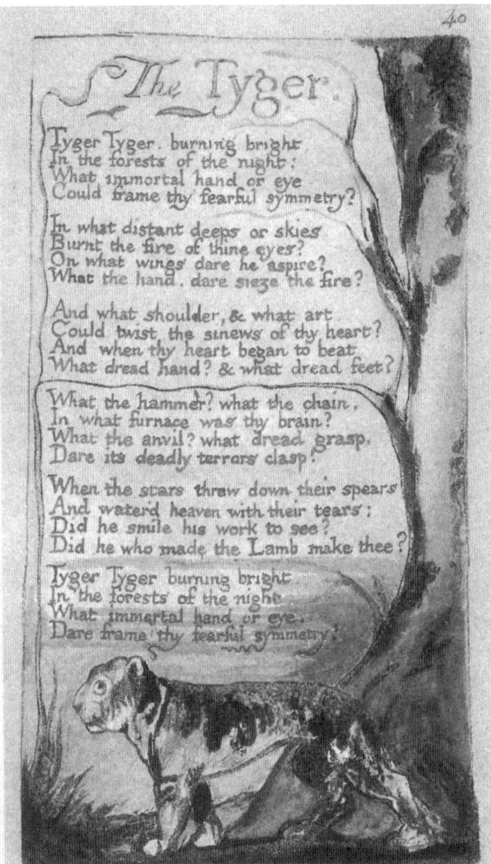

Figure 29. "The Tyger," *Songs of Innocence and of Experience,* copy E, plate 40.

9. On the question of artistic competence, see Charles Harrison's interesting discussion in "On the Surface of Painting," *Critical Inquiry* 15 (winter 1989): 292–336. Harrison questions the "straightforward antithesis between intentional competence and involuntary incompetence" (p. 298), suggesting that judgments of competence and technical success are often made retrospectively without regard to the historicity of technical criteria. It might be "salutary," in Harrison's view, "to conceive of a possible world in which the grounds of judgement never did change in Cezanne's favour, a history of art in which he remained incompetent and unregarded" (p. 299).

When questions about the formal competence and coherence of Blake's art were raised in the nineteenth century, the assumption was that they were also questions about his mental competence as an individual. One can be a sane person and a bad artist, but in Blake's case the character of the art doesn't look like mere technical inability to handle the crafts required for visual or verbal coherence. Blake clearly *intended* his art to look the way it did (though occasionally he confesses limitations, as in his admission that he has been trying to "paint round" all his life but has never been able to do so).[10]

In general, Blake's own remarks on his art reject any notion of chaos, formlessness, or madness. He uses these terms in the same way as his antagonists, to bring things down in the world. He generally characterizes his own work as controlled and competent, with an execution perfectly appropriate and adequate to his imaginative conceptions. He regarded his choice of a highly linear graphic style, moreover, not simply as appropriate to his own intentions but as the only aesthetically and scientifically correct mode of composition. His famous polemics against the painterly and coloristic tradition embodied by Rubens, Rembrandt, Titian, and Tintoretto are not measured or qualified by any concessions to different intentions or artistic metiers. Blake asserts dogmatically that his own artistic style is the one true path, and that the choice of paths is between an art of organized clarity and distinctness (his own) and an art of disorganization and chaos: "the unorganized Blots & Blurs of Rubens & Titian are not Art nor can their Method ever express Ideas or Imaginations any more than Popes Metaphysical Jargon of Rhyming."[11]

The choice Blake forces on questions of artistic style is not merely a question of aesthetics, a debate about the beautiful. It is a moral, political, and metaphysical issue. The painterly, coloristic style signifies imitative, derivative "mental weakness" and "imbecility," the corruption of art by "Commerce" and the flattery of corrupt governments. Blake regarded the brown shadows and chiaroscuro of Rubens and Rembrandt as a kind of painterly excrement and staged his attack on color as an act of aesthetic hygiene: "To My Eye Rubens's Colouring is most Contemptible His Shadows are of a Filthy Brown somewhat the Colour of Excrement" (E 655). This sort of polemical hygiene, of course, comes dangerously close to producing or projecting the very filth it wants to cleanse. Rubens's coloring is excrement "to Blake's eye"; he knows that it is not seen that way by

---

10. Quoted in Geoffrey Keynes, *Blake Studies*, 2d ed. (London, 1971), 86.
11. *The Poetry and Prose of William Blake*, revised ed., ed. David V. Erdman (Berkeley and Los Angeles, 1982), 576; hereafter cited as "E" after quotations.

others, and he writes as one whose first principle of vision is "As the Eye, Such the Object" (E 645). It isn't just that Blake wants to make the general point that Rubens and the painterly schools are "bad"; he also challenges us to see their sumptuous, luxurious tonalities as excremental, to understand their art within an aesthetics of anality and "filthy lucre." Blake didn't see himself as "above" this filth, only as more clear-sighted and explicit about it, "sitting down to shite" in his poetry and representing the act of defecation graphically. See, for example, plate 23 of *Jerusalem* (figure 30); and compare the figure on all fours with *Nebuchadnezzar* (color plate XVI), discussed below.

Blake issues a similar kind of challenge at the level of mental hygiene when he insists on framing these aesthetic judgments as a choice between sanity and madness. English engraving, in Blake's view, had been corrupted by its neglect of the true style embodied by Durer and the "old engravers" of Italy, and had gone whoring after false gods in attempting to work within coloristic and painterly modes: "Ye english Engravers must come down from your high flights ye must condescend to study Marc Antonio & Albert Durer. . . . It is very true what you have said for these thirty two Years I am Mad or Else you are so both of us cannot be in our right senses Posterity will judge by our Works" (E 573).

Blake's immediate posterity, by and large, took his challenge literally and dismissed his work as the chaotic productions of a madman. Or (in much smaller numbers) it chose to ignore the challenge and to find artistic merit and spiritual wisdom in his artistic productions, while pretending that Blake's dogmatic opinions—his attempt to force an absolute choice between sanity and madness, true linear art and false coloristic painting—could be set aside. And the subsequent canonization of Blake as a major artist has, in general, continued this latter tradition, choosing to bracket Blake's opinions about art, or to explain them away, while finding ways to appreciate his works, usually in relation to mainstream Romantic aesthetic categories like "organic form," "originality of invention," and "imaginative coherence."[12] The issue of Blake's sanity, which he himself chose to raise, has by and large been ignored as a serious question in Blake studies, along with the related issues of obscenity and chaos.

I would like to reopen the question of Blake's sanity, not in order to demote him from his status as a major artist or to dismiss his works as mere symptoms of

---

12. The best effort in this mode remains Morris Eaves's *William Blake's Theory of Art* (Princeton, N.J., 1982).

Figure 30. (opposite page) *Jerusalem,* copy F, plate 23 (Pierpont Morgan Library, PML 953).

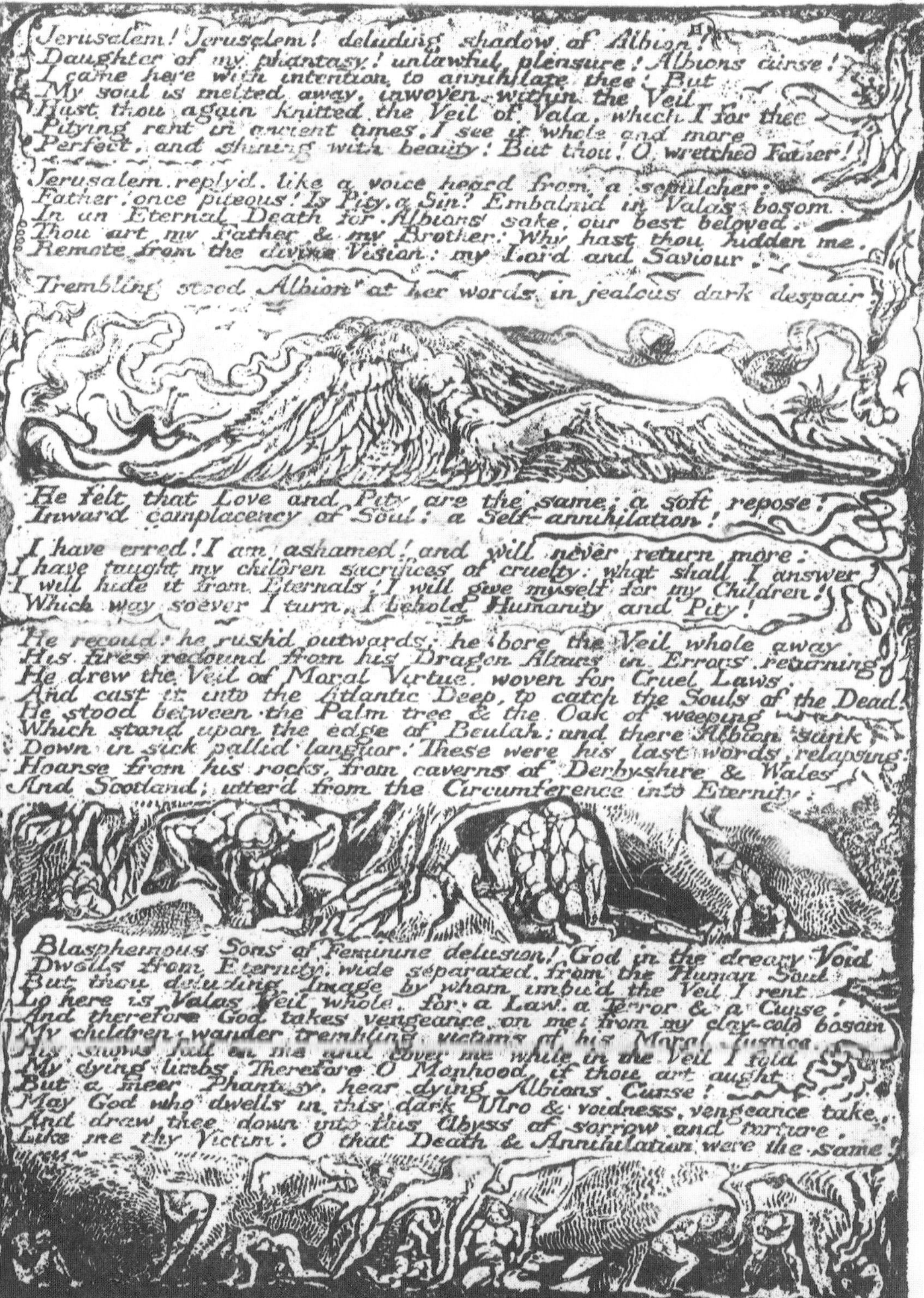

Jerusalem! Jerusalem! deluding shadow of Albion!
Daughter of my phantasy! unlawful pleasure! Albions curse!
I came here with intention to annihilate thee! But
My soul is melted away, inwoven within the Veil
Hast thou again knitted the Veil of Vala, which I for thee
Pitying rent in ancient times. I see it whole and more
Perfect, and shining with beauty: But thou! O wretched Father!

Jerusalem replyd, like a voice heard from a sepulcher:
Father! once piteous! Is Pity, a Sin? Embalmd in Valas bosom.
In an Eternal Death for Albions sake, our best beloved.
Thou art my Father & my Brother: Why hast thou hidden me,
Remote from the divine Vision: my Lord and Saviour.

Trembling stood Albion at her words, in jealous dark despair:

He felt that Love and Pity are the same; a soft repose!
Inward complacency of Soul: a Self-annihilation!

I have erred! I am ashamed! and will never return more:
I have taught my children sacrifices of cruelty: what shall I answer?
I will hide it from Eternals! I will give myself for my Children!
Which way soever I turn, I behold Humanity and Pity!

He recoild: he rushd outwards; he bore the Veil whole away
His fires redound from his Dragon Altars in Errors returning
He drew the Veil of Moral Virtue, woven for Cruel Laws
And cast it into the Atlantic Deep, to catch the Souls of the Dead.
He stood between the Palm tree & the Oak of weeping
Which stand upon the edge of Beulah; and there Albion sunk
Down in sick pallid languor! These were his last words, relapsing!
Hoarse from his rocks, from caverns of Derbyshire & Wales
And Scotland; utter'd from the Circumference into Eternity.

Blasphemous Sons of Feminine delusion! God in the dreary Void
Dwells from Eternity, wide separated from the Human Soul
But thou deluding Image by whom imbu'd the Veil I rent
Lo here is Valas Veil whole, for a Law, a Terror & a Curse!
And therefore God takes vengeance on me: from my clay-cold bosom
My children wander trembling victims of his Moral Justice.
His snows fall on me and cover me, while in the Veil I fold
My dying limbs. Therefore O Manhood, if thou art aught
But a meer Phantasy, hear dying Albions Curse!
May God who dwells in this dark Ulro & voidness, vengeance take,
And draw thee down into this Abyss of sorrow and torture,
Like me thy Victim. O that Death & Annihilation were the same!

incapacity to which we can feel superior, but to provide a frame in which the fundamental issue of artistic chaos (and its relation to form) can be situated, both in Blake's work and in the context of more general aesthetic questions. My aim in doing this is not to decide, once and for all, whether Blake was mad or not, or whether his art makes sense or doesn't, but just the opposite: I want to make it harder to decide these questions, and to undermine the confidence that allows us to draw firm boundaries between form and chaos, sanity and madness, the "hygienic" and the "excremental," or to see the one as containing or controlling the other. I also want to render problematic the ready association between formal order and sanity (on the one hand) and chaos and madness (on the other). Part of my argument here will be that the association can go quite the other way, that madness is often linked with the most rigorous, inflexible forms of order, while sanity is quite compatible with a high degree of disorganization. Above all, I want to suggest that terms like form and chaos, sanity and madness, are dialectical categories that are mutually necessary to one another for their meaning: that they cannot be understood abstractly but must be placed in their precise discursive situation; and (most important) that they cannot be resolved in some higher synthesis (Hegelian or otherwise) but are continually reinscribed as the boundaries of the thinkable.[13] Indeed, I'm tempted to put this in more radical terms and suggest that the form/chaos, sanity/madness binaries are the limit of Blake's dialectic, the place where the difference between contraries (which mutually coexist) and negations (which are mutually destructive) can no longer be sustained. Unlike the contraries of good and evil, love and hate, reason and energy, the interplay of chaos and form may not necessarily produce "progression," and if it is "necessary to human existence," it may also threaten to destroy it.[14] Form and chaos, madness and sanity, in short, are incommensurable, irreconcilable, and inimical to all totality. They push the rule of dialectical contrariety into the realm of what Blake called Negations, dualisms or abstract antitheses, the border of Blake's art that opens onto a void of meaninglessness, a chaos without form and a form without chaos that comes, perhaps, to the same thing.

Another, less apocalyptic way of putting this is just to allow the possibility that Blake was a bit mad some of the time, in different ways on different occasions, and that he was equally sane (also in different ways) on others. As a pre-

13. For an argument that Blake's dialectic is in many points compatible with Hegel's, see David Punter, *Blake, Hegel, and Dialectic* (Amsterdam, 1982), chap. 2.
14. On Blake's contraries, see *The Marriage of Heaven and Hell*, pl. 3–4; E 34. On the distinction between Contraries and Negations, see *Jerusalem*, pl. 17; E 160.

liminary road map to this subject, let me suggest three basic types of madness that Blake explicitly acknowledges and represents in his own art. The first might be called "Blake's own madness," those moments in the record of Blake's personal life where he testifies to being "out of his senses," in the grip of higher (or lower) forces such as divine inspiration, demonic possession; or in a kind of empty depression. The second might be called "world madness," the vast cosmic allegory of psychic conflict that comprises Blake's "system" and his master-narrative of the nightmare of history. The third I will simply call the "dark forces," the specific figures and states of mind within Blake's mythological system that personify or embody uncontrollable passions or disruptive, chaos-producing elements in an otherwise orderly world.

Blake's own madness is, of course, a sensitive subject, since he felt persecuted by an "aspersion of Madness" and vigorously denied that his art was anything but the expression of "Mental Health" (*Milton*, plate 41:8 [E 142]; E 481). At the same time, Blake's frequent expressions of doubt about his own direction; his apologies for his "perhaps too great enthusiasm"; his reports of emerging "from a Deep pit of Melancholy, Melancholy without any real reason for it" (E 706) cannot be ignored. Even Blake's conviction that he was "under the direction of Messengers from Heaven" is "not as some suppose. without trouble or care. Temptations are on the right hand & left behind the sea of time & space follows swiftly he who keeps not right onward is lost. . . . Who can describe the dismal torments of such a state" (E 724). Blake's comparison of himself to the legendary mad king Nebuchadnezzar is not, one suspects, a casual matter, but testimony to his deep anxiety about mental health. "Nebuchadnezzar," he tells Hayley, "had seven times passed over him" before his "understanding" was restored: "I have had twenty" (E 756).[15] The figure of Nebuchadnezzar in Blake's 1795 color print reveals the extent to which Blake imagines this pathological form of madness as antithetical to the integrity of the human form itself. Nebuchadnezzar is reduced to a a beast crawling on all fours, living in caves (color plate XVI).

The figure of Nebuchadnezzar shows us madness as an eruption from the interior of the body, expressing itself outwardly in an excess of hair and claws that overwhelms the human form. Blake's accounts of "inspiration" or "poetic furor,"

---

15. Letter to William Hayley, 23 October 1804, in *The Complete Writings of William Blake*, ed. Geoffrey Keynes (London, 1966), 850. Blake goes on to "thank God I was not altogether a beast as he was; but I was a slave bound in a mill among beasts and devils." These "beasts and devils," Blake reports, "are now, together with myself, become children of light and liberty." This narrative of slavery and freedom, madness and sanity is, of course, being constructed for the benefit of a man whose ideas about sanity, normality, and order had been experienced by Blake as slavery for the previous three years.

by contrast, show the artist possessed by something outside himself. Blake claims that his words and images come to him when he "is drunk with intellectual vision," producing an art that is not strictly "authored" or "intended" by himself as a private individual but is "dictated" by spirits over which he has no conscious control (E 729). "I pretend not to be the author," he says in *Milton,* "but merely the secretary. The authors are in eternity." This does not mean, however, that we can rely on spatial figures of outer and inner origin to distinguish poetic from pathological madness. The muses of *Milton* "come into" Blake's hand, not from an external heaven, but "down the Nerves of [his] right arm / From out the Portals of [his] Brain"; and they are not credited with unquestionable authority, presiding rather over "Realms / Of terror & mild moony lustre in soft sexual delusions" (*Milton,* bk. 1; E 96). Similarly, Blake's figure of the "Spectre" or "Selfhood" often appears as an externally located phantom or vampire that hovers over the artist's scene of labor, acting as a kind of skeptical counter-muse who raises doubts about the work and leads the artist astray.

The tradition of poetic inspiration as a form of madness had, of course, become a hollow convention in the eighteenth century, the grand, inflated claims of divine dictation reduced to a mere convention. "Hail muse, etcetera" says Lord Byron in *Don Juan,* reflecting a century's worth of skepticism about claims to artistic inspiration, a skepticism expressed in the writings of Collins and Gray at the end of the century, and by Keats during Blake's own time—a skepticism tinged with sadness for the passing of the heroic, prophetic age of poetry and what Keats called "the fond believing lyre." Blake's invocations to the muse claim, by contrast, to be literally true; his poetic madness claims to be actual, not just a convention to be repeated. At the same time, Blake shares the eighteenth-century skepticism about a God or gods in some transcendent heaven dictating words and images to artists. There is no God, Blake insists, except "the intellectual fountain of humanity," the human genius: "God only Acts & Is in existing beings or Men" (E 40). Blake's inspiration, then, comes with a very severe constraint on its claims to authority. His inspiration comes from "eternal authors," but those authors are not located in a religiously sanctioned heaven, nor in any publicly acknowledged, socially legitimated set of doctrines about the true, the beautiful, or the good. His "inspiration" comes from an "eternity" that can only be found in himself—within his physical body, and his actual, phenomenal consciousness as a specific historical individual. "Where hadst thou this terrible Song" (E 107), ask the eternals of the Bard in *Milton: A Poem,* and the answer is a tautological appeal to the authority of inspiration as such: "The Bard replied. I am Inspired! I know it is Truth! for I Sing / According to the inspiration of the Poetic Genius / Who is the eternal all-protecting Divine Humanity / To whom be Glory & Power & Dominion Evermore Amen" (E 107–8). Blake's defense against a skepticism that he himself has invoked and dramatized in his poem is to give an answer that ignores the question of "Where" his authority comes from, making a dogmatic assertion that turns into a prayer.

At the level of rhetorical form, then, Blake insists on an authority equivalent to the ancient prophets; at the level of content, he adopts a thoroughly skeptical, post-Enlightenment account of religious inspiration. He makes Isaiah admit that "I saw no god. nor heard any, in a finite organical perception; but my senses discover'd the infinite in every thing" (E 38); he locates the inspiration of *Milton* in the physical organ of the brain; he defines the prophet simply as a man who speaks his mind on public and private matters, and he equates "the voice of God" with "honest indignation." The net effect of these strategies is to produce what might be called undecidability without equivocation. That is, Blake isn't hedging or rendering his authority ambiguous or uncertain. He claims the full authority of the ancient prophets. But he redefines and reclaims that authority in a modern idiom, one that dislocates it from its traditional site in an allegory of political, social, or religious authority—king, father, priest, god—who speaks by virtue of his position in a worldly hierarchy.

Blake is very close to Bataille's notion of a "headless allegory," an acephalic symbolic system without a hidden transcendental signified to regulate the flow of meaning.[16] So where Blake says he is inspired, we might paraphrase this as: "I am speaking my mind, but that doesn't mean I know what I'm going to say or what I'm talking about." We would now say that Blake is conjuring with a notion of the unconscious; that in fact his sense of poetic possession and divine madness is a conjoining of his own unconscious with a set of firmly held convictions, both religious and secular, and a vast body of traditional poetic and visual tropes, figures, and narratives. As we know from Blake's letters, even these firmly held convictions were subject to doubt: the relation between "Duty & Reality" and an "Abstract folly" that lures Blake from his work into a land of spectres is never fixed in a stable structure but becomes instead the very content of his narrative and dramatic poems.[17]

This brings us to Blake's second form of madness, what might be called world madness, an encyclopedic "schizoid psychodrama" or mythopoeic psychosis. This is the basic schematic content of his major prophetic books, the system within

16. See Stoekl's introduction to *Visions of Excess*, xiii–xiv.
17. See Blake's letter to Butts, 11 September 1801 (E 685).

which the conflicts among the psychological forces, passions, drives, interests, and desires that animate the human soul are articulated. One might think of these "systems" in Blake's allegory (the "States," spaces, relationships, and genealogies) as the Blakean equivalent of Freud's metapsychology, with its "dynamic, topographical, and economic coordinates." Freud saw his own system as a kind of headless allegory—"no more than a torso"—that remained radically incomplete.[18] Readings of Blake's poetic mythology tend to assume (perhaps necessarily) that his chaotic psychodrama *is* complete, contained spatially by system and temporally by the form of utopian narratives, an eschatological framework that is "headed" toward closure and resolution of conflict. But it's also widely recognized that Blake's millennial, apocalyptic narratives always conclude with some kind of sublated form of chaos—a state of struggle, a scene of drastic swervings from one order of being to another. It is clear, moreover, that Blake himself does not claim to be above or beyond the psychomachias he narrates: the space of the poem is his own mind and his immediate field of concrete circumstances. He has been called a "poet without a mask," but he might equally be thought of as a mask without a face behind it, playing across the boundary between scenes of divine madness, the traditional melodramas of the gods, the chaotic scenes of contemporary history, and the field of his own immediate sensations, memories, and fantasies. To write sublime, headless allegory, the poet must "lose his head," and his heading, risk castration, abjection, and "Self Annihilation," submitting himself to the destructive element.

This continual swerving in Blake's text from private psychodrama to public theater to cosmic struggle is visually actualized in the physical scale and proportions of his images. One of the keys to the visual effect of Blake's art is its constant playing on the antitheses of miniaturization and monumentality, the

18. Sigmund Freud, "An Autobiographical Study" (1924), in *The Freud Reader*, ed. Peter Gay (New York, 1989), 37. Bataille questions the application of psychoanalytic categories, understood as a fixed system, to Blake's work: "What can we find in psychoanalysis, whether it be that of Freud or Jung, other than the data of psychoanalysis itself? Thus the attempt to elucidate Blake through Jung tells us more about Jung's theories than about Blake's intentions. . . . It seems to me that analysis is merely cancelling out a remarkable work and that it is substituting a somnolent heaviness for awakenness. The real answer is the harmony which Blake arrives at in a lacerated condition, while for Jung . . . it is the harmony—the end— of the journey which matters, rather than the agitated journey itself" (p. 88). Bataille seems to sense here that the real problem is Jungian, not Freudian, interpretation (he cites W. P. Witcutt's *Blake: A Psychological Study* [London, 1946], a Jungian reading). Freud's insistence on the incompleteness of psychoanalytic theory and practice, his commitment to intransigent, accidental empirical data over the closure of systematic deduction, and above all his literariness make him far more interesting for Blake studies (or for anything else) than Jung.

disjunctive senses of scale appropriate to "Fairies" and "Giants" respectively. The clearest symptom of this play is the strange appropriateness of Blake's images to slide projection. The contorted figures of *The Book of Urizen*, for instance, often seem to find their best visual realization when magnified to many times their actual size. This is an art in which loss of proportion is quite literally the desired effect on the beholder.

Within Blake's psychodrama there are, finally, those "dark forces" that have abundant names in modern psychology: paranoia, depression, fixation, obsession, compulsion, regression, rage, narcissism, melancholia, hysteria, mania, delusions of grandeur, fetishism. Blake does not have these names.[19] He gives his symptoms the concrete bodies, spaces, and "English names" that come to him, spaces such as "the petrific abominable chaos," "the abomination of desolation," "the Void outside existence," "the Abyss of the Five Senses"; human forms and bodies such as the Spectre and Emanation, the Abstract Folly, Thel, Oothoon, Los, Orc, Urthona, Urizen, Hand. These figures and places hover on the threshold between private obsessions and publicly recognizable forms and fantasies, including the "national imaginary" of Albion, the collective mind/body of England and of humanity, whose nightmares are the drama of the illuminated books.

The most famous of the "dark forces" in Blake's art is, of course, the figure of Urizen, the very personification of sanity and proportionality in his time. Urizen's rage for order, system, control, and law is consistently represented by Blake as producing the most pathological forms of madness, a "petrific abominable chaos" in both the subjective mental life of the reasoner and the political sphere of rational social management—whether it is the authoritarian reason of traditional patriarchal societies or the mathematical, utopian rationality of modern revolutions.

The mythological system that Frye educed as the chief evidence of Blake's sanity could easily, of course, be used as a text to analyze his madness. I'm not going to argue that way—only to emphasize again that it seems to be the specific nature of Blake's art to deconstruct the difference between sanity and madness, to render it undecidable as the framing concept of his art while invoking it continually as the authority for that art. It's not so much that Blake doesn't

---

19. Actually, Blake *does* have the terminology of melancholy, inherited from Renaissance humor theory and faculty psychology, and the categories of lunacy, mania, and delirium. Youngquist (in *Madness and Blake's Myth*, 28) adopts a Foucauldian take on the historical status of Blake's madness as a pure negation or nothingness, an "unreason" in the Age of Reason. My sense is that the detailed historical investigation of the language of Blake's madness remains to be done.

believe in a difference between sanity and madness, but that the difference itself "swerves" through different applications that involve reversing the meaning
of the key oppositions, sanity vs. madness, and also form vs. chaos. That is,
Blake says he is mad (that is, divinely inspired); he generally rejects any notion
that he is mad in a pathological sense, but he also portrays himself as sicker than
Nebuchadnezzar and admits to fits of melancholy—delusional states of abstraction and obsession that we would call madness. He tries to force a choice between himself and the mainstream of what for him was modern art as a choice
between sanity and madness. This last form, "public madness," is the point at
which Blake's work comes to ground in its claims of authority and legitimacy.
It is the place where he defends himself against the "aspersions of madness" made
in the public press and levels counteraccusations. I'm not suggesting that Blake
seems maddest (in the bad sense) in his public statements (though he often does
seem delusional and paranoid in his polemics against the Venetians): I'm only
pointing out that Blake himself tries to force the category sanity/madness as a
choice in these writings, or he finds it forced upon him. We have a higher tol-
eration for chaos, formlessness, and nonsense in the prophetic books and poems
than we do in his prosaic, public declarations. The latter statements, presumably, were not written in a state of inspiration. But much of what Blake writes
is not inspired, doesn't even claim to be. He nods all the time, no matter how
much he protests that every word & letter is studied and put in its fit place.

These swervings between an art of public monuments and private fantasies,
prophetic vision and uncontrolled symptom, divine and demonic madness are, as
I've suggested, the performative aspects of Blake's dialectic, the working through
of non-Hegelian contraries to a non-synthesis. The visual, graphic image of this
"swerve" is Blake's characteristic line, the "style" of drawing that cuts the metal
spaces of the engraving plate. Blake calls it his "bounding line" to indicate its double character, simultaneously forming, inscribing, and leaping over boundaries.
The schematic figure of the bounding line is, of course, the vortex or arabesque,
traditionally the signature of the master draftsman. It also appears as the line of
beauty, a form that signifies (for Hogarth) the uncontrollable variety, curiosity,
and passion that strains against the rectilinear pyramid of "Order." The vortex is
also associated in traditional atomistic and materialist thought (compare
Cartesian vorticism) with the phenomenon of chaos, understood as a swerve in
the structure of reality that disrupts a structure or generates a new one.[20]

20. See W. J. T. Mitchell, "Metamorphoses of the Vortex: Hogarth, Blake, and Turner," in Richard Wendorf,
ed., *Articulate Images* (Minneapolis, 1983), for a more comprehensive discussion of this form.

An image that concentrates many of these issues in a single gestalt is the famous color-printed portrait of Newton that Blake designed and first executed around 1795 (color plate XVII). Newton, of course, epitomizes the regime of rationality, scientific objectivity, and lawful order we call the Age of Reason. The first thing that may strike us about Blake's treatment is that it is not straightforwardly satiric or critical, certainly not a caricature of the sort he sometimes deploys for his own figure of Urizen. Newton is presented as a heroic, beautiful, and idealized nude. His facial expression conveys the most intense concentration, an obsessive absorption in his own project of intellectual creativity. His compasses, the traditional emblem of rational measurement and abstract philosophy, are not alienated instruments but (as in the famous portrait of the Ancient of Days) extensions of his hand.

And yet two features of the print make it clear that this is not the whole story Blake wants to tell about Newton. The most obvious is the gorgeous array of coloristic splashes that adorns Newton's seat; this color field, along with the mysterious dark aquamarine atmosphere that envelopes Newton's upper body, stands as a stark contrast to the enamel-like clarity of the figure. Where everything about Newton's body is clearly delineated and articulated, everything about the space he occupies is left ambiguous, shadowy, and indeterminate. Are we beholding a nocturnal meditation or an undersea tableau, a coral reef adorned with luminous vegetation washed by invisible tides? The process by which Blake produced these color effects is also the direct antithesis of the linear drawing procedures that produced the figure of Newton. This sort of color printing involved the application of colors to a piece of millboard that was then pressed against the paper and pulled away, leaving an unpredictable and random pattern of mottled impressions.[21] Blake could then leave these impressions in the accidental state produced by the print or delicately "touch up" the chaotic impressions with his brush, revealing the ambiguous, emergent vegetative forms that seem to wave in the undersea medium of Newton's world.

The other feature of the print that resists the geometric, linear economy of Newton's science is the coiled spiral of the scroll on which he inscribes his diagrams. This spiral suggests, in a quite literal way, the materiality of the medium in which Newton's ideal conceptions must be embodied: the diagrams may refer

---

21. Robert N. Essick reminds me of Frederick Tatham's comment that this way of color printing had "a look of accident about" it. See his letter of 6 November 1862 to W. M. Rossetti in *Rossetti Papers,* comp. W. M. Rossetti (London, 1903), 16–17.

to purely abstract, immaterial conceptions, but they are inscribed by an instrument that is an extension of the human hand, and on a material surface that obeys its own laws of motion, coiling up in the form of a vorticular swerve that suggests geometries beyond those of the two-dimensional plane and the structures of stable triangulation, division, and encompassing.

It may seem odd to characterize this image as "about chaos," much less as chaotic in itself, but I want to suggest that this is exactly the way to see it. The closest thing to a positive or literal rendering of chaos in the picture is, of course, the random splatters of color. It seems to be presented as graphically antithetical to the order of Newton's body, which is all clarity and delineation.[22] What the picture really shows us, however, is the "swerve" between two antithetical conceptions of the world, depicted as contrasting regions—the human form and the world of nature, the body and its spaces, the hyperorganized armored self and the random flux of reality it encounters. The picture does not offer any mediation between these spaces: Newton ignores everything around him, concentrating himself on the ideal, fictional space he is bringing into being. All mediation between form and chaos in this picture is left to the beholder, who must perform an act of concentrated meditation on a gestalt that defies resolution into a single formal whole. The beholder's vision, in short, must continually "swerve" in the presence of this image, continually revising its sense of what order, coherence, and rationality consist in, and what sort of chaos and madness it is that stands over against this order, generating it and being generated by it. The figure of this swerve is the vorticular shape of the scroll that links the world of Newton's ideal forms to the material realities they address.[23]

But the tiny detail of the scroll is still only a kind of emblem of the motion required of the beholder by the composition, only a way of graphically tracing the alternation between two regions of the picture that might be labeled by binary oppositions such as chaos and form, nature and the human, materiality and ideality. The link suggested by the scroll does not in itself show concretely how we move from Newton's sculpted, linear body to the setting or "ground" in which he is depicted. To see this movement we need to temporalize the picture, reading it

22. Essick notes that "this body was also color-printed, but then Blake worked over it—in an almost Newtonian passion for abstract order?—to clarify outline and delineate musculature. So the 'chaos' of color printing lies hidden beneath the Newtonian order of Newton's body. Does that inner disorder excrete itself in the form of the encrusted rock? We see on that rock what lies hidden beneath the false covering of the Newtonian body-order" (correspondence with the author).

23. Essick notes that the maculated textures of Blake's color printing are also vorticular, although this only becomes apparent when they are magnified.

as a scene of the mutual production and consumption of chaos and form. A helpful way to accomplish this is to reverse figure and ground and see the picture's *subject* as the coral reef on which Newton sits. As it happens, the scientific understanding of coral formations was undergoing a transformation in Blake's time. No longer seen as a vegetative form, coral was being redescribed as a mass of animal forms whose hard exterior substance is formed from excretions of lime. The visible "coral reef" is, according to Rees's *Cyclopedia* (for which Blake engraved seven plates), "the structure and habitation of certain sea animals, . . . designed for their protection and support." The living coral animal is soft, diaphanous, and invisible to the naked eye. When the animals die, according to Rees, "they corrupt and communicate to the water the smell of putrid filth. This juice or liquor . . . little by little becomes fixed and hard and is changed to stone."[24] The ancient name for coral was *gorgonium*, an implicit comparison of the hydra-like polyp's properties with the power of Medusa's severed head to turn living beings into stone.

But it is not the dead or petrified bodies of coral animals that actually form the gorgeous, colorful reefs that we know today and that were first being explored in Blake's time. It is the *excrement* of the coral animal that serves as its habitation, housing the living organism, Rees notes, in a manner analogous to the shell around the vulnerable flesh of a turtle or the liquid nakedness of a snail. In this light Newton must be seen as sitting on—indeed, inhabiting as his ground and dwelling place—a gorgeous mound of excrement that he himself has produced.[25]

Before you dismiss this as a merely outrageous suggestion, recall a few relevant associations. First, Blake's own linkage of chaos with excrement, especially in the coloristic style of the Flemish painters; in this light Newton's environment may actually be seen as divided into two distinct forms of chaos, the "petrific," excremental coral reef, and the empty void or nothingness that surrounds both Newton and his encasing seat. Second, the unavoidable association of pictorial figures of contemplative philosophy, from Durer's *Melencolia* (which hung above Blake's workbench) to Rodin's *Thinker,* with images of anal retentive self-absorption.[26] And third, the unavoidable association of the coral reef in Blake's

24. Rees's *Cyclopedia,* s.v. "Coral." Essick suggests further analogues in Blake's engravings for Earle's *Practical Observation on the Operation for the Stone* (1793), which depict the surface of urinary tract stones as similar to the lichens or undersea creatures on Newton's rock. "Perhaps," Essick speculates, "Newton's rock is a 'passed' stone—another form of excrement." Correspondence with author. See Essick's *Blake's Commercial Book Illustrations* (Oxford, 1989), p. 61 and pl. 123.
25. Essick notes that the use of excrement was a staple of political caricature in the 1790s.
26. See Freud's "Character and Anal Erotism" (1908), *Standard Edition,* 9:68, for a discussion of the obsession with order associated with the anal character.

time with a whole series of swerves in the very understanding of the natural order, a renegotiation of the boundaries between living and dead matter, between living form and excremental chaos, between nature understood as a divine, rational order and nature as a mad chaos of irrational drives and destructive forces.

But what is the point of this sort of "excremental" reading of *Newton?* Does it make the picture a scatological Swiftian satire on the great rationalist? Does it simply turn the appearance of beauty into the reality of shit? Or does the swerve induced by the picture go in the other direction as well—toward a recognition of the reality of the appearance, the beauty of shit? My own sense is that the beauty and dignity of Newton is ultimately deepened, not defaced, by Blake's rendering of the contradiction between his cerebral, formal abstractions and the absorption of his body in the chaotic materiality of nature. In this sense, the picture epitomizes the way Blake's art deconstructs the very preconceptions about proportion, order, cleanliness, and sanity that it evokes.

Blake's art becomes not just intelligible, then, but also identifiable as truly itself only if we give full play to the problematics of chaos and madness in his work. We have to see him as occupying a specific threshold in the history of madness as an institutional discourse: he speaks from a time before the medicalization of madness, its mapping by the form of chaos theory we call psychoanalysis. He speaks from within a moment when madness is associated with irrationality, formlessness, incompetence, possession by hidden forces—a time before the unconscious but after the spirits and deities that had played their role. He asks us to believe in the possibility of artistic and human emergence from the chaotic slime of materialism, but always with a reminder that this emergence is grounded in— always runs aground on—the reef of history, blindness, and contingency. We can only hope to read and see his work from a moment that is aware of both the Wolf Man and Nebuchadnezzar, Lacan and Bedlam; a moment when we can say with historical certainty that Bataille read Blake, and with another kind of conviction that Blake reads Bataille.

University of Chicago

Contributors

David Bindman, Durning-Lawrence Professor of the History of Art at University College London, is the author of *The Complete Graphic Works of William Blake* (1978). His most recent book (with Malcolm Baker) is *Roubiliac and the Eighteenth-Century Monument* (1995).

Morris Eaves, a professor of English at the University of Rochester, is the author of *William Blake's Theory of Art* (1982)and *The Counter-Arts Conspiracy* (1992). Currently a Guggenheim Fellow, he is completing a book on the posthumous power of audiences over artists. With Robert N. Essick and Joseph Viscomi, he edited *The Early Illuminated Books* (1993) in the Blake Trust series. Also with Essick and Viscomi, he is working on "The William Blake Archive" (http://jefferson.village.virginia.edu/blake>), an electronic edition cosponsored by the Getty Fund and the Institute of Advanced Technology in the Humanities (University of Virginia).

Anne K. Mellor is a professor of English and Women's Studies at the University of California, Los Angeles. She is the author of *Blake's Human Form Divine* (1974), *English Romantic Irony* (1980), and *Mary Shelley: Her Life, Her Fiction, Her Monsters* (1988). She edited *Romanticism and Feminism* (1988) and coedited *The Other Mary Shelley* (1995). Her most recent book is *Romanticism and Gender* (1993), and she is now completing a study of the political writings of British women in the Romantic era.

W. J. T. Mitchell, Gaylord Donnelley Distinguished Service Professor of English and Art History at the University of Chicago, has been editor of *Critical Inquiry* since 1978. His books include *Blake's Composite Art* (1977), *Iconology* (1986), and *Picture Theory* (1994), recently awarded the College Art Association Prize for art history. He is now at work on "The Last Dinosaur Book: or the Totem Animal of Modern Culture, 1840–2000."

Tilottama Rajan is a professor of English at the University of Western Ontario and director of the Centre for Theory there. Her books include *Dark Interpreter: The Discourse of Romanticism* (1980) and *The Supplement of Reading: Figures of Understanding in Romantic Theory and Practice* (1990). She is coeditor of *Intersections: Nineteenth-Century Philosophy and Contemporary Theory* (1995), and of a forthcoming volume, "Romanticism, History, and the Possibilities of Genre."

Joseph Viscomi, a professor of English at the University of North Carolina at Chapel Hill, is the author of *Blake and the Idea of the Book* (1993), and with Robert N. Essick edited *Milton: A Poem* (1993) in the Blake Trust series. With Eaves and Essick, he edited *The Early Illuminated Books* and is now working on "The William Blake Archive."

William Blake: Images and Texts

Edited by Susan Green
Formatted by Karen Harms and Kathleen Thorne-Thomsen
in Adobe Garamond and Adobe Garamond Expert fonts
using QuarkXPress for Macintosh
Printed by Publishers Press, Salt Lake City, Utah